Coverscaping

Cover

scaping

Discovering Album Aesthetics

edited by

Asbjørn Grønstad and Øyvind Vågnes

Museum Tusculanum Press
University of Copenhagen 2010

Asbjørn Grønstad and Øyvind Vågnes (eds.).
Coverscaping: Discovering Album Aesthetics

Copy editors: Christian Falden and Jordy Findanis
Layout, typesetting and cover design: Pernille Sys Hansen, Damp Design
Printed by Narayana Press, www.narayanapress.dk
ISBN 978 87 635 0774 5

This book is published with financial support from
The Department of Information Science and Media Studies, University of Bergen
The Faculty of Humanities, University of Bergen
The Reasearch Council of Norway

Museum Tusculanum Press
126 Njalsgade
DK–2300 Copenhagen S
Denmark
www.mtp.dk

Contents

Acknowledgements

The editors wish to thank the staff at Museum Tusculanum Press, Jordy Findanis and Marianne Alenius in particular, for seeing this project through to its completion. We are also grateful to Christian Falden for his input and editorial efforts at an earlier stage of the process. This book would not have been possible without the generous support of The Research Council of Norway, The Faculty of Humanities and the Department of Information Science and Media Studies at the University of Bergen. Finally, we would like to extend our thanks to our authors, for creating this book with us as well as for their patience in seeing it brought to fruition.

Introduction

Asbjørn Grønstad & Øyvind Vågnes

> Then I decided that this disorder and this dilemma, revealed by my desire to write on Photography, corresponded to a discomfort I had always suffered from: the uneasiness of being a subject torn between two languages, one expressive, the other critical; and at the heart of this critical language, between several discourses, those of sociology, of semiology, and of psychoanalysis – but that, by ultimate dissatisfaction with all of them, I was bearing witness to the only sure thing that was in me (however naïve it may be): a desperate resistance to any reductive system.[1]

Confronted with this passage from Roland Barthes' *Camera Lucida*, the reader might envision the avid collector of pictures perusing through her box of sepia-tinted images, occasionally taking out one to scrutinize it more closely. Or she might be led to think of a collector of books, running her fingers across the shelves, carefully taking out one only to hold it in her hands for a moment, remembering when it was bought, when it was read, "seeing through them into their distant past as though inspired",[2] as Walter Benjamin once wrote about that particular sense of magic.

But, as the collective effort of the essays in this anthology demonstrates with clarity, the desire of that heavily mythologized figure of popular culture – the record collector – to write about album covers reveals dilemmas similar to those Barthes describes. Torn between the expressive and the critical, she is bound to arrive, with Barthes, at what he calls a "curious question": "why mightn't there be, somehow, a new science for each object?"[3] In a sense, this book is about such a search: the search for the album cover, if not for its "science", then at least for a much needed movement from the expressive to the critical.

Equally a part of popular musical history and of visual culture, as well as straddling both the sphere of art and that of advertising, album art – we would like to suggest – seems deserving of a phenomenology of its own. While the cur-

1 Roland Barthes, *Camera Lucida: Reflections on Photography*, trans. Richard Howard (New York: Vintage, 2000), p. 8.

2 Walter Benjamin, "Unpacking My Library", *Illuminations*, ed. Hannah Arendt, trans. Harry Zohn (New York: Schocken, 1969), p. 61.

3 Barthes, p. 8.

rent volume is not to be confused with a comprehensive, textbook-style introduction to this topic, nor with an exhaustive reader in record cover aesthetics, it is nevertheless our hope that this book can be conceived as a starting point from which further work in this field may be instigated. There are evidently a number of critical and theoretical perspectives, running the whole gamut from the unflinchingly sociological to the unapologetically aesthetic that may be brought to bear on the analysis of album art. Richly heterogeneous in method, subject matter and point of view, the essays in *Coverscaping* represent an eclectic array of approaches to their occasionally elusive object, thus reflecting at once both a healthy lack of dogmatism and the embryonic, provisional state of the emerging field of album art studies. Although the dearth of any previous efforts in this particular area makes the engagement with the object an exceptionally unpredictable one, the absence of that pre-existing "reductive system" so cautiously shunned by Barthes also indicates that the mostly unprecedented exploration of album cover art may yield insights less calcified than those which emanate from more familiar textual encounters.

Peculiarly, perhaps, the genre of album art is both iconic and precarious. There are, on the one hand, sleeves so emblematic that they have inscribed themselves indelibly into the visual lexicon of popular culture; so much so, in fact, that they are immediately and profusely evocative of historical events, cultural moods, aesthetic contexts, or personal biographies quite independently of the accompanying music. Album covers such as *A Love Supreme*, *Abbey Road*, *Sticky Fingers*, *Dark Side of the Moon*, *Born in the U.S.A.*, and *Nevermind*, to name just a few, circulate rhizomatically in our post-historical economy of images and have long since acquired a symbolic significance which exceeds the music they once contained. On the other hand, there is also a certain precariousness to the textual genre of album sleeves, and this is due to the fact that such images may not actually constitute a separate genre or medium in the first place. The standard perception of a record cover, after all, is that it is something which *supplements* the music stored on the disc. Thus, what defines the object, or – in the parlance of poststructuralism – text of for instance *Abbey Road* is not its cover but the songs found on the album. At best, the album art is a surface manifestation, a visually rendered metonym perhaps, of the compositions it enfolds. More often a record cover is simply music's wrapping paper, the favored method of packaging and marketing a commercial product. In any event, album art is usually regarded as a phenomenon akin to Gérard Genette's notion of paratext; "a zone between text and off-text, a zone not only of transition but also of transaction".[4] Like the paratext that frames and introduces a work of literature, an

4 Gérard Genette, *Paratexts: Thresholds of Interpretation*, trans. Jane E. Lewin (Cambridge: Cambridge University Press, 1997), p. 2.

album cover is external to the "text itself" yet also clearly a part of it, however enigmatically.[5]

An underlying premise for this collection of essays is that a record is a composite medium, made up not solely of the music itself but also of graphic material and printed text. As such, the music disc is a cultural form which lends itself remarkably well to interdisciplinary and intermedial types of analyses. However, not only have there hitherto been few – if any – scholarly publications devoted to the examination and interpretation of cover art, there has also been scant critical awareness of the difference between music as an art form and the album as a unique medium that, in transmitting that art form, simultaneously engenders a semiotic configuration and an aesthetic experience that is not reducible to music alone. W.J.T. Mitchell's pronouncement that "all media are mixed media",[6] therefore, seems no less pertinent to the analysis of compact discs and vinyl records than it does to more obviously heterogeneous forms such as theatre, film and graphic novels. When we set out to produce an anthology of essays that in diverse ways address the issue of the album cover, we did not assume that this was a separate, visual entity that could be easily detached from the musical object. Rather, it was precisely the realization that cover art should in fact be considered an inextricable part of this composite medium that convinced us that a concerted effort to expand our knowledge of the pictorial aspect of recorded music was much needed. On the whole neglected both by the disciplines of art history and cultural studies, the subject of the album cover has generally been relegated to the genre of coffee table books and to non-academic publications that for the most part seem content merely to present a given canon of cover art rather than engage critically with it.[7]

So far, then, it appears that no academic discipline has staked a territorial claim to the highly visible yet strangely unacknowledged genre of the record cover. It falls beyond the purview of introductory remarks like these to probe the causes of this neglect; suffice it to say that the era of interart studies now emerging may be more conducive to studies of those manifestations of our shared culture of images that have been institutionally marginalized, such as that of album art. Its status, we would like to suggest, may not be paratextual only, as there is undoubtedly a strong sense of continuity between the musical, visual and textual compound that constructs the album as a multi-faceted but also curiously coherent phenomenological entity. Although the primacy of the music seems so instinctively warranted that one hardly ever pauses to reflect upon it, we would still maintain that there is no good reason why the album sleeve should have any lesser impact in the overall expressivity of the work as a

5 The objection could of course be raised that the relation between a record and its sleeve design is becoming increasingly irrelevant in an age of downloadable music and iPods, but presently there are few indications that enterprises such as the iTunes Music Store will make the record as a physical object obsolete (and even the iTunes store features virtual album covers as part of its design). Moreover, the somewhat unexpected longevity of the vinyl format would seem to imply that album art is more integral to the experience of music than has so far been acknowledged.

6 W.J.T. Mitchell, *Picture Theory: Essays on Verbal and Visual Representation* (Chicago: University of Chicago Press, 1994), p. 5.

7 For a selection of this literature, see for instance Brad Benedict and Linda Barton, *Phonographics: Contemporary Album Cover and Art Design* (New York: Collier Books, 1977); Graham Marsh, Felix Cromey, and Glyn Callingham (eds.), *Blue Note: The Album Cover Art* (San Francisco: Chronicle Books, 1991); Martin Pesch, *Techno Style: The Album Cover Art* (London: Collins & Brown, 1995); Michael Ochs, *1000 Record Covers* (London: Taschen, 1996); Graham Marsh and Barrie Lewis (eds.), *The Blues: Album Cover Art* (London: Collins & Brown, 1996); Burkhardt Seiler (ed.), *The Album Cover Art of Punk* (London: Collins & Brown, 1998); Takumi Matsui, *In Search of the Lost Record: British Album Cover Art of 50s to 80s* (Tokyo: Graphic-Sha, 2001); Charlotte Rivers, *CD Art: Innovation in CD Packaging and Design* (Hove: RotoVision, 2003); and Intro, *Radical Album Cover Art: Sampler 3* (London: Laurence King, 2003).

whole. In studying the culture of recorded music, one should be careful not to emulate an anti-pictorial bias already discernible in the *Poetics*. In his discussion of the six elements that are constitutive of the form of tragedy, as one may recall, Aristotle places visual adornment – judged to be narratively and aesthetically inferior not only to plot and diction but also to song and dance – at the bottom of the compositional hierarchy.[8] *Coverscaping* aims to carve out a makeshift analytical space, however nascent, from which to re-appraise the ever mutable relation between the visual and the auditory.

Among the burgeoning family of visual artifacts, the album cover as we know it today is a fairly recent arrival, younger than the commercial ad, the postcard, the comic book, and the movie poster. Its immediate precursor was the sheet music cover, but in the early stages of the recording industry the sleeves were not illustrated and featured a standardized design which displayed the name of the record company rather than the artist. Even though the wholesale manufacture of records was in full swing by the early twentieth century, leading record companies like Columbia and Victor did not apprehend the advertising possibilities inherent in personalized covers. By the 1930s, radio had become a more significant medium than records for transmitting music to the masses and in 1929 Victor was acquired by RCA. It was not until 1940 that Alex Steinweiss, then Columbia's art designer, persuaded his label to have four 78 rpm records of *Smash Song Hits by Rodgers & Hart* appear with a graphic front cover (Steinweiss was also credited with inventing the LP cover eight years later). The attempt was a success, and RCA Victor and Decca followed Steinweiss' example within a year.

A genre just a little over half a century old, the record cover has always been an indissoluble part of the larger realm of popular culture, often epitomizing vital trends or offering a visual shorthand for the cultural zeitgeist. In his book about album art, Nick de Ville emphasizes the subcultural aspect of design for music and defines it as a kind of folk art whose practitioners purposely disowned the conventions of mainstream designers.[9] In terms of its position within the broader image culture of the post-war era, cover art was certainly an alternative and perhaps even oppositional genre with regard to the more established forms of art design. Drawing initially on styles and motifs from available traditions of illustration for music, as well as on book design, posters and the painting of the 1920s and '30s, album art soon developed its own distinctive iconographies, fashioned by an individual designer or a small group of designers and often inspired by the musical innovation of artists under contract to niche labels such as Blue Note (and, later, ECM and 4AD). Throughout the 1950s

8 Aristotle, *Poetics*, trans. Malcolm Heath (London: Penguin Books, 1996), pp. 12–13.

9 Nick de Ville, *Album: Style and Image in Sleeve Design* (London: Mitchell Beazley, 2003), pp. 8, 83.

sleeve designers came to rely increasingly on photography, with illustration becoming fashionable again in the days of the counter-culture. The 1960s was also the decade in which the recording artists themselves started to influence the aesthetics of their record covers by hiring their own designers.

Disciplines committed to the study of artistic texts, like for instance literature or film, are often divided up into three separate but overlapping areas of research: criticism, history, and theory. As an aesthetic object worthy of academic interest, album art can boast neither of those. So in lieu of an existing tradition or methodology, new theoretical work on the politics of the album cover needs to begin, maybe tentatively and heuristically, with a few generalized assumptions which may be derived from examining the evolution of the LP, and later CD cover as both a tangible cultural object and as a symbolic intertext, an iconography machine in the Benjaminian ecology of popular music culture. But this introduction is not the place to summarize even cursorily the short history of album art, so we shall remain content to delineate a mere handful of key characteristics which may serve to encapsulate some essential functions of album art.

The album sleeve, first of all, is inescapably a product of the record companies' desire to promote their music; the art of sleeve design originated as a feat of advertising. As de Ville points out, prior to the advent of MTV the cover was the industry's principal marketing device. Secondly, the album sleeve is a crucial vehicle for conveying the identity of the artist and the distinctiveness of the music. This is in itself a process of interart poetics, of the act of capturing the *noeme* of a text in a different medium. The album cover, furthermore, is a form that, like photography, seems particularly adept at seizing the singularity of the instant, at distilling the aesthetic reality of a specific cultural moment. Perhaps it is this snapshot quality which contributes to the perception that record covers "are more powerfully inscribed in the memory of popular culture than any other single class of images", as de Ville puts it.[10] Iconicity may be the exchange value of a skillful condensation of the contingency of the instant.

Not the least important of the fundamental attributes of the album sleeve is its exquisitely wrought narrative canvas. As kids we pored over a motley compilation of record covers as opaque and unfathomable as Pink Floyd's *Wish You Were Here* (1975) or Led Zeppelin's *Presence* (1976), making up elaborate, private stories from the cryptic evidence provided by the cover's frozen diegesis. Lastly, to return momentarily to Genette's concept, the album sleeve is marked by a subtle ambivalence of relation and reference, an ambivalence that envelops the charged, transitional space of the paratextual zone. As a form of

10 de Ville, p. 9.

wrapping, the album sleeve conceals its content even as it purports to represent it. It is the deceptive mask of recorded music, its arbitrary signifier, the specular preamble to the stories told by the music, the attention-grabbing facade, music's other, its totem. If a record possesses something comparable to the Barthesian *punctum*, the album cover may be its distorted blow-up, as semiotically fuzzy as the images David Hemmings' photographer develops in Antonioni's film.

The album cover, then, simultaneously embodies commercial, indexical, ekphrastic, narrative, and paratextual qualities (in addition, obviously, to broader artistic, historical, and political ones). At the same time both a form of graphic design and of art, moreover, the record cover seems to offer itself up as a particularly suggestive object for the quietly yet rapidly expanding field of visual studies. As an indivisible part of a larger aesthetic object, the form also destabilizes the traditional art historical notion of the unity and purity of the image.

Back when the idea for this book was first articulated, we envisaged a rather catholic and, no doubt, impossibly wide-ranging investigation into the myriad facets of our chosen topic; inviting issues such as genre and genealogy, group style and iconography, intertextuality and quotation, self-referentiality and parody, aesthetic hybridity, fashion, designers' oeuvres, liner notes, remediation, and censorship to name a few. This incipient excursion into the largely uncharted territory of album cover aesthetics cannot – for evident reasons of scope and space – broach, and much less resolve, all of these issues, but we hope that the following essays will provide a beginning of sorts and that they can help bolster a sustained critical interest in the album cover as an art historical medium.

According to de Ville, album art can be construed as "a field of design in which complex stylistic tropes are regularly deployed; half authentic, half bent on complex missions of (re)contextualization".[11] In the first essay of this book, Colleen Sheehy unravels the semiotic intricacies of just such a process of figural re-appropriation. In her analysis of the cover image of Bruce Springsteen's 1984 album *Born in the U.S.A.*, Sheehy explains how the juxtaposition of the artist's dorsal pose and the American flag produces a layered and rather ambiguous discourse on the themes of patriotism and masculinity in post-Vietnam American culture. Both the front and back of the album feature the same Annie Leibovitz photograph of Springsteen's backside, facing an enormous American flag. Like the arguments over the meaning of the song "Born in the U.S.A.", the album image is open to varied interpretations. Was Bruce waving the flag?, Sheehy asks, or was he "exploiting the flag imagery of the Reagan era?" Or was

11 de Ville, p. 8.

something else altogether going on in this representation? Sheehy analyzes this image, paying particular attention to the diverse and sometimes conflicting connotations which accrue to it, and connects it with other images that help illuminate its possible meanings, with particular attention to flag imagery. She examines the album cover's art historical allusions to an ideal masculinity, looking closely at the stance that Springsteen assumes – called "contrapposto" in art historical terms. Sheehy also reassesses notions of masculinity as expressed in Springsteen's music and considers how nationalism constructs the military body, which is often represented by the flag, and relates it to what she calls the "ecstatic body", envisioned and embodied in rock and roll and in Springsteen's performances.

In her essay on Neil Young's *Greendale*, Nicole Brown explores the various ways in which the release can be considered an entirely new kind of "concept album", as our very sense of "concept" shifts when we navigate our way through the range of visual-, audio-, and text-based commentary that accompanies the record. Not only does the artwork of the cover extend the metaphorical reach of its lyrics and its exploration of political, social, and environmental issues. According to Brown, *Greendale* also manages to engage the listener in a contemporary form of "communal" activity, one that lends extra force to Young's story of a small town and its residents, as the listener keeps on returning to the ethical questions raised by this group of songs. It could perhaps be argued that the *Greendale* album is a materialization of what Peter Lunenfeld has named a *gesamtkunstmedium*,[12] a concept which may be just as applicable to the work of the design collective Tomato, the digital German trio Oval and the graphic designer Michael Schaeffer. How the tools and practices of digital technology effect representation, design, and consumption, as well as the relationship/s between text and image, is the central question Anne Galperin wrestles with in her essay "Envisioning Music in the Digital Environment". How, she ponders, has technology altered the production, representation and consumption of music, and the relationship/s between music and image? Noting that it has become increasingly commonplace for younger graphic designers to move from print to video work to sound, Galperin underscores the extent to which significant segments of contemporary music culture are defined by media convergence. Today's musicians and designers share digital technologies, and the DIY (Do It Yourself) merger of aural and visual is exponentially more expressive than either one alone. And while in the album era the production of music and design belonged to separate domains, the advent of digital aesthetics has ensured the ascendancy of more hybridized practices. Galperin's essay, moreover, also

12 Peter Lunenfeld, *Snap to Grid: A User's Guide to Digital Arts, Media, and Cultures* (Cambridge, Mass.: The MIT Press, 2000).

dispels the popular myth that the graphic aspect of music has become less salient in the iPod age. In fact, quite the opposite is true, as "digital technologies have also made music's visual component more portable and broadly available". Artist/fan/label websites go beyond the album cover's promotion of a particular set of music to create an equally distinctive, but much more comprehensive environment. One conclusion to be drawn from the digitalization of the spheres of music and design, Galperin suggests, is that the power over the music and its images is increasingly reallocated from the media corporations to the performers, artists and their audiences.

Eve Klein's astute discussion of the culture of the self-made CD zooms in further on the operations of the DIY aesthetic in relation to music and design. Where Galperin's emphasis is on artistic convergence and the proliferation of hybridized texts within the fluid realm of the digital, Klein accentuates the potential inherent in the DIY tradition for a de-commodification of the artwork. The DIY moniker signals an ideological continuity with subcultural movements and with the principles of oppositional art-making. "Small production runs of CDs, and the creation of unique one-off CDs for special events and library collections", Klein maintains, "promote an economy of exchange which can fetishize rarity". Drawing in part on Walter Benjamin's seminal essay on textual reproduction, Klein makes use of case studies from Sydney to explore how the strategies of DIY – always "usurping technologies and modes of production to tell the stories of *its* production" – interact with the politics of aesthetic authenticity and expose the cultural morphology of the aura.

Sharing music offers distinct ways of communicating and creating bonds between listeners, and many readers of this book are likely to have both made and received mixes over the years. In "Re-presenting Mixed Tapes and CDs", Gavin Steingo addresses the visual as well as the tactile character of the object that is the mix compilation, arguing that this aspect of a venerable tradition of exchange has been sorely neglected, in spite of the fact that presentation undeniably plays a significant role in such an exchange. Contributing valuable insights from his research on the topic, Steingo deconstructs the various interrelated creative processes involved in mixing and problematizes notions of what is "inside" and "outside" a mix.

Lou Thomas' photograph of the bodybuilder George O'Mara, on the cover of The Smiths' single "Hand in Glove", evokes the muscular masculinity of classical sculpture. Perhaps we have been blinded by its marble-like whiteness? In his reading of a number of the band's record sleeves, Andrew Warnes addresses these well-known pictures in terms of racial representation. O'Mara's skin, according to Warnes, dazzles while "paralyzing all inquiry into The Smiths' African-American influences". In an analysis bound to seem provocative to some readers, the author claims that the cover negates the "debt that The Smiths owe to the Blues". Thus, the essay keenly reminds us how vital it is to reconsider the various implications of album covers that seem to have become iconic; indeed, a systematic reading of such images can very well be the starting point of a more systematic revision of a music group's musical roots. Of course, a reconsideration of a band's identity can also be an intended effect of our first meeting with a record and the cover that contains it. In his essay, Jonathan Silverman demonstrates how the cover of *De La Soul is Dead* can be considered a forceful statement that invites De La Soul's audience to rethink their apprehensions about the band's identity, and, furthermore, about "rap identity". Among the many meanings ascribed to the word "image", W.J.T. Mitchell writes in his introduction to *Iconology*, we find "image" not only as "mental image", but also as "public image".[13] On the De La Soul sleeve, these meanings are brought into play. Contrary to the title's pronouncement, the object that we are holding in fact speaks loudly of De La Soul's existence. The songs on the album thus leave the listener pondering what is in fact dead – our image of, or, perhaps rather "the image" of, De La Soul as we knew it? As a narrative construction, the album demands that the listener reconsiders its semiotic interplay, as we look at its images and listen to its songs. A declaration of death only masks the opposite, as the band communicates their re-invigoration through a clever play with negations. As Silverman points out, the success of this particular communal engagement with a shifting fan base depends on an analysis of "the image" of a band, in both the most and less obvious sense of the phrase.

How album design ambiguously configures artistic identity is also the focus of Ian Chapman's essay, which places the cover of the KISS album *Alive!* (1975) firmly within an art historical tradition of pictorial exegesis. Chapman's analysis takes as its point of departure a situation familiar to many a record collector and music lover; the seductive and slightly suspenseful moment when we become temporarily transfixed by the serendipitous encounter with a band whose music we know nothing about at the time. Who hasn't at one point bought a record solely on the strength of the promise its cover holds? In adopting an iconographical method for the interpretation of album imagery, Chapman suggests that Erwin Panofsky's three-step approach to visual hermeneutics represents a precious way in which further to pursue the textual ramifications of that first charged encounter. Through a close reading of the KISS album cover in conjunction with Panofsky's insights into the interpretation of pictorial signs,

13 W.J.T. Mitchell, *Iconology: Image, Text, Ideology* (Chicago: University of Chicago Press, 1986), p. 10.

Chapman is able to tease out of the image a range of implications that are shown to revolve around the performance of identity and fantasy.

That the album cover is a genre that often gravitates toward the vicissitudes of appearance and the refashioning of identity is something yet again affirmed by Sigrid Lien's essay on the rock portrait aesthetics of photographers Pennie Smith and Anton Corbijn. By considering their work for artists like The Clash and Captain Beefheart respectively, Lien shows how the star portrait in the hands of photographers like Smith and Corbijn can become a sign of authenticity. Arguing that the portrait of the music industry displays a continuity with the modern character portrait, she discusses the photograph collections *The Clash: Before and After* (Smith) and *Famouz: Photographs 1976–88* (Corbijn), as well as both the photographers' works for *New Musical Express*, with an eye toward finding an answer to the crucial question posed by her essay: "what brings a specific photograph – for instance Smith's portrait of the bass-smashing Simonon or Corbijn's desert photograph of Van Vliet – to the record cover?" Through her analysis, Lien arrives at the quite captivating notion that the star portrait takes on a different communicative function when placed on a record cover. "Isolated and torn loose from other flows of images", she writes, the portrait attains its new status as monument.

Drawing from his analysis of a number of goth sleeves, Jeffrey A. Weinstock shows us how the profanation of the sacred – of debased nuns, angels, saints, and Christ himself – can have not only the immediate capacity to shock, but also to serve as a critique of religious ideology. In a world where images travel at a higher speed than ever before, the iconoclastic image can potentially have a reverberant effect to the unprecedented degree that it not only comments on or reinforces large-scale cultural conflicts, but also instigates them, as in the case of the controversial Muhammad caricatures printed in the Danish newspaper *Jyllands-Posten*.[14] "Cartoon language is mostly limited to deploying a handful of recognizable visual symbols and clichés", the cartoonist Art Spiegelman claims, in an essay in *Harper's* about the "Cartoon war".[15] Spiegelman stresses the point that the cartoon itself is only a *medium*, a "symptom", not "the cause".[16] In terms of staging ideological struggle, however, popular art forms can enter our public sphere and our domestic lives with tremendous ease. Like newspapers, record sleeves are spread across the tables of our living rooms, they are not hung on gallery walls: their impact is neither framed by nor confined by the borders of any given institution. Perhaps it is not so strange, then, that album art makes for a brilliant site for ideological critique, a site where, in the words of Weinstock, "the goth subculture enacts its challenge to the dominant culture".

14 This controversy began after twelve editorial cartoons, most of which depicted the prophet Muhammed, were published on 30 September 2005, in the Danish newspaper. In the aftermath of this incident, muslims who were offended by the images protested the publication by staging impassioned demonstrations in cities like Damascus, Beirut and Istanbul.

15 Art Spiegelman, "Drawing Blood: Outrageous Cartoons and the Art of the Outrage", *Harper's*, June 2006, p. 45.

16 Ibid., p. 43.

"Rhythm appears as music when it invests the auditory level, and as painting when it invests the visual level", Gilles Deleuze wrote in a book on the paintings of Francis Bacon.[17] The final essay in this volume, Hilary Moore's attentive analysis of two major works of art, Ornette Coleman's *Free Jazz* and Jackson Pollock's *White Light*, advises the reader to explore further the often neglected parallels between artistic expressions that upon closer inspection are less different than we routinely are led to believe. In a chapter that convinces us to look as well as to listen anew, a record and the painting that is reproduced on its cover are scrutinized. Pollock described his painting as "energy and motion made visible", Moore points out, and suggests that "*White Light*'s near disregard for metanarrative, along with its focus upon individual gestures of overlapping color" resembles the approach of Coleman's ensemble. "On closer inspection", W.J.T. Mitchell claims, "all the so-called visual media turn out to involve the other senses".[18] Whatever perspectives the individual essays in this book bring to bear on the analysis of the album cover, they all ultimately address and affirm this multi-sensory, synaesthetic aspect that characterizes the form. And in the process these analyses may very well have contributed to a keener appreciation of the essence of that peculiar challenge which defines the art and craft of the genre, a challenge eloquently formulated by graphic artist Dan Nadel (whose interview also concludes this anthology): To come up with an image "as indelible and affecting as the music it was representing".

17 Gilles Deleuze, *Francis Bacon: The Logic of Sensation* (London: Continuum, 2004), p. 44.
18 "There Are No Visual Media", *Journal of Visual Culture* 4.2 (2005), p. 257.

Bruce's Butt

Masculinity, Patriotism, and Rock's Ecstatic Body

Colleen J. Sheehy

In fall 2004, Bruce Springsteen took an unprecedented leap into the political fray of American presidential politics in the race between Democratic Senator John Kerry and incumbent Republican George W. Bush. Springsteen's music had carried a political charge for some time, championing and giving voice to working class Americans, mostly men, who found themselves frustrated by thwarted dreams and broken civic promises.[1] His 2002 release, *The Rising*, captured the new conditions and consciousness of a post 9/11 America haunted by the towers of death and sacrifice, immersed in loss and grief, not knowing what lay ahead. Although Springsteen had cautiously avoided full immersion in electoral politics, 2004 was different. Like so many other Americans, Springsteen was convinced that the Bush administration had to be stopped. Outraged by the administration's whipping up of national fear through exaggerated intelligence or, as some thought, outright lies about Iraq's weapons of mass destruction and their imminent threat to the United States, used to justify invading Iraq, Springsteen no longer felt that he could remain neutral or uninvolved in the presidential battle.

The artist stepped forward in a big way, fully realizing the risks of angering and alienating some fans. In an August 2004 editorial piece for the *New York Times*, he announced his opposition to the current administration and his plans to work for the Kerry campaign through a series of concerts under a new banner, Vote for Change:

> I've tried to write songs that speak to our pride and criticize our failures. These questions are at the heart of this election: who we are, what we stand for, why we fight. Personally, for the last 25 years I have always stayed one step away from partisan politics. Instead, I have been partisan about a set of ideals: economic justice, civil rights, a humane foreign policy, freedom and a decent life for all of our citizens. This year, however, for many of us the stakes have risen too high to sit this election out.[2]

1 A version of this paper was presented at the Pop Conference at Experience Music Project in April 2003. I thank those who provided comments and suggestions at the conference, including Greil Marcus, Steve Waksman, David Cavicchi, Ann Powers, Andrew Ross, and others. Jefferson Cowie and Lauren Boehm offer an astute discussion of the equivocal meanings of "Born in the U.S.A." and its relationship to the changing status of working-class men in "Dead Man's Town: 'Born in the U.S.A.', Social History, and Working-Class Identity", *American Quarterly* 58.2 (2006), pp. 353–378. I am grateful to Professor Cowie, who teaches at Cornell University's Department of American Studies, for sharing this with me.

2 Bruce Springsteen, "Chords of Change", *New York Times*, 5 August 2004, Section A, p. 23.

Springsteen played a central role in the Vote for Change concerts, which took him, the E Street Band, and other major groups and singers to election swing states. Ticket proceeds supported America Coming Together (ACT), a group campaigning for John Kerry. At the Vote for Change concerts, Springsteen shared arena stages with other musical acts, something he had not done in large venues since the 1988 Amnesty International Tour, this time with alt rock favorites R.E.M. and newcomer Bright Eyes. He began his own VFC set with a solo, souped-up, twelve-string, Jimi Hendrix-style "Star Spangled Banner". In interviews and from the stage, the singer called for "a deeper patriotism" that involved holding elected officials accountable, asserting our rights to criticize government actions, in other words, remaining true to democratic ideals.[3] By the end of the campaign, Springsteen appeared at Kerry's final rallies in Madison, Wisconsin and Cleveland, singing "The Promised Land".

As Springsteen anticipated, some fans expressed dismay over their hero's partisan coming out. The right wing Republican governor of Minnesota, Tim Pawlenty, for instance, commented that he was "heartbroken" about Springsteen's work for the Kerry campaign, stating that he would not attend the concert.[4] Yet, should the singer's political sympathies have been surprising to anyone who had followed his musical career? Twenty years earlier, during the reign of Pawlenty's first political hero, President Ronald Reagan, Springsteen had released his most popular album in terms of sales, *Born in the U.S.A.* At that time, many considered the title tune politically equivocal, and the album cover featured a huge American flag, corresponding to the increased flag imagery employed by Reagan. Springsteen's flag presentation was a bit different, however. The singer's body, notably his rear end, blocked the flag.

During the many years of my Springsteen research, which led in one form to the exhibition *Springsteen: Troubadour of the Highway*, I found that comments on Bruce's butt had been frequent, becoming almost predictable. It struck me that in my nearly a lifetime of rock and roll participation, fandom, and study, I had never heard so many comments on that part of a performer's anatomy – not about Prince with the buttless pants, not about Jennifer Lopez. The closest connection I could recall was the preoccupation with Elvis' hips in the fifties.[5] Today, when butts frequently are found in lyrics and featured prominently in rock and hip-hop videos, Bruce's butt calls for more serious consideration, particularly in relation to ongoing arguments about the singer's politics.

Springsteen himself fostered this interest in his rear end. In 1984, he unveiled a newly buffed physique, having enlisted a trainer, adopted a serious fitness regiment, and sworn off his usual fast food diet. Known for his three to

3 At the first Vote for Change concert in Philadelphia on 1 October 2004, Springsteen's brief comments from the stage were: "We remain a land of great promise. But it's time we need to move America towards the fulfillment of its promises that she's made to her citizens: economic justice, civil rights, protection of the environment, respect for others and humility in exercising our power at home and around the world. These core issues of American identity are what's at stake on November 2. I believe that Senator Kerry and Senator Edwards understand the important issues and I think they're prepared to help our country move forward. America is not always right. That's a fairy tale that you tell your children at night before they go to sleep. But America is always true. And it's in seeking those truths that we find a deeper patriotism. Don't settle for anything less. So we've got some work to do between now and election day – if you share our concerns, find the best way to express yourself, roll up your sleeves, and get out there and do something. And remember, the country we carry in our hearts is waiting". Cited on www.backstreets.com, "Set Lists 2004".

4 See Dave Aasen, "A Ballad about Squandered Credibility", *Twin Cities Star Tribune*, 9 October 2004, A25; and Phil Kuntz, "What's Changed for Springsteen Fans", *Wall Street Journal*, 5 October 2004, C15.

5 Greil Marcus commented that there is a little-known fan fascination with Elvis' rear end, evidenced by buttons of the King's butt worn by fans at Graceland. Email correspondence with author, 13 July 2004.

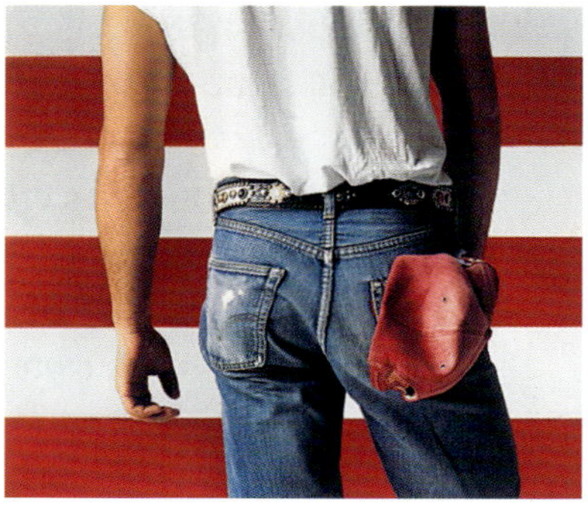

Bruce Springsteen, New York City, 1984 (*Born in U.S.A.* cover photo) Cibachrome photograph. © Annie Leibovitz (Contact Press Images), courtesy of the artist.

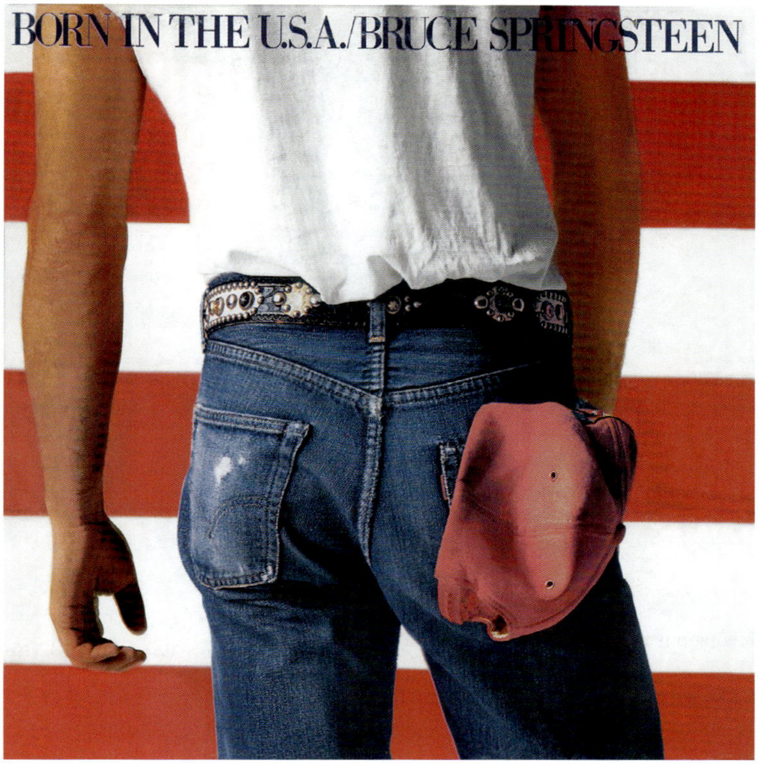

Bruce Springsteen, *Born in the U.S.A.*, album cover, 1984. © Annie Leibovitz (Contact Press Images), courtesy of the artist.

four hour, physically demanding performances, Springsteen had trained like an athlete to be ready for his upcoming world concert tour. Wearing his usual skin-tight jeans, the singer showed off his body on this tour, with his well-toned rear and bulging biceps.[6]

The tour, of course, was for his new album *Born in the U.S.A.* And it was this album cover that put Bruce's butt front and center in his visual culture. The album featured the same photograph by Annie Leibovitz on both its front and back, showing the back of Springsteen's torso as the singer stands facing an enormous American flag. In considering the comments on Bruce's butt, it was this image that my interests centered on.

The *Born in the U.S.A.* cover presents a conundrum, which makes it particularly rich to analyze. On the one hand, it has an easily read beefcake kind of come-on, which is interesting in itself in terms of the display of the male body that is such a prominent element of rock and roll. The image also employs a graphic simplicity that makes it particularly powerful in its juxtaposition of two major elements: a man's body and the flag. Both images are fragmented. The

6 For a fascinating discussion of pumped up bodies and masculinity and their relationships to Reagan's politics, see Susan Jeffords, *Hard Bodies: Hollywood Masculinity in the Reagan Era* (New Brunswick, NJ: Rutgers University Press, 1994). Her study begs a consideration of Springsteen's body of this period, which, although in superficial ways aligned with other images such as Sylvester Stallone in the popular Rambo films, acted as an oppositional image of masculinity.

body could be anonymous, but we know it is Springsteen himself. The white t-shirt and worn blue jeans signify American working class or youth culture, with rock star flamboyance thrown in by the bejeweled belt. The colors of the clothing – red, white, and blue suggest a completion of the fragmented flag.[7] (There is no need for stars; Springsteen is the "star"). The image also has chutzpah.[8] It can cause a jolt by juxtaposing this body part with a symbol that has sacred connotations. All of these elements help to create an uncertainty of meaning.

Like the debates about the meaning of the song "Born in the U.S.A.", the album's signature image has also been questioned: was Springsteen exploiting the flag imagery of the Reagan era? Was he participating in a jingoistic patriotism? Or was this Bruce a product, in a pop art-like expression? Was Springsteen disrespecting the flag by plastering his butt on it? Was he pissing on the flag, as many conjectured, in a rock version of Andres Serrano's controversial 1989 photograph *Piss Christ*? The combined power and ambiguity of the image make it intriguing to consider more fully.

The record cover's continued power and circulation, along with Springsteen's recent, more direct political commentary, make it an opportune time to reconsider this image. Its iconic status was reflected by its inclusion in the Simpson's parody covers for a November 2002 *Rolling Stone* with Homer Simpson as the Springsteen figure.[9] In 2001, young upstart Ryan Adams referenced the image in the cover for his CD *Gold* in an image he called a "slouchy" parody of *Born in the U.S.A.* As recently as February 2003, a reporter for *Entertainment Weekly* commented in an interview with Springsteen that in the mid 1980s, the singer had "the most famous ass in America".[10] Furthermore, on his tour for *The Rising* in 2002–2003, Springsteen revived the full E Street band version of "Born in the U.S.A." from the original album recording, after resolutely performing the song as a mournful acoustic blues tune ever since the 1988 Amnesty International tour. Intersecting with all this is the fact that a revival of displays of American flags in public spaces and in many vernacular memorials occurred across the nation after the 9/11 attacks and launching of the Iraq war.[11] With these flag displays came renewed questions about what the American flag can mean, a conversation and debate that continues today in relation to the war in Iraq and the use of flags in public and private realms, in both peace and protest demonstrations and pro-war gatherings.

To explore these questions, the cover art for *Born in the U.S.A.* serves as my key object of analysis. In examining it, I argue for the critical importance of the visual culture of rock and roll to our understanding of this art form and the ways in which it operates. Conversely, I also argue for the importance of rock

7 The red baseball cap stuffed into one of Springsteen's back pockets was given to him by friend Lance Larson, owner of the Wonder Bar in Asbury Park, N.J. When Larson's father died, Springsteen helped him to deal with the loss, and Larson gave Springsteen his father's red baseball cap. Springsteen said that they would do something to remember Larson's father. It's Larson's father's cap that appears on the *Born in the U.S.A.* album cover. According to Larson, Springsteen called him after the album came out and said that his father's cap is part of history now, memorialized on the album cover. He told Larson, every time you see that album, you'll think of your father. This story was told by Lance Larson during a tour of Asbury Park for the "Glory Days: A Bruce Springsteen Conference" held at Monmouth University on 8–11 September 2005. The tour took place on 8 September 2005.

8 "Chutzpah" is a Yiddish word meaning "nerve, gall, or supreme self-confidence" accordring to Merriam-Webester's Collegiate Dictrionary, 10th edition (Springfield, MA: Merriam-Webster, Inc. 1999), p. 206.

9 See *Rolling Stone*'s Simpson parodies on the cover of the 28 November 2001 issue. Other covers parodied were Nirvana's *Nevermind* and The Beatles' *Abbey Road*. In June 2004, the Springsteen fansite www.backstreets.com noted the 20th anniversary of *Born in the U.S.A.*'s release with "FIRESTARTER: 20 years of Born in the USA": "One score years ago, Bruce Springsteen brought forth on this continent a little record called Born in the U.S.A. (And we do mean record, not CD.) Yes, this week – specifically Friday, June 4 – marks 20 years since Springsteen's radio-ready follow-up to Nebraska, since the bandwagon started rolling, since the buttshot heard 'round the world captivated an icon-hungry planet'".

10 See Hugo Lindgren, "America Rocks", *New York Times Magazine*, 4 November 2001, p. 15. In this interview, Ryan Adams says of his *Gold* album cover shoot, "... we did a lot of different poses and everything. One of the things

and roll to an understanding of our broader visual culture, and in this case, our political culture as well. I employ a range of art historical and interdisciplinary methods to explore this image and its meanings, to relate it to concepts of masculinity, patriotism, nationalism, and the body in rock and roll. A close reading that pulls apart this image but also considers the connection of the two main images – flag and body – has continuing import today in terms of the meaning of the body, primarily the male body; of the flag and patriotism; of the ongoing impact and unsettled meanings of the Vietnam War, and of ongoing military conflicts and the individual's relationship to nation, nationalism, and community. This examination goes beyond re-assessing Springsteen's work, ideas, and political values to address broader American values concerning militarism and masculinity, and it explores the role of rock and roll in disrupting, countering, and offering alternative embodiment to performers and audiences.

The decision to put Bruce's butt with the flag on *Born in the U.S.A.* was not a calculated marketing plan but came about in a creative evolution of ideas, photo shoots, and design decisions, recounted by Springsteen and his art director at that time, Andrea Klein.[12] After hearing the music for the record, Klein recommended that this release have a bold color cover, particularly to follow the stark black-and-white landscape used for Springsteen's previous release, the somber 1982 *Nebraska* album, which Klein had also designed. At first, Springsteen suggested working from a Joseph Szabo book of photographs of teenagers, but they abandoned that approach early on. Klein suggested that they try some studio shots, and both she and Springsteen had the idea that they wanted to use a flag in some way, because of the title song. Manager Jon Landau suggested they use a flag image by American artist Jasper Johns, but the others decided to go ahead with studio work, using both painted flags and real flags.

For the photography, Klein enlisted Annie Leibovitz, who was well known for her gutsy, unexpected poses of musicians and actors in *Rolling Stone*. Klein had an artist paint a Jasper Johns-like flag as a backdrop in the studio. At a later point, graffiti artist Keith Haring painted another flag that was used for some shots.[13] At a late point in the process, they tacked a huge American flag to the wall. It may have been one that Springsteen himself owned or one Klein bought. They shot hundreds of photos.[14]

Springsteen went back and forth on what direction to go with the cover image, and even considered, to Andrea Klein's dismay, starting from scratch. Klein mocked up possible album designs from the existing photos. In one version, she took a detail from one of Leibovitz's photos with Bruce's bum as the focal point. While they had taken many photos of the singer facing the cam-

we had was this big huge flag, and I thought it looked powerful that's what attracted me to it. I also kind of wanted to tweak the whole Bruce Springsteen 'Born in the U.S.A.' thing. Instead of me standing there all tough like Bruce, I'm in my slouchy, twitchy position, my head down, my hair a mess. We thought it looked cool, but it was also meant to be a bit of a goof". See Ken Tucker, "Springsteen Speaks", *Entertainment Weekly*, 28 February 2003, pp. 14–18.

11 These images can be seen in Colette Gaiter's online media project called "The Flag Code", which was instigated in response to the plentiful displays of flags following 9/11. The url is www.digidiva.net/FC.

12 See Arlen Schumer, "Cover Me: Behind the Design of the Bruce Springsteen Image: An Interview with Andrea Klein", *Backstreets*, Winter/Spring 1986, no. 16, pp. 28–30; and Arlen Schumer, "Cover Me: The Birth of Born in the U.S.A. Part Two: An Interview with Andrea Klein", *Backstreets*, Summer 1986, no. 17, pp. 26–28; and Kurt Loder, "The Rolling Stone Interview: Bruce Springsteen", *Rolling Stone*, 6 December 1984; reprinted in *Bruce Springsteen: The Rolling Stones Files* (New York: Hyperion, 1996), p. 154.

13 According to Leibovitz's archivist Michael Fisher, the Haring flag is now displayed in the Carriage House Restaurant on 19th Street in New York City. Author's phone conversation, 10 April 2003.

14 I was able to see a large variety of images from this photo shoot in Annie Leibovitz's archive while doing research for the exhibition *Springsteen: Troubadour of the Highway*, which opened at the Weisman Art Museum, University of Minnesota in Minneapolis in September 2002.

era, Springsteen felt, as Klein put it, that "he looked schlumpy". Leibovitz liked other shots better, including Springsteen with fire burning behind him, and another of a Springsteen jumping, taken in the basement of his New Jersey home (these were used as sleeves for single releases from *Born in the U.S.A.*). Springsteen, however, kept going back to the image of his rear end with the flag, and finally made the decision to go with that, despite some concerns about having his butt on the cover.[15] Rock critic Kurt Loder later told Springsteen in an interview for *Rolling Stone* that some people had conjectured that he was pissing on the flag. Springsteen denied that intention, saying "In the end, the picture of my ass looked better than the picture of my face".[16]

Springsteen's butt is not the first one to appear on an album cover though frontal shots are the favored pose. Nor was his the first to use an American flag. Butts have appeared fairly frequently. A 1950s album for Johnny "Scat" Davis and his Dixieland Band features two women, dressed in tight pants and high heels, walking down a street, rear ends at the cover's dead center. Or one could point to the brutally honest John and Yoko back cover for the 1968 *Two Virgins*, with the two singers naked, looking back at the camera. (Famously, the record cover showed them in frontal view, also naked. The cover was banned in most countries.) The 1979 best of album for Average White Band features a woman's naked body, her rear end acting as the letter "W". Loverboy's 1981 *Get Lucky* album shows a close-up of a man's rear in skin-tight red leather. Other album designs have fragmented the male body, most notably the Andy Warhol cover for the Rolling Stones 1971 album *Sticky Fingers*. That cover offers a potent sexual come-on, with its invitation to unzip the real zipper on the album cover, followed by slipping out the sleeve to reveal the male figure in briefs. All of these (and more) appeared before Springsteen's 1984 release.

In general, bodies are a key element of album design in rock and roll, in part as a means of first identifying the musical artists and then encouraging identification between the viewer and the singer or band. Bodies also promote rock's sensuality and its recognition of bodily experience that are so central to the musical form. Even if the cover does not feature the performer's body, the display of a body, often female, asserts the eroticism of the music, sometimes raising questions about the sexist treatment of women in rock. American flags have appeared on many album covers, ranging from Kate Smith's modest mailbox flag on her *U.S.A.* album to Sly Stone's *Greatest Hits*, where he is literally wearing the flag.[17] In talking about the *Born in the U.S.A.* flag image with Kurt Loder, Springsteen said, "We had the flag on the cover because the first song was called 'Born in the U.S.A.' and the theme of the record kind of follows the

15 Schumer, *Backstreets*, Summer 1986, pp. 26–28.
16 Kurt Loder, "The Rolling Stone Interview: Bruce Springsteen", *Rolling Stone*, 6 December 1984; reprinted in *Bruce Springsteen: The Rolling Stones Files* (New York: Hyperion, 1996), p. 154.
17 Many of these album covers can be seen in Michael Ochs, *1000 Record Covers* (Cologne, Germany and New York: Taschen, 2002).

themes I've been writing about for the last six or seven years. But the flag is a powerful image, and when you set that stuff loose, you don't know what's gonna be done with it".[18]

Stuff was, indeed, set loose. Springsteen's use of the flag coincided with Ronald Reagan's presidency. His campaign for "Morning in America" aimed to shore up American pride and stifle criticism of the government after the national crises brought on by the Vietnam War, Watergate, economic recession, and the Iran hostage crisis of the 1970s. Reagan's conservative economic policies retrenched social programs and blatantly protected and further enriched the wealthy. His presidency took on greater official formality than President Carter's, and the flag became a more prominent element of his administration as an assertion of renewed American self-assurance and power.

Then, of course, there was the matter of the chorus for "Born in the U.S.A.", with its infectious beat and dance-ability, which also "set stuff loose". Many listeners and concert goers rallied around the anthemic qualities of the chorus, "I was born in the U.S.A.; I was born in the U.S.A.", singing along as a statement of their birthright and skipping or overlooking the critique expressed in the song's verses. *Born in the U.S.A.* sold 24 million copies worldwide, the most of any Springsteen release to this day, and his concert tour attracted larger crowds as he played in larger venues than ever before. In most stadiums on the tour, Springsteen and the band performed against a backdrop of a huge American flag. The flag was an inescapable part of the song.[19]

1984, the year of *Born*'s release, was an election year, and Springsteen became something of a political football in presidential campaigns, as pundits and politicians appropriated Springsteen and his American imagery, hoping for a hold on the singer's followers. Ronald Reagan's campaign invited Springsteen to appear with him at a campaign stop in New Jersey, but the invitation was declined. Reagan, nonetheless, invoked Springsteen in his speech in that state, aligning his own dream for America with Springsteen's.[20] Democratic candidate Walter Mondale also joined in, trying to wrestle Springsteen to the Democratic ticket. To all this, Springsteen responded primarily by using his concert performances to make statements distancing himself, particularly from Reagan. Even earlier, in 1980 when Reagan was first elected, Springsteen stated from one concert stage the day after the election that he thought Reagan's election and policies were "pretty frightening". After Reagan's statement in 1984, Springsteen said at another concert, "I don't think the president's listened to my *Nebraska* album". The singer commented further on Reagan's lack of concern for working people in an interview, saying that in many parts of America,

18 Loder, p. 154.

19 It is interesting to note that the American flag frequently has been used in musical performances. See, for instance, John Cohen's photograph of Bill Monroe and his Blue Grass Boys (1962) in his book *There is No Eye* (New York: Powerhome Books, 2001), p. 143; the musical and political Detroit radicals, MC5, used flags in their performances, see photo in Steve Waksman, *Instruments of Desire: The Electric Guitar and the Shaping of Musical Experience* (Cambridge: Harvard University Press, 1999), p. 218. I thank Steve for pointing this out to me. Interestingly, Jon Landau, Springsteen's longtime manager, also managed the MC5. Recently, the punk band Green Day sang their hit song "American Idiot" in front of a veiled, green American flag on the Grammy Awards show, 13 February 2005.

20 Dave Marsh, *Glory Days: Bruce Springsteen in the 1980s* (New York: Pantheon Books, 1987), pp. 261–263.

not only wasn't it "morning", but "It's midnight, and there's a bad moon risin'".[21]

It was the conservative columnist George Will, who, after seeing part of a Springsteen concert in Baltimore, wrote a column, "A Yankee Doodle Springsteen", and also recommended to Reagan's campaign circle that the president seek the singer's endorsement. Will thought "Springsteen and his merry band" a fine example of American verve and noted that "a lot of American flags got waved at Springsteen's concert".[22]

In Will's mind, and for many others still today, the flag can only mean one thing: devout loyalty and unquestioned support for the government and its actions. But if one studies the history of the American flag itself and of flag imagery, what becomes apparent is exactly the opposite. Rather than having a fixed meaning, the flag's meaning is contentious and uncertain. In fact, the American flag activates ongoing argument and debate about how it can look and what it can mean, and, to some extent, that is a significant role it plays in contemporary society.

Scott Guenter documents this debate over 150 years of American history in *The American Flag, 1777–1924: Cultural Shifts from Creation to Codification*. He notes the ongoing transformation of the flag itself, from Continental Colors of the Revolutionary period to the standardization of its design throughout the course of the nineteenth century. He also details the changing meaning of the flag, as it acquired significance as a symbol of insistent national unity by Union forces during the Civil War (in opposition to the Confederate flag), to its role in the 1880s as a symbol of American culture as flags entered school rooms to Americanize immigrants. Debate over the flag's meaning wax and wane, taking on greater urgency during any time of military action. Arguments accompany these surges of interest in the flag – about its design, its proper display, and its use according to ritualistic codes.[23]

Despite official flag codes, Americans have used the image of the flag with great glee. In no other nation does one find such a range of popular applications of a national flag. One place we see the American flag used outside of government is in products and advertising. From the 1880s and well into the twentieth century, American flags were popular means to decorate and promote products. Flags were used to sell everything from potato chips to cod liver oil to soap. Flag designs were incorporated into all kinds of products like napkins, hammocks, pillows, awnings, hosiery, and many forms of clothing.[24] As early as the 1880s, efforts were made to ban the use of the flag on products and alteration of the image of the flag in any way.[25] Bills presented to Congress were not passed. In 1907,

21 Christopher Sanford, *Springsteen: Point Blank* (New York: Da Capo, 1999), p. 195. For analysis of Springsteen's politics, *Born in the U.S.A.*, and Reagan's America, see Susan Mackey-Kallis and Ian McDermott, "Bruce Springsteen, Ronald Reagan, and the American Dream", *Popular Music and Society* (Winter 1992), pp. 1–10; and Jim Cullen, "Bruce Springsteen's Ambiguous Musical Politics in the Reagan Era", *Popular Music and Society* (Summer 1992), pp. 1–22.

22 Marsh, p. 257.

23 Scott Guenter, *The American Flag, 1777–1924: Cultural Shifts from Creation to Codification* (Cranbury, NJ: Associated University Presses, 1990). For a chronicling of the meaning and use of the flag and flag imagery that comes up to current times, see Karal Ann Marling, *Old Glory: Unfurling History* (Hawkhurst, United Kingdom: Bunker Hill Publishing in conjunction with The Library of Congress, 2004). The stringent codes for use of the flag are documented in official booklets such as *The American Flag: Everything a Patriotic American Should Know About Our Country's Flag* (New York: New York Army National Guard, 1990).

24 For examples of how the flag has been used in products and advertising, see Kit Hinrichs and Delphine Hirasuma, *Long May She Wave: A Graphic History of the American Flag* (Berkeley: Ten Speed Press, 2001).

25 Guenter, p. 138.

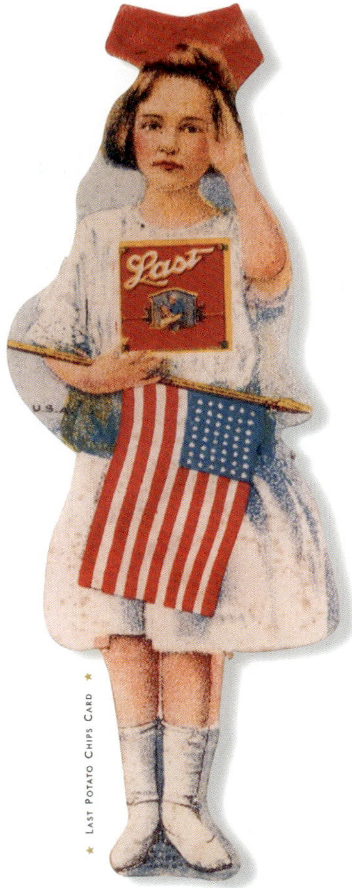

Last Potato Chips Card

"Flag Girl" advertisement.

the Supreme Court ruled that states could set their own legislation about proper use of flag imagery within their borders.[26] Not until 1968, in response to the Vietnam War protests, did Congress pass a federal law against flag desecration. Not until 1990 did the Supreme Court overturn that law as unconstitutional. The role of the flag as a means of protest, as a vehicle of free speech, and therefore as a means of *activating* the principles of the Constitution, along with official rulings on legal cases, make a fascinating history told by Robert Justin Goldstein in *Desecrating the American Flag*.[27]

Springsteen's use of the flag juxtaposed with his backside *was* really something new under the sun. The most common way of representing bodies with flags shows people standing at attention or in a ritualistic pose in front of the flag. For instance, in 1942, the covers of over 100 popular magazines fea-

26 Ibid., p. 146.

27 Robert Goldstein (ed.), *Desecrating the American Flag: Key Documents of the Controversy from the Civil War to 1995* (Syracuse, NY: Syracuse University Press, 1996).

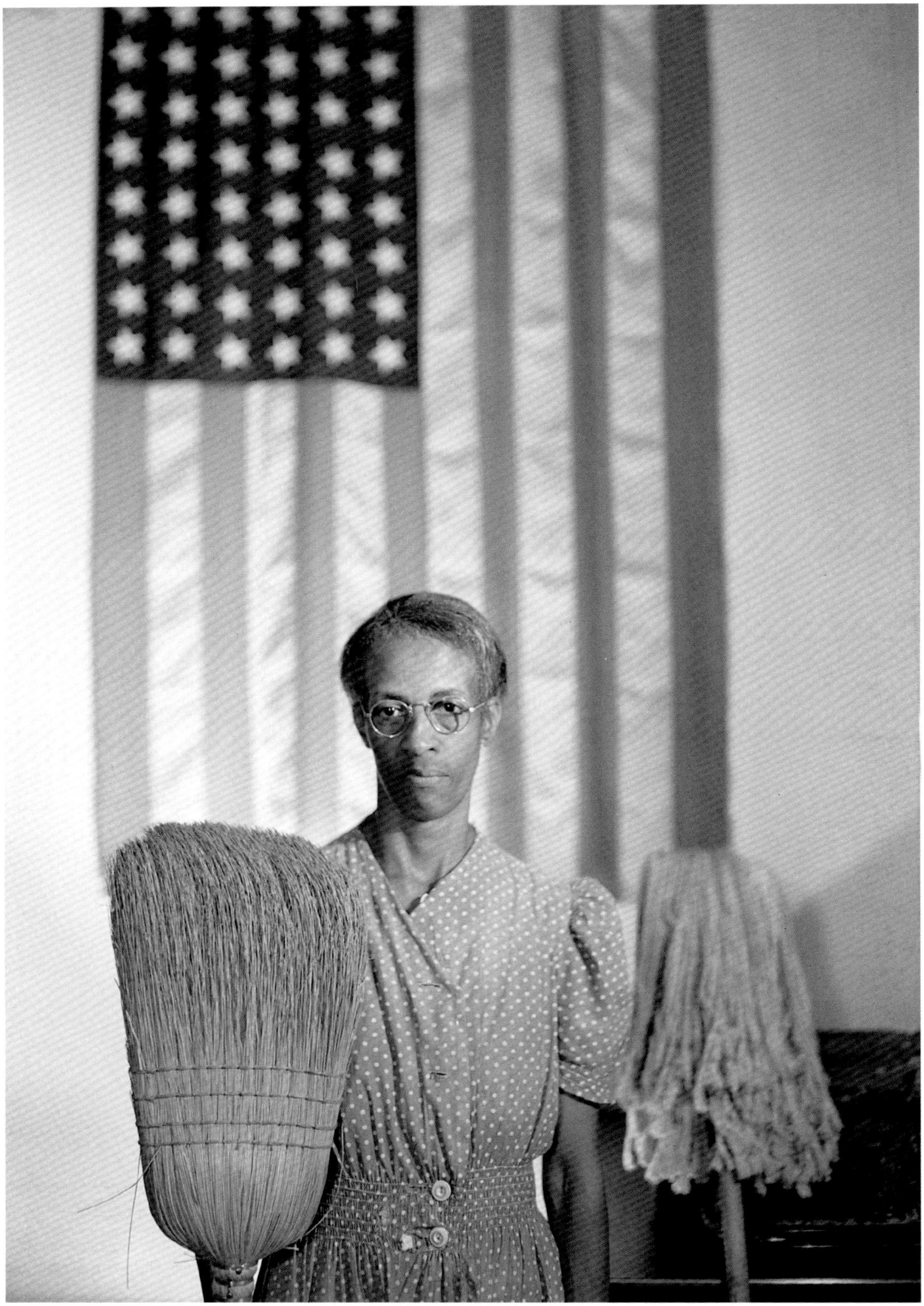

Gordon Parks, "Ella Watson, charwoman, Washington, D.C., 1942". Library of Congress, Prints & Photographs Division, FSA/OWI Collection.

tured the flag or citizens with flags, showing them standing at attention.[28] In another arena, Carl Van Vechten's 1935 photograph of Gertrude Stein, author of the groundbreaking literary work *The Making of Americans* (1925), presents the writer in a solemn pose with an American flag behind her. She stares straight into the camera, as if to assert, "I too belong to America, Jewish lesbian that I am". Similarly, Gordon Park's signature photograph, *American Gothic, Washington, D.C.* (1942), shows an African-American cleaning woman in a government building, proudly but wearily standing in front of a huge flag, broom and mop in either hand. The closest referent for Springsteen's image may be the flag patch sewn onto the seat of blue jeans in the 1960s and 1970s, a practice that became the focus of desecration laws, and people were, indeed, prosecuted for that offense.[29] Despite all of the efforts to control and codify the flag, the social, visual, and legal history of the flag tells us that the flag is extremely malleable. It is an object and image that citizens and artists feel some license to manipulate, despite the rules of the official flag code.

The flag appears frequently in American art. Entire exhibitions have been done on this subject.[30] In its long history in art, the flag has been shown in battle scenes, such as Emmanuel Leutz's *Washington Crossing the Delaware* (1851). Or it appears as symbol of the nation as in Childe Hassam's painting *Allies Day, May 1917*, where the U.S. flag flies prominently along Fifth Avenue in New York City among the flags of other Western nations, after the U.S.'s pivotal role in World War I. The flag also frequently appears in American folk art, reflecting its accessibility and appeal as an image across classes and levels of artistic training.[31]

American artist Jasper Johns made the flag his most enduring subject in over ninety paintings, drawings, and sculptures from 1954 to the present. His 1954/55 piece, entitled simply *Flag*, paved his way into the postwar New York art world. In this work, Johns raised questions in a subtle yet provocative way: what does the flag as image and object mean? Is a painting of a flag a flag? How are abstraction and subject related? How do we imbue images with meaning? In the context of the Cold War nationalism of its time, Johns' flag coolly connected with the prevalent display of the flag in politics of the day.[32]

An important element of Johns' 1954/55 *Flag*, and one not commented on much by critics, was the fact that his first flag is a painted collage, not just a painting. To create this piece, Johns painted over a surface created from a collage of small, torn bits of newspaper. He used the small print articles from inside and back pages, not the headline stories of the front page. If you get close to this object (now in the collection of the Museum of Modern Art), you can

28 These covers were collected in Peter Gwilliam Kreitler's *United We Stand: Flying the American Flag* (San Francisco: Chronicle Books, 2001).

29 Goldstein, pp. 100–101.

30 See, for instance, *The American Flag in the Art of Our Country* (Allentown, PA: Allentown Art Museum, 1976); David S. Rubin, *Old Glory: The American Flag in Contemporary Art* (Cleveland: Cleveland Center for Contemporary Art, 1994).

31 The Museum of American Folk Art holds many works in their collection featuring the flag, as in their Flag Gate by an unidentified artist, Jefferson County, New York, created circa 1876. For other examples, see *The American Flag in the Art of Our Country*, cited above.

32 On Johns, see *Jasper Johns Flags, 1955–1994* (London: Anthony d'Offay Gallery, 1996); and Jill Johnston, *Jasper Johns: Privileged Information* (London: Thames and Hudson, 1996) pp. 55–100.

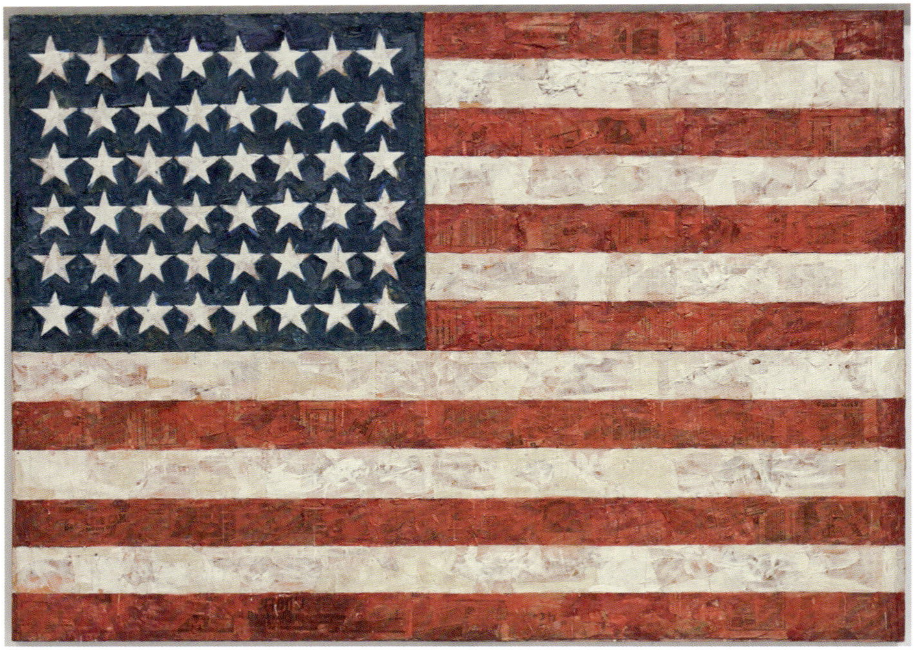

Jasper Johns, *Flag*, 1954 (dated on the reverse). New York, Museum of Modern Art (MoMA). Encaustic, oil and collage on fabric mounted on plywood (107.3 × 153.8 cm). Gift of Philip Johnson in honor of Alfred H. Barr, Jr. 106.1973. © 2009. Digital image, The Museum of Modern Art, New York/Scala, Florence.

see the newsprint leaking through the stripes like a ghostly whisper of history. His flag has a voice and it was the voice of people's everyday stories, not of the government. In his *Flag*, the image seems to be oozing, dripping with its use of encaustic, a medium of wax mixed with pigment. The flag here is like something biological and living, about to erupt, and, while seemingly stationary, it is also moving, in an act of forming and dissolving at the same time. Along with Robert Rauschenberg, Johns re-introduced everyday objects into American art, bringing a subconscious or surreal perspective to common imagery.

Following Johns and Rauschenberg, pop artists treated the American flag as an aspect of popular culture, an image closely aligned to our commercial interests as much as to our political system. In works such as Tom Wesselman's *Still Life Number 36* (1964), and James Rosenquist's *President Elect* (1960), only fragments of the flag need appear to signify the entire object. Since the 1960s, African-American artists have used the flag to indict American society for the gap between our ideals and our practices in relation to African-American society.[33] In Faith Ringgold's painting *The Flag is Bleeding* (1967), the flag is superimposed on three figures, a white woman and man and an African-American man, who lock arms in a show of solidarity. Blood-like drips ooze from the red stripes, suggesting the violence aimed at civil rights demonstrations and the

33 See the discussion, "The Flag: A Symbol of Repression", in Samella Lewis, *African-American Art and Artists* (Berkeley: University of California Press, 1990), pp. 165–172.

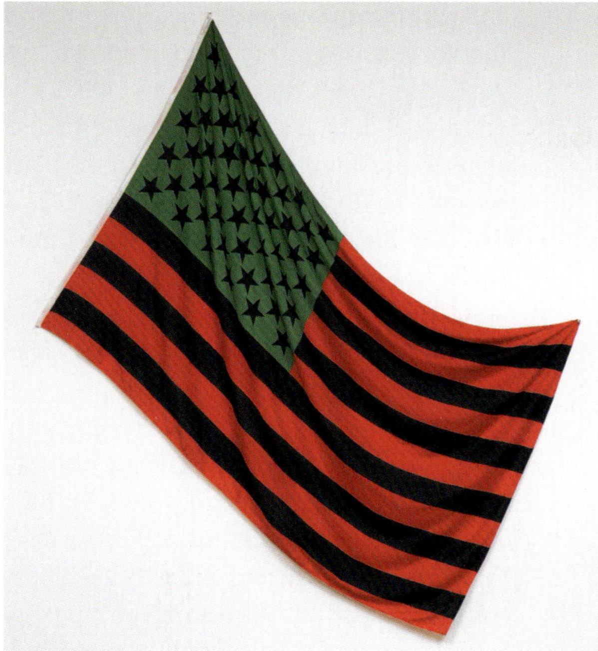

David Hammons, *African-American Flag*, 1990. New York, Museum of Modern Art (MoMA). Dyed cotton (142.2 × 223.5 cm). Gift of The Over Holland Foundation. 296.1997. © 2009. Digital image, The Museum of Modern Art, New York/Scala, Florence.

urban unrest of the period. David Hammons' monoprint *Injustice Case* (1970) is a chilling x-ray-like image of a woman bound to a chair and gagged, reminiscent of Bobby Seale's treatment at the 1969 trial of the Chicago Eight. An American flag serves as the border to Hammons' large image.[34] In 1990, Hammons reclaimed the American flag as a symbol of transformation and possibility in *African-American Flag* by altering its colors to the orange, black, and green of the African National Congress.[35]

As in the work of American artists, many groups have appropriated the American flag as both object and image to convey expanded notions of its political meanings. Perhaps best known is its use in protests during the Vietnam War, when it was hung upside down as a sign of distress and sometimes burned in protest of the military violence of war and to assert protestors' rights to free expression and critique of the government. The Civil Rights Movement made potent use of the American flag, documented in photography. Marchers commonly carried American flags, reclaiming an object that had become a symbol of the Ku Klux Klan in the South. In this context, the flag represented the ideals of the U.S. Constitution and Declaration of Independence, the documents that formed the bedrock of the Civil Rights Movement. Many photographs show a confluence between the flag and the body in images of African Americans and flags, as in

34 See Samella, p. 271.

35 See Rubin, *Old Glory*, copyright page.

Bruce Davidson's photograph *Three Youths on the Selma to Montgomery March, March 21–25, 1965*. One famous poster, created just after the assassination of Dr. Martin Luther King, Jr., shows a black man with an American flag painted across half of his face, the words of the Pledge of Allegiance appearing above him.[36] These images remind us that the black body is something upon which to inscribe the ideals that African Americans were seeking. It was the black body that bore the brunt of the violations of those principles in lynchings, beatings, rapes, and physical segregation.

Bruce Springsteen certainly knew about varied meanings conveyed by the flag by the time he created the *Born in the U.S.A.* cover, at least through his familiarly with the work of the Swiss-born émigré photographer Robert Frank. In 1955, Frank drove across the United States in an old car and created a powerful portrait of the American landscape, physical and social, in his classic book *The Americans*. Springsteen had shown Frank's book to art director Andrea Klein when they were working on the cover design for *Nebraska*.[37] The photograph by David Michael Kennedy that became the album cover, a highway stretching out to nowhere, resembles one of Frank's photographs. From *The Americans*, Springsteen would have known Frank's recurring interest in flags in the landscape, where flags cover or fragment bodies. In Frank's work, the flag appears as a veil or barrier. In *Parade, Hoboken, New Jersey*, for instance, a flag hanging from a building obscures a woman standing in the window, and in *Fourth of July – Jay, New York*, a large flag bisects the space of the social gathering, dividing some picnickers from others. Frank's photographs eloquently document 1950s America, showing the disparities between an official America, represented by political rallies and politicians, and an unofficial America of black funerals, motorcycle clubs, beauty pageants, bars, the street, and the highway.

Springsteen's *Nebraska* album is key to understanding "Born in the U.S.A." The song was originally recorded as a quiet acoustic tune during the creation of the *Nebraska* album, an album he recorded on a simple sound system set up in his bedroom.[38] *Nebraska* tells stories of those left out of Reagan's mornings in America. This landscape is so bleak that, as Greil Marcus commented in one essay, nihilistic acts makes sense as a form of rebellion.[39] Springsteen has said that *Nebraska* is his most autobiographical work, drawing from memories of his own childhood and the lives of his parents and grandparents.[40] His was an American family left out of the grand narrative of postwar prosperity. Springsteen took these songs into the studio to record with the E Street Band, but he eventually decided to use the original cassette tape from his bedroom recording for *Nebraska*.

36 See Gary Yanker, *Prop Art: Over 100 Contemporary Political Posters* (New York: Darien House, 1972), p. 152.

37 Arlen Schumer, *Backstreets*, Winter/Spring 1986, p. 30; see also a discussion of the song "Nebraska" and its relationship to Frank's work in Howard Hampton's "Nebraska", in Sean Wilentz and Greil Marcus (eds.), *The Rose and the Briar: Death, Love, and Liberty in the American Ballad* (New York: Norton, 2005), p. 335. See also Dave Marsh, *Glory Days*, pp. 140–141.

38 For an account about the creation of *Nebraska*, see Marsh, *Glory Days*, pp. 81–147.

39 Greil Marcus, *In the Fascist Bathroom: Punk in Pop Music* (Cambridge, MA: Harvard University Press, 1993), p. 238.

40 Bruce Springsteen, *Songs* (New York: Avon Books, 1998), p. 136.

"Born in the U.S.A." was left off. The full band version of that song became the title track of Springsteen's next album. Nonetheless, the song must still be read in relation to *Nebraska*, its original home. The musical evolution of the song makes it clear that Springsteen did not intend the song as an anthem of unexamined patriotism but as a critique of the nation's treatment of Vietnam vets.

"Born down in a dead man's town, the first kick I took was when I hit the ground", the song starts out in a cry of anguish and anger. On his 1975 classic *Born to Run*, Springsteen's character could race out of that dead man's town, taking to the highway. Here, he has "no where to run, nowhere to go".[41] Mobility itself is problematic. The young man can be sent to Vietnam and return to his country, but otherwise he's bounded by a profound sense of inertia. "Ten years burnin' down the road" only marks time from Vietnam, not movement to a new place.

The structure of the song is based on a kind of slippage – an ellipsis – with lyrical phrases trailing off into unfinished ambiguity. "Went down to my VA man, he said, 'Son, don't you understand now...'". And "Come back home to the refinery/Hiring man says, 'Son, if it were up to me...'". Slippage, in fact, is a major subject of Springsteen's songs, a fault line running between promises and realities, whether about romance or about what your county stands for or owes you. One slip –"a little hometown jam" – and you can end up in Nebraska territory: "they put a rifle in my hands and sent me off to a foreign land to go and kill the yellow man". In this context, the chorus "I was born in the U.S.A." sounds like a prison sentence, a burden as much as a statement of fact.

"Born in the U.S.A." is the centerpiece of a whole cycle of Vietnam songs by Springsteen, beginning with "Lost in the Flood" from the 1973 album *Greetings from Asbury Park*.[42] Later songs include "Shut Out the Light", also recorded during *Nebraska*, about a vet trying to readjust after returning home; and "A Good Man is Hard to Find", recorded during the *Born in the U.S.A.* period but not available until Springsteen's 1998 box set of unreleased music. In the mid 1990s, during his Tom Joad work, Springsteen wrote one of his most affecting, if little known, songs, "Brothers Under the Bridge", about a homeless vet living in the desert near Los Angeles. At the song's end, the narrative shifts, as the vet addresses his daughter. He tells her about coming back from Vietnam and standing at attention on Veterans' Day, wearing his uniform, as the color guard pass by. The song ends with the man trying to offer some explanation about how he's ended up destitute and homeless. He says, "One minute you're right there ... then something slips...". He can't go on, but the music finishes the line.

41 Jefferson Cowie in "Dead Man's Town" (cited above) also notes the line's reference to Martha Reeves and the Vandellas' song "Nowhere to Run". The line also ties to lyrics of Laura Nyro's "Eli's Coming". For a lengthy discussion of the making of *Born in the U.S.A.* see Geoffrey Himes, *Born in the U.S.A.* (New York: Continuum, 2005).

42 I hadn't listened to "Lost in the Flood" as a song about a Vietnam vet until this was pointed out to me by Dave Marsh; phone conversation with the author, July 2002.

By the time Springsteen resumed writing Vietnam songs in the early 1980s, he had already become involved with the Vietnam Veterans of America and had met and become friends with Vietnam vet Ron Kovic. Their meeting was true serendipity. On a cross-country road trip, Springsteen stopped at a motel in Los Angeles, where Kovic also happened to be staying. The singer had picked up Kovic's 1976 memoir, *Born on the Fourth of July*, at a drugstore bookrack and had read it during the trip. At poolside, Kovic recognized Springsteen and struck up a conversation. Springsteen learned that he was the author of the book he just had finished reading. Springsteen's friendship with Kovic eventually led him to connect with the Vietnam Veterans of America, a group lobbying the federal government for fair benefits and help for veterans with disabilities.[43] In 1981, Springsteen did a benefit concert that virtually saved the organization.

It bears noting that in the 1960s, Springsteen had registered for the draft, as required of young men at the time, but didn't pass the physical because of a concussion suffered in a motorcycle accident. Like many other draftees at the time, he tried to act crazy at his physical and checked all the boxes about having various illnesses and being homosexual. Though not involved in Vietnam era politics, Springsteen was deeply affected by the death of Bart Hayes, the drummer from his first band, who enlisted in the army and was killed in Vietnam.[44]

Kovic's memoir is central to a reading of "Born in the U.S.A." as song and image. He was, literally, born on the 4th of July, in 1946. Growing up in a small town on Long Island, he dreamed of playing for the Yankees and of the exploits of John Wayne and the U.S. Marines. In his memoir, Kovic chronicles his movement from an All-American Boyhood in the fifties to his stint as an enlisted Marine in Vietnam in 1964. During his round of duty, Kovic was seriously wounded, resulting in him being paralyzed from the chest down. Returning home, Kovic went through harrowing experiences at inadequate medical facilities and suffered from feelings of alienation from his family and society. He experienced a growing conviction that his sacrifice had been needless and that the killing he did in the war violated his ideas of what was just and heroic. Kovic eventually became an anti-war protestor and joined Vietnam Vets against the War.

Kovic's body and his changing awareness of it plays a central role in his story. As a boy, he admired the ideals and mythological figures of America, even making his First Communion wearing a cowboy hat and holster. As a teenager, Kovic worked hard to create an ideal male body by working out and joining the high school wrestling team. He describes his discovery of his strength and his sexuality as an adolescent, as he strove to attain an ideal masculinity in terms of physical appearance, deportment, and action. In a poignant scene, he writes

43 For the story of their meeting, see Will Percy, "Rock and Read: Will Percy's Interviews with Bruce Springsteen", *Doubletake*, Spring 1998, p. 36. Ron Kovic's book maintained visibility through Oliver Stone's 1989 film, starring Tom Cruise. Kovic has continued his activism in fighting for veterans' benefits and an end to military conflict.

44 Loder, pp. 152–153. There are some discrepancies in the Springsteen literature about the bandmate's name, which was most likely Bart or Barton Hayes. That is the name inscribed on a cross in a memorial to U.S. veterans in Freehold, New Jersey, where Springsteen grew up. In Loder's interview, the friend is named as "Bart Hanes". This may have been a transcription mistake. In my text, I have used Hayes.

about his last night at home before he leaves for the Marines, when he stands at attention before his TV with his hand over his heart as the American flag waves and the "Star Spangled Banner" plays for the station's broadcasting sign off.[45]

Art historian Abigail Solomon-Godeau has argued in *Male Trouble: The Crisis in Masculinity* that masculinity is a constructed idea, and, of course, this idea owes great debt to feminist studies about the construction of gender.[46] She distinguishes gender from biological sex, with gender being a socially constructed identity. Solomon-Godeau argues that visual imagery plays a key role in gender construction. Though she applies these ideas to eighteenth-century French painting, tracing changing attitudes about masculinity and its relationship to the new French state, they are useful in relation to other representations of masculinity. As Kovic demonstrates in his autobiography, visual images informed his notions of manhood, particularly the films of John Wayne and of the U.S. military.

This notion of a visual ideal in the representation of masculinity can inform Springsteen's *Born in the U.S.A.* image. In the cover photograph, Springsteen bears his weight on one leg, while the other leg bends casually beside it. In art historical terms, this pose is called "contrapposto" and is associated with idealized masculinity as represented in Western culture. As an artistic device, contrapposto originated in ancient Greek sculpture, departing from earlier frontal and more stilted depictions of the body. Its use continued in Roman statuary, the only remaining evidence of the Greek developments, and it was revived in sculpture during the Renaissance. This statuary represented the ideal man and the ideal citizen.

The contrapposto pose remains very familiar to American eyes today due in large part to the iconic status and circulation of images of Michelangelo's 1501 sculpture *David*. Depicting David of the Bible story – the young boy who wins against his stronger adversary, Goliath – this heroic figure remains the most famous representation of the contrapposto stance in Western art. Art historian Herbert W. Janson describes David's posture as "vibrant with pent-up energy", "at once calm and tense", showing "action-in-repose".[47]

This pose still can convey similar ideas. Historian Garry Wills recognized as much in his study of John Wayne's appeal in *John Wayne's America*. Wills notes that one thing that made Wayne a riveting presence was his use of his body. He had an uncommon grace for such a large man. Part of his physical ease was conveyed through his frequent pose in contrapposto, both on and off the set, and his signature swagger was a kind of loping contrapposto.[48] Wayne's posture conveys casualness and ease that can readily turn into action. By adopt-

45 Kovic, p. 62.

46 Abigail Solomon-Godeau, *Male Trouble: A Crisis in Representation* (London: Thames and Hudson: 1997).

47 Janson is the great canonmaker of world art history with his major surveys of *History of Art*, required in college art history classes everywhere for several decades. For his commentary on David, see *History of Art*, 5th edition revised (New York: Prentice Hall and Harry N. Abrams, Inc. 1997) p. 461. He comments further that Michelangelo's *David* embodies "fortitude" and that without the head of Goliath depicted, "here is not the victorious hero but the champion of a just cause ... here the figure has a civic-patriotic rather than moral significance".

48 Garry Wills, *John Wayne's America* (New York: Simon and Schuster, 1997), pp. 15–22, 48. Wills connects Wayne's posture to Michelangelo's David. See his illustrations at the center of the book (n.p.).

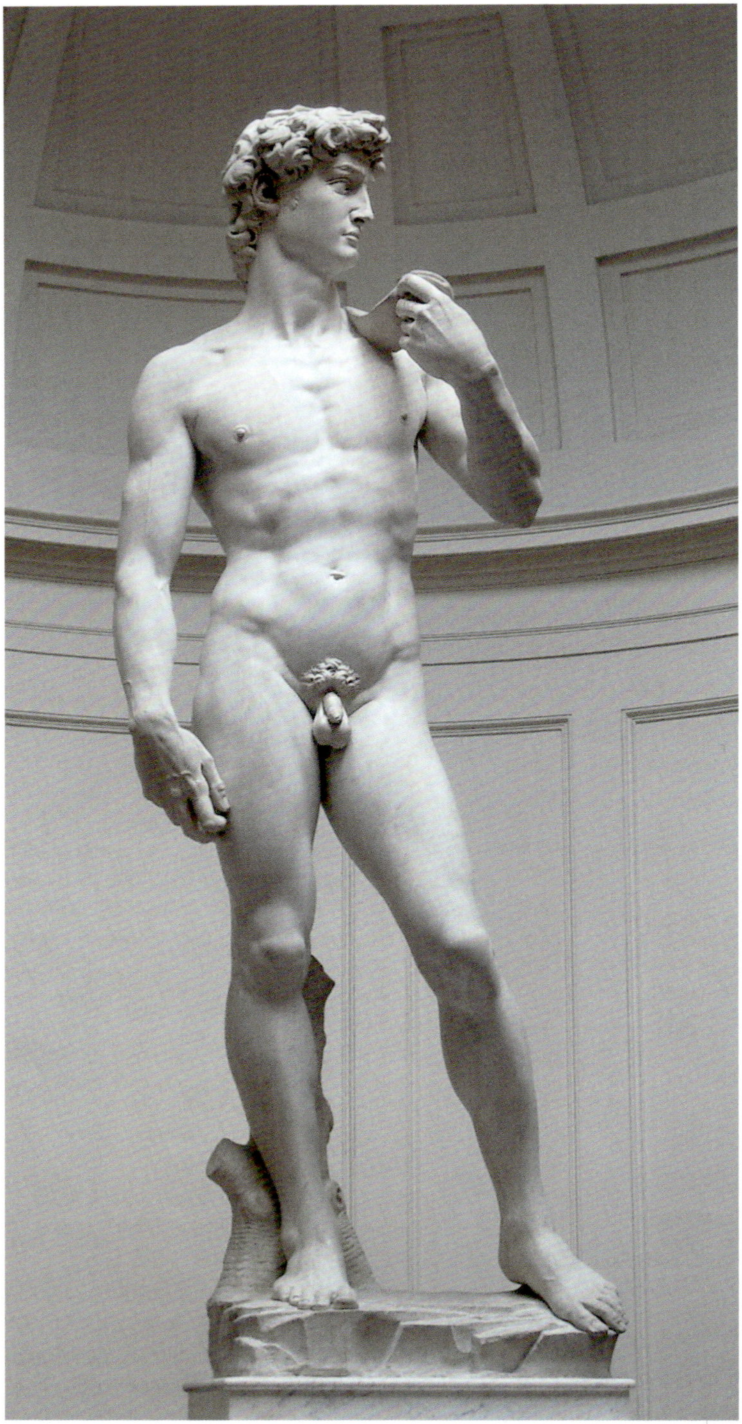

Michelangelo's David sculpture.
Photo: David Gaya.

ing this pose for the *Born in the U.S.A.* cover, Springsteen invokes our cultural associations with masculinity, strength, and restraint. In this context, his pose becomes more confrontational, more of a poised standoff between his body and the flag.

Springsteen's body can also be read as a stand-in for the body of Ron Kovic. The center of the body is represented – the loins: the very part of Kovic's body wounded in the war. Kovic's memoir is marked by an acute sense of his body. He writes about his adolescent years, "I was a natural athlete, and there wasn't much of anything I wasn't able to do with my body back then. I was proud and confident and there was a tremendous bounce to the way I moved".[49] But after returning from the war, Kovic agonizes over his disabled condition and the indignity of his medical treatment:

> The aide pushed me into the line-up in the hallway. There are frames all over the place now, lined up in front of the blue room for their enemas. It is the Six O' Clock Special. There are maybe twenty guys waiting by now. It looks like a long train, a long assembly line of broken, twisted bodies, waiting for deliverance. It is very depressing, all these bodies, half of them asleep, tied down on their frames with their rear ends sticking out.[50]

Later, he mourns his inability to have sex or to father children, saying with great anger,

> And it is gone for America. I have given it for democracy... I have given my dead swinging dick for America. I have given my numb young dick for democracy. It is gone and numb, lost somewhere out there by the river where artillery is screaming in. Oh God Oh God I want it back. I gave it for the whole country. I gave it for every one of them. Yes, I gave my dead dick for John Wayne and Howdy Doody...[51]

Kovic goes on to detail his growing political involvement against the Vietnam War, eventually deciding to use his broken body as a physical testimony against the war. Reading Kovic in relation to Springsteen's image, the album cover becomes a statement about the sacrifice of the male body in military actions.

Yet Springsteen doesn't necessarily leave us there. His bejeweled belt on *Born*'s cover invokes the rock and roll body at the same time as it references Kovic. If the military body is muscled, erect, at attention, and in service, it is also dispensable, able to be sacrificed. The rock and roll body is one of pleasure

49 Kovic, p. 54.
50 Ibid., p. 23.
51 Ibid., p. 98.

and transcendence, something that might be called "rock's ecstatic body". In performance, physical exertion and movement along with extremes of volume and emotion can move both performers and listeners to altered states (with or without the use of other substances). This corresponds to Robert Palmer's invocation of the Greek god Dionysus as the patron saint of rock and roll in his "unruly history" of the music.[52] The experience of ecstasy is one of the compelling attractions to rock and roll; it's part of the ritualistic experience of rock performance.

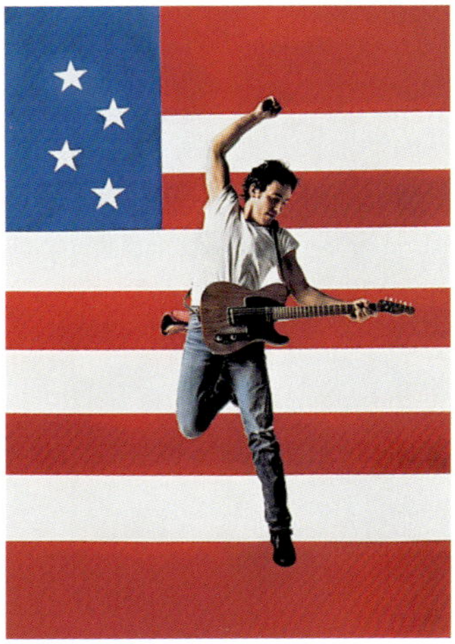

Bruce Springsteen, New York City, 1984. Cibachrome photograph. © Annie Leibovitz (Contact Press Images), courtesy of the artist.

This state of mind, spirit, and body is well represented in visual images of Springsteen's body in performance. Many images show him lost in the moment of performance or pushing himself to physical extremes for an intense experience of bodily pleasure.[53] This is muscle in the service of fun. His marathon performances can create similar responses among fans in the audience, who stand and cheer and dance for hours, reaching similar states of joy and exhaustion as the singer. In talking about his concerts and audiences, Springsteen has said, "If you get their asses moving, their spirits will follow".[54]

The twin image for *Born in the U.S.A.*'s rump shot, also taken by Leibovitz in the same studio session, reinforces this point. Appearing on the cover of the *Born in the U.S.A.* tour booklet and widely reproduced through the present, this image features Springsteen leaping like a rock and roll super hero, guitar in hand. His body is whole. He's triumphant, ecstatic. His guitar is his "choice of weapons", to borrow a phrase from photographer Gordon Parks. In this image, Springsteen has become the "cool rockin' daddy in the U.S.A.", of the song's final lyrics. He asserts himself as "the long gone daddy in the U.S.A.", harking back to the hip cats and outcasts of the Beat Generation. Here freedom is not a principle or an intellectual construct. It is literally embodied.

Political theorist Benedict Andersen theorizes that nationalism required an act of imagination to envision a broad entity of connected citizens, something he calls an "imagined community". The nation, he argues, was a concept that required connections to be forged among individuals far beyond the familiar face-to-face, local, or regional contacts during the periods when nationalism arose – late eighteenth and nineteenth centuries in the West, later, for other nations. Because the nation is an abstraction, Andersen argues, it required symbols, such as flags, and networks, such as national publications, to foster a sense of connection and commitment to a larger entity. This imaginary construct could become so compelling that men risk and even sacrifice their lives in military service to defend the nation.[55]

In contrast to Benedict's ideas about an amorphous if powerful nation-

52 Robert Palmer, *Rock and Roll: An Unruly History* (New York: Harmony Books, 1995), pp. 147–155.

53 For examples, see illustrations in Dave Marsh's *Glory Days*, n.p.

54 Sandford, p. 177.

55 Benedict Anderson, *Imagined Communities: Reflections on the Origin and Spread of Nationalism* (London and New York: Verso, 1983; reprint 1990).

alism, Springsteen's notions of a community are close and immediate. In his songs, characters strive to break away from but also to return to family and community connections. Those who remain outside of community bonds often become criminals, as in "Nebraska" or "Highway 29" from *The Ghost of Tom Joad*. Springsteen speaks of his concerts as events that bring him and his audience together in a temporary community. He has worked hard to foster this sense of direct connection and commitment with his fans, something that has evoked intense devotion to the singer among his followers.[56] Springsteen also commented that in concert even the individual alienation that he sometimes sings about can be overcome if people experience it together in a shared event, an idea he found corroborated for him by Walker Percy's essay "The Man on the Train".[57] Beyond Springsteen's direct efforts to foster connections, his fans acknowledge very meaningful relationships among kindred souls, a phenomenon documented in Daniel Cavicchi's valuable ethnography of Springsteen's fans.[58] By the time of Springsteen's participation in the 2004 presidential race, he could articulately express a broader, more abstract set of ideas that generated his notion of a nation, an imagined community, committed to "economic justice, civil rights, a humane foreign policy, freedom and a decent life for all of our citizens". Yet at the same time, Springsteen still brought the demands of nationalism and patriotism close to home in interviews with *Nightline* journalist Ted Koppel. When questioned about why he, as a pop singer, should comment on politics, Springsteen replied that his son was fourteen and, as a father, Springsteen anticipated his son having to deal with a possible Vietnam-style war in Iraq, a possibility that also echoed the times Springsteen had lived through as a young man.[59]

As this examination of Springsteen's *Born in the U.S.A.* record cover argues, the singer's work can be read as one long meditation about masculinity and American mythologies, the individual and our civic life. If masculinity, as Solomon-Godeau has argued, is unstable and constantly in flux, images can try to pin it down. Springsteen explores the *instability* of masculinity as well as the uncertain meanings of patriotism and allegiance in both song and image. His loaded imagery – the flag, the car, the highway – is multivalent. Despite their familiarity, these images are not always easily read and require the kind of complex analysis that other works of art receive.

If we return to Bruce's butt again, one final question that must be asked involves where our position as viewers exists. Where do we stand? We stand behind him. Springsteen insists that we join him in reflecting on masculinity and American ideals. The album image insists that a consideration of body and flag, individual and nation, pleasure and sacrifice is inescapable. You can turn the

56 See, for instance, Springsteen's comment in Paul Nelson's "Springsteen Fever", *Rolling Stone*, 13 July 1978, reprinted in *Bruce Springsteen: The Rolling Stone Files* (New York, Hyperion, 1996), p. 72.

57 Walker Percy, "The Man on the Train", in *The Message in the Bottle: How Queer Man Is, How Queer Language Is and What One Has to Do with the Other* (New York: Farrar, Straus, and Giroux, 1975), pp. 83–100. In this essay, Percy writes about an imaginary commuter on a train and the way in which art can break through the loneliness of existence: "The nonreading commuter exists in true alienation, which is unspeakable; the reading commuter rejoices in the speakability of his alienation and in the new triple alliance of himself, the alienated character, and the author".

58 See the chapter "Belonging Together: Fandom, Community, and Connection", in Daniel Cavicchi, *Tramps Like Us: Music and Meaning Among Springsteen Fans* (New York: Oxford University Press, 1998), pp. 158–193.

59 Bruce Springsteen, "Chords of Change", *New York Times*, 5 August 2004, Section A, p. 23. Koppel's interview was broadcast on 4 August 2004.

album over, but it's still there. Today, as the Iraq war wages on, at a time when the flag-draped coffins of dead American soldiers remain invisible, banned from appearing in the news,[60] Springsteen's *Born in the U.S.A.* image and the issues it raises revive the need to examine bodies and flags.

60 On 26 February 2009 this ban was lifted by President Obama.

Remediation of Album Art

Neil Young's *Greendale*

Nicole R. Brown

meanwhile across the ocean
living in the internet
is the cause of an explosion
no one has heard yet
Neil Young, "Leave the Driving", Greendale

To consider the visual-rhetorical functions of album covers, one would likely assign close attention to the elements of graphics, colors, and themes. Album covers are historical artifacts; the images and titles sponsored by artists simultaneously document and create social and historical contexts. For instance, a genealogical analysis of Neil Young's thirty-nine albums constructs a timeline of hippy culture that moves from psychedelic Woodstock to include a more recent album, *Greendale*. The songs and images of *Greendale* tell the story of the Green family – Woodstock-era folks finding their way as contemporary grandparents and citizens living in Northern California in the small (seemingly fictional) town of Greendale. There is another layer, however, to Young's attention to *time* that is made visible through a simultaneous analysis of *Greendale* and the influence of emerging visual and multimedia technologies on our lives and the ever-shifting music industry.

A stroll through most music stores reveals that things have changed dramatically since 1939, when graphic designer Alex Steinweiss augmented the music industry by inventing the illustrated album cover.[1] Steinweiss' approach to attracting people to music through the mode of the visual followed other industry trends at the time, taking advantage of product packaging that could serve the dual purposes of protecting and advertising products. Prior to this

1 Jennifer McKnight-Trontz and Alex Steinweiss, *For the Record: The Life and Work of Alex Steinweiss Inventor of the Album Cover* (New York: Princeton Architectural Press, 2000), p. 1.

time, the music industry's visual-based traditions were limited to promotional posters and booklets for live musical acts. The incorporation of art onto album covers became a means for attracting people to music through the medium of the visual, as well as providing potential listeners with a hint of what to expect from the record inside. Along with protecting the easily scratched vinyl, album covers became a genre worth analyzing, collecting, and enjoying with the music. Stated simply, the album cover has evolved from the carrier of music to becoming an integral part of the music experience and social history.

Due to the diminished canvas size and the subsequent demise of the artwork that comprised the album's sleeve, the music industry's shift to cassettes and compact discs was a disappointment to most fans of album art. Some music critics, however, weighed the scaled-down size of the canvas against evolving visual technologies and computer graphic programs that allow both large and independent labels to incorporate the visual with words in their cover designs. In an age of one-song downloads and the online trading and pirating of music, initial concerns over the diminished canvas size seem moot. As claims are being made for a new semiotics to account for a text-based culture gone visual,[2] the visual experience associated with music may be at an all time low. To address the possible connection between the loss of advertising space and decreasing revenues, the music industry is employing innovative and resourceful ways for creating visual experiences around music that feels "real" to potential audiences.[3]

In considering the remediation of album art in an age of multimedia options and digital delivery systems, there are other variables to be considered alongside the seemingly diminished canvas size. According to Jay David Bolter and Richard Grusin, multimedia technologies are creating a culture around media being perpetually remediated.[4] For Bolter and Grusin, acts of remediation involve older media being refashioned by new media, resulting in (1) the act of mediation becoming more transparent and/or (2) the inter-media relations becoming more visible.[5] As Bolter and Grusin note:

> The idea of excess has been part of the popular music culture for decades. At first the excess was achieved simply by turning up the volume, until the sound could be felt as well as heard. More recently, the stage production of popular musicians has emphasized the visual spectacle and the acknowledgement of multiple media. The excessive, highly self-conscious video style of MTV is one result, and the music spectacle CD_ROMS obviously remediate MTV. The excess of media becomes an authentic experience, not in the sense that it corresponds to an external reality, but

2 Gunther Kress, "English at the Crossroads: Rethinking Curricula of Communication in the Context of the Turn to the Visual", in Gail E. Hawisher and Cynthia L. Selfe (eds.), *Passions, Pedagogies, and 21st Century Technologies* (Logan, UT: Utah State University Press/NCTE, 1999), pp. 66–88.

3 John Forss, Jo March, Graham Coxon, and Scott Burnett, "Creative Design and Packaging: Wear Your Art on Your Sleeve", *Music Week*, 2 October 2004.

4 Jay David Bolter and Richard Grusin, *Remediation: Understanding New Media* (Cambridge, MA: The MIT Press, 2000).

5 Ibid.

rather precisely because it is does not feel compelled to anything beyond itself.[6]

In the case of the multimedia package that makes up Neil Young's *Greendale*, the viewer is asked to look beyond the excess of media to discover how remediated texts construct versions of reality in complex and relevant ways. As John Walker and Sarah Chaplin note, in their introduction to *Visual Culture*, visual culture is reproduced in various forms – books, magazine, television, music video, etc. While transformations of color, scale, texture, etc. are certainly enabled through the refashioning of images in different mediums, for Walker and Chaplin, access to a diverse range of mediums for delivering visual artifacts not only creates a *visual* experience but a *material* experience as well.[7]

The story of *Greendale* is told through complex integrations of image, text, video, and sound that produce cultural and technological artifacts that embrace and even complicate Jean Baudrillard's notion of *simulacra*.[8] For Baudrillard, simulacra are signs or artifacts that come to be known as the real, while in actuality they have no representational relationships to the real or to the assumption that there is no real. Over time, simulacra become known as real by negating themselves as signs or artifacts. Contemporary society is one dominated by image-based simulacra, and in *Picture Theory* W.J.T. Mitchell makes a case for a critical interpretation of how "texts act like pictures or 'incorporate' pictorial practices and vice versa".[9] Keeping these contextual premises in mind, the *Greendale* package raises important questions regarding the interplay between (1) the origins of production and delivery through multiple forms of media and (2) representational practices.

Forms of Media

The cover image on the *Greendale* album declares little about the Green family and the album's political commentary on small-town America, contemporary media, political and corporate power, and the erosion of civil liberties and the environment. Rather, the album cover is a simple, two-tone, aerial sketch of the town. Demanding active participation on behalf of the viewer, the map is annotated with text on the album's corresponding web site and viewers are encouraged to "orient" themselves with the visual rhetorics that construct *Greendale*. Likewise, the online map highlights locations relevant to the town's story – such as the local art gallery [the "L" Gallery] and the Green family farm [the Double "E" Rancho]. Inside the CD booklet are two-toned sketched drawings of par-

6 Ibid., pp. 54–55.

7 John A. Walker and Sarah Chaplin, *Visual Culture: An Introduction* (New York: St. Martin's Press, 1997), p. 198.

8 Jean Baudrillard, *Simulations* (New York: Semiotext[e], 1983).

9 W.J.T. Mitchell, *Picture Theory: Essays on Verbal and Visual Representation* (Chicago: University of Chicago Press, 1994), p. 4.

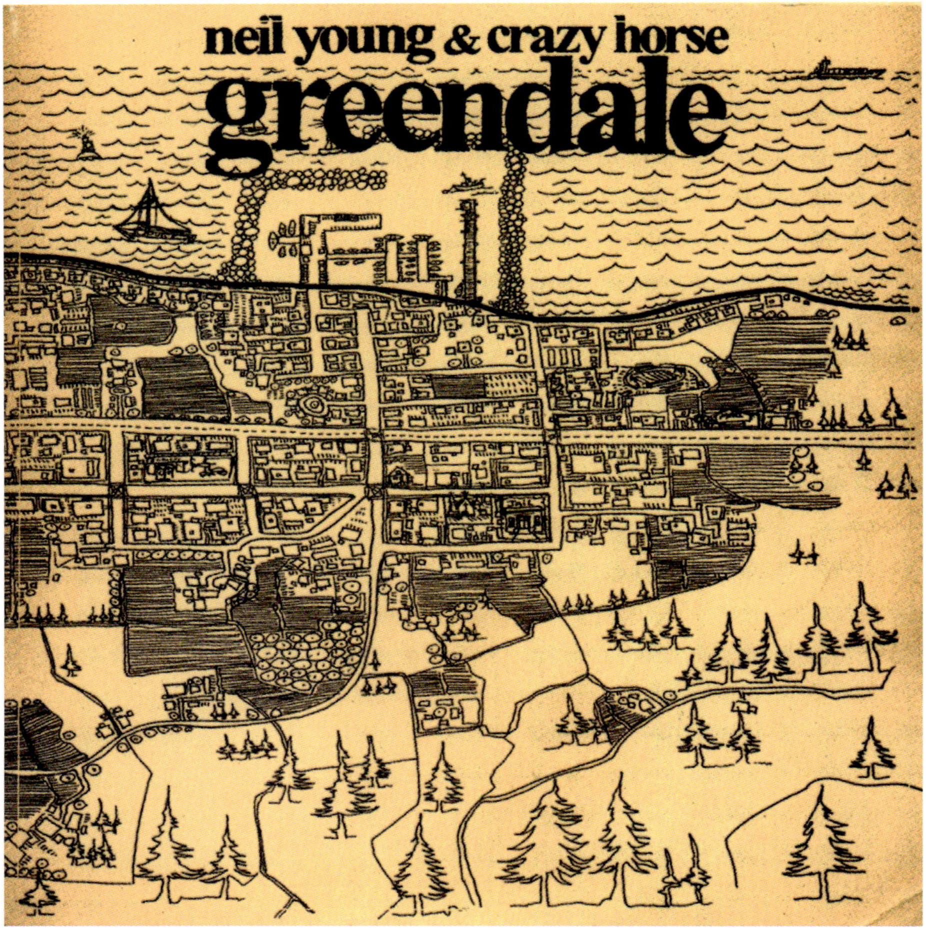

Captain John Green's boat (left of the left hand pier) · Jed's seafish apartment (to the right of the boat) · Scene of the crime (on the far left, where the road that dissects Greendale enters the map) · Carmichael's house (between the road and the ocean, near the centre of the map) · John Lee's bar, Greendale Mortuary (scene of Carmichael's service), Sun's room at rooming house (scene of FBI raid), Greendale High School, Motel (all near the pier and ocean, between the pier and the far right of the map) · Double 'E' Ranch (in the bottom left corner of the map) · Jail, grandma and grandpa's house, gallery (all below the main road, near the center of town).

Greendale Map. Neil Young & Crazy Horse, *Greendale*, album cover (U.S.A., Reprise Records, 2003).

ticular Greendale residents, which create a visual experience around the song titles and the stories written beneath. In the *Greendale* CD booklet, there is a clear absence of lyrics, despite its pages well exceeding the number of songs on the album. Instead, song titles are accompanied with portrait-like images and text-based narratives about the songs, the town, its residents, and important life-events. While the images that comprise the CD's packaging appear undemanding, the overall visual experience of the *Greendale* album, developed through various modes of multimediated representation, is quite complex.

The artwork for the *Greendale* CD cover, which is also the index of the web site and the cover of the trade publication book, establishes the centralizing image of the Greendale multimedia package – the illustrated map of the fictional California town. Viewed independently from the diverse scope of media employed to create the overall visual and interpretive experience of the album, the cover, at first glance, doesn't leave much for analysis.

Upon further study, however, one might conclude that this map could be a map of any small town, which seems to be Young's point. Despite the universality of the image-map, however, any subsequent interpretation of *Greendale* must also consider the following combinations of media made available to its viewers:

1. the recorded music of Neil Young and Crazy Horse published on CD;
2. the CD cover and booklet with sketched drawings and a narrative telling the story of the town and its residents;
3. a DVD of Neil Young's acoustic performance of Greendale at Vicar Street, Dublin, Ireland [included as part of the CD purchase];
4. a live performance of a multimedia rock opera/concert, consisting of several stages, 30+ actresses/actors, cardboard set designs, and a video screen broadcasting images also displayed in the CD booklet, the Greendale movie, and trade publication book;
5. a low-production film shown in theaters and available on DVD [and the text-based script for producing it, which is available through the web site];
6. a highly developed web site enabling users to zoom in and pan around Young's invented world;
7. a series of original artwork by James Mazzeo and Lou Grappi, integrated as an important part of the Greendale story;
8. a written and recorded narrative on the web site about the town, its residents, and their stories/histories otherwise absent from the music experience, including a range of image-based genres such as a Green family tree;
9. a trade publication book that compiles the images, narrative, lyrics, and artwork of Greendale into a print resource apart from the music.

While a scan of this list will show how the contemporary influence of multimedia on the music industry is undeniable, to reduce the *Greendale* project to an example of album art being remediated alongside the changing music industry does not represent the project's rhetorical complexities.

Utilizing the media capabilities of the World Wide Web, the *Greendale* web site includes elements taken from each part of the *Greendale* package listed above. Through the use of Flash media, visitors to the site can zoom-in to relevant locations situated spatially on the sketched map that comprises the CD cover. The image of the map functions as a semantic reference useful for spatially situating and recalling the events of the Greendale story. Beneath the animated map that is also the centralizing image on the web site, there are a series of ten smaller images linked to index pages on the web site for: the Book; the Music; the Album Tracks; the Lyrics; a High Resolution Map; the DVD Chapters (including the script and series of still-framed images); a Narrative of the Greendale story [text and audio]; an image- and text-based Green Family Tree; the "L" [art] Gallery; and the Movie Premier.

Throughout the *Greendale* web site, the image-experience for the viewer is created in distinguishable ways. The images on the site move between high- and low-resolution, three- and two-dimensional, static and animated, two-toned and full-spectrum color, and audio and textual. For example, a visitor to the DVD index can, with selections from the album playing, select from ten DVD chapters organized in the order of the songs on the album. Once selected, a chronological slideshow of frames captured from the Greendale movie are viewable in color. In addition, visitors to the site can view the text-based script for each DVD chapter, making visible the writing behind the production of the story and images that create the town and its residents.

Similarly, visitors to the fictional art gallery – "L" Gallery – are greeted with photographs, web-cam video, and operating hours and directions, as well as an opportunity to visit The Redwood Wing – a virtual gallery of artist Earl Green's [a lead character in the Greendale story] paintings. Visitors to the "L" Gallery's Redwood Wing can take a virtual tour of Earl's paintings that in "reality", showcase work done by psychedelic artist James Mazzeo. In the story of *Greendale*, Mazzeo, a psychedelic artist and long-time friend of Neil Young, is Earl Green – a Vietnam veteran, artist, and primary character in the Greendale story. The character of Earl Green occupies a complex space between a representation of nonfictional reality and a production of fictional reality.

In the tradition of film-based acting, Mazzeo characterizes Earl Green through a series of images that range from Mazzeo's performance of Earl Green in the *Greendale* movie, to a photographic image of Earl Green/James Mazzeo available on the web site, to a series of sketched images available in the CD, the trade publication book, and online. Mazzeo is the author of these sketched images, as well as the artist behind the paintings done by Green currently on display in the "L" Gallery. These paintings are viewable in the context of *Greendale* through the movie, the "L" Gallery node of the web site, and the trade publication book. Earl's artwork (aka Mazzeo's) is on display at the "L" Gallery along with another artist's, Lou Grappi's. A photo of Grappi with Earl/Mazzeo and the "L" Gallery's fictional owner, Lenore, is posted on the gallery's web site. While

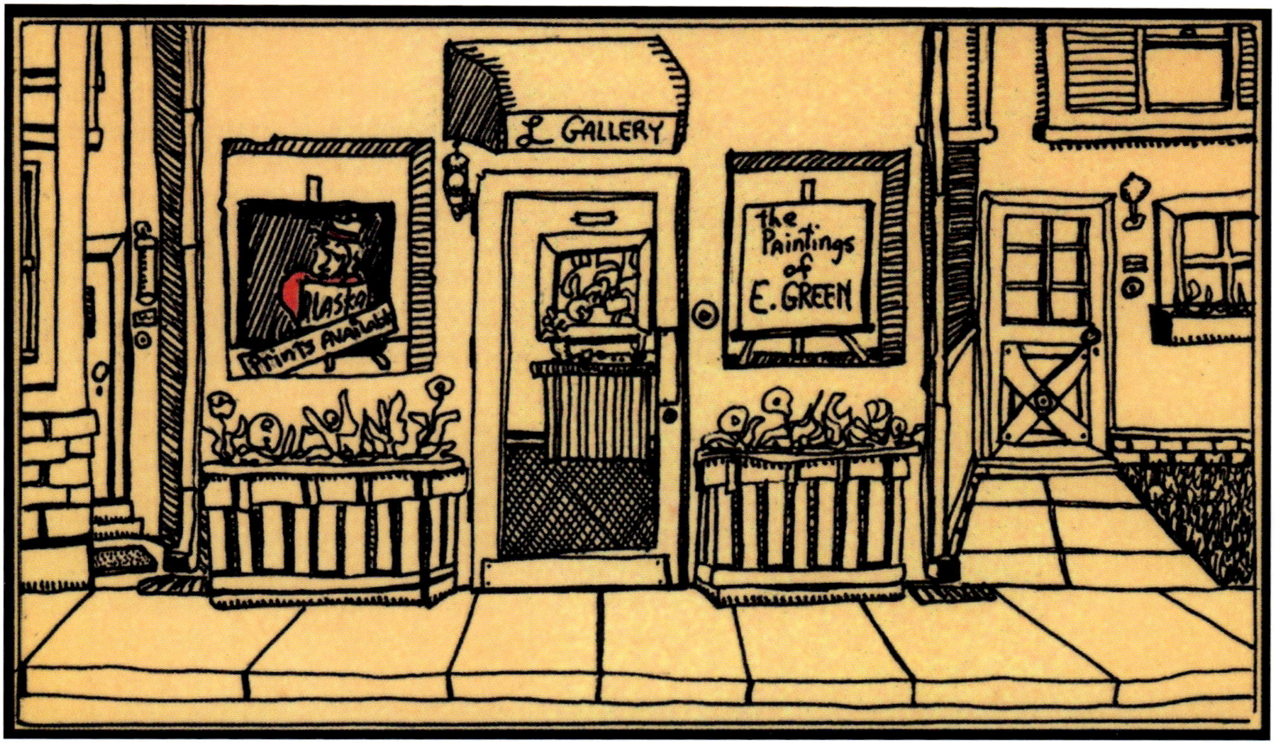

The "L" Gallery. Neil Young, *Greendale* (London U.K.: Sanctuary Publishing, 2004). Courtesy of James Mazzeo.

it is not uncommon for artists to be petitioned for creating album covers, such as Andy Warhol's famous banana cover from *The Velvet Underground featuring NICO*, it was not the cover art that was the job of Mazzeo. In fact, Neil Young created the centralizing image – the map of Greendale – and Mazzeo signifies a much more complex relationship between character, image, and reality.

The sketched image of the "L" Gallery is remediated throughout the Greendale package to include streaming video and high-definition images on the *Greendale* web site.

Online, visitors can view photographs of actual paintings and print postcards from home. The photographic images of the paintings and streaming video of the gallery opening signifies for the viewer a material reality that exists apart from the *Greendale* package. The photographic images emerge as simulacra by juxtaposing the sketched image of the Redwood Wing with the photographic images available on the web site. As Jean Baudrillard, drawing on Borges, notes in "Photography, or the Writing of Light", "the photographic image materially translates the absence of reality which 'is so obvious and so easily accepted because we already have the feeling that nothing is real' (Borges)".[10]

10 Jean Baudrillard, "Photography, Or the Writing of Light", *ctheory.net* 12 (April 2000), www.ctheory.net/articles.aspx?id=126 (accessed 1 December 2005), p. 4.

Photographic images that complicate representations of the real in album art are quite common. Take, for example, the cover of *Sgt. Pepper's Lonely Hearts Club Band*. Drawing on an even more diverse range of [re]mediations, the *Greendale* package, through the continuous juxtaposition of image, text, and multiple forms of media, demands viewers to question mediated representations and their relationships to the construction of basic reality.

Narratives recorded and transcribed from live performances by Neil Young that construct the town and residents of Greendale through story and song are also available on the *Greendale* web site through audio- and text-files. Speaking about Earl's paintings, Young encourages viewers of the Greendale package to participate in an interactive process of meaning making and to consider images this way:

> When you look at Earl's paintings, first of all you just see a kind of blur of lines and colors. The longer you look at them, the more you see – until finally you can see people talking and making love and fighting and kicking each other and playing cards, doing all kinds of things. All Earl's paintings are like that.[11]

Throughout the *Greendale* package, the cyclical process of producing, distributing, and consuming media is made visible for viewers to consider how we – even as listeners of music – participate in the social construction of reality. Simultaneous to this, through the integration of sound, photography, text, web, painting, music, as well as other image- and text-based genres, the *Greendale* package represents how multi-mediated realities are ubiquitous in our lives. The argument that Neil Young uses media to raise attention to and even critique media is further supported through a discussion of the representational practices in the *Greendale* package.

Representational Practices

Telling the story of a small town and its residents, *Greendale* is a visual-, audio-, and text-based commentary on political, social, and environmental issues. Because the *Greendale* multimedia package is structured around a theme-based story, it may be considered a concept album. Music critics often view concept albums as pretentious, since they frequently deal with political issues where some believe the entertainment industry does not belong. More recently, however, music critics have been discussing the comeback of the concept album as an at-

11 Neil Young and Crazy Horse, "Telling the Story", *Greendale CD* (Reprise Records, 2003).

tempt by artists to discourage one-song downloads in an era of digital listening. In either situation, concept albums can be viewed as a representational practice being redeveloped in chord with the contemporary socio-political climate.

In *The Great Good Place*, Ray Oldenberg critiques how spaces for the creation of community are no longer available in modern life where there has been an overall decrease in shared, public space.[12] For many, like Oldenberg, new technologies offer mediums for social exchange by creating opportunities for community-life online – i.e. online communities. In his discussion of the online community *The Well*, Howard Rheingold states that logging into a particular online community or message board is "similar to the feeling of peeking into the cafe, the pub, the common room, to see who's there, and whether you want to stay around for a chat".[13] Through the multimedia construction of *Greendale*, Neil Young takes the metaphor of community online to another level by constructing Greendale around "conceptual modes of representation rather than pictorial duplication of visible reality".[14]

The visual, textual, and audio representations of the town of Greendale and its residents do not participate in an intrusion of reality on existing community structures as much as an establishment of a [re]mediated reality. These image-based representations reveal something about the voyeuristic experience advanced through the larger hyper-mediated times within which we live. The voyeuristic desires and duties of contemporary American culture that the *Greendale* package relies upon are summarized by Young in the lyrics of *Leave the Driving to Us* – "and we'll be watching you/no matter what you do/and you can do your part/by watching others too".[15] Along with developing an understanding of just how partial such an experience is, these lyrics represent exactly what viewers of the *Greendale* package are being asked to do. These lyrics, when considered alongside the voyeuristic feel of the images associated with Greendale, offer perspectives on what Walker and Chaplin refer to as "the magnifying power of modern media".[16]

Through the use of image-based media, the *Greendale* package uses media to critique the intrusion and false representations advanced by an overabundance of media in our lives. Young draws upon our desires towards both community and voyeurism while exposing the overwhelming access to media as simultaneously empowering and destructive. For instance, early in the *Greendale* story the listener/viewer experiences the death of Grandpa that follows the Green family becoming a "human-interest" story. Commenting on the events that eventually lead to Grandpa's passing, Young states in an interview with Ted Greenwald from *Wired*,

12 Ray Oldenburg, *The Great Good Places: Cafes, Coffee Shops, Community Centers, Beauty Parlors, General Stores, Bars, Hangouts, and How They Get You Through the Day* (New York: Paragon House, 1989).

13 Howard Rheingold, *The Virtual Community: Homesteading on the Electronic Frontier* (Reading: Addison Wesley, 1993), p. 26.

14 Leslie Devereaux, "An Introductory Essay", in Leslie Devereaux and Roger Hillman (eds.), *Fields of Vision: Essays in Film Studies, Visual Anthropology, and Photography* (Berkeley: University of California Press, 1995), p. 12.

15 Neil Young and Crazy Horse, "Leave the Driving", *Greendale CD* (Reprise Records, 2003).

16 Walker and Chaplin, p. 201.

> The media wants to know how it feels to have a cop killer in the family. Why is it OK to ask that question? The TV guys think everybody has a right to know, but the fact is, nobody has a right to know anything other than whether Jed is guilty or innocent.[17]

In the *Greendale* film, as well as through a series of images published online and in the trade publication book, the Greendale audience is presented, in ways similar to Grandpa, with a series of images that remediate media sources – ranging from newspapers to news cameras. The overabundance of media in Greendale, which is too much for Grandpa to handle, promotes an understanding that nothing is private and everything is available for the consumption of others, including the town and the Green family. This premise is further supported in the caption written over the image of the town map on the web site, which reads "this town is now available".

Young makes an additional, perhaps even contrasting, point about the role of contemporary media in our lives by raising attention towards relationships between social agency and media access. Available in the trade publication book and on the *Greendale* web site (as a frame captured from the *Greendale* film) is an image of Sun Green – the young, radical and environmentalist granddaughter to Grandpa. In the still-frame available on the web site, Sun is lying on her bed watching the news on television with books lying next to her. The cover of one book reads *Use Media*. In the sketched remediation of the same image published in the trade publication book, the titles of two additional books lying on Sun's bed are visible: *Saving the Earth* and *Alaska Paradise*. In addition, the title of one of the books shown in the trade publication book reads *How to Use the Media* rather than *Use Media* as shown on the web site. The book *How to Use the Media* is layered over another book presumably on the '60s – the decade that television and newspapers became distinctly separated and the roots of the Internet were established.

An analysis of the frame turned sketch (or vice versa), shows the planning and complexities of the images captured during the filming of the movie and Young's overall argument regarding the relationship between advocacy and the critical use of contemporary media even in contexts related to saving the planet, where many might feel that the mis-use of technology is to blame.

To show contradictions in the use of media, Young, operating under his pseudonym Bernard Shakey, used Super 8 film blown up to 35 millimeter for the production of the *Greendale* movie. Super 8 filming is reminiscent of classic films because it reflects light and, therefore, provides more grainy and textured

17 Ted Greenwald, "The Reinvention of Neil Young, Part 6", *Wired Magazine*, 12 March 2004, www.wired.com/wired/archive/12.03/young (accessed 17 January 2005), p. 7.

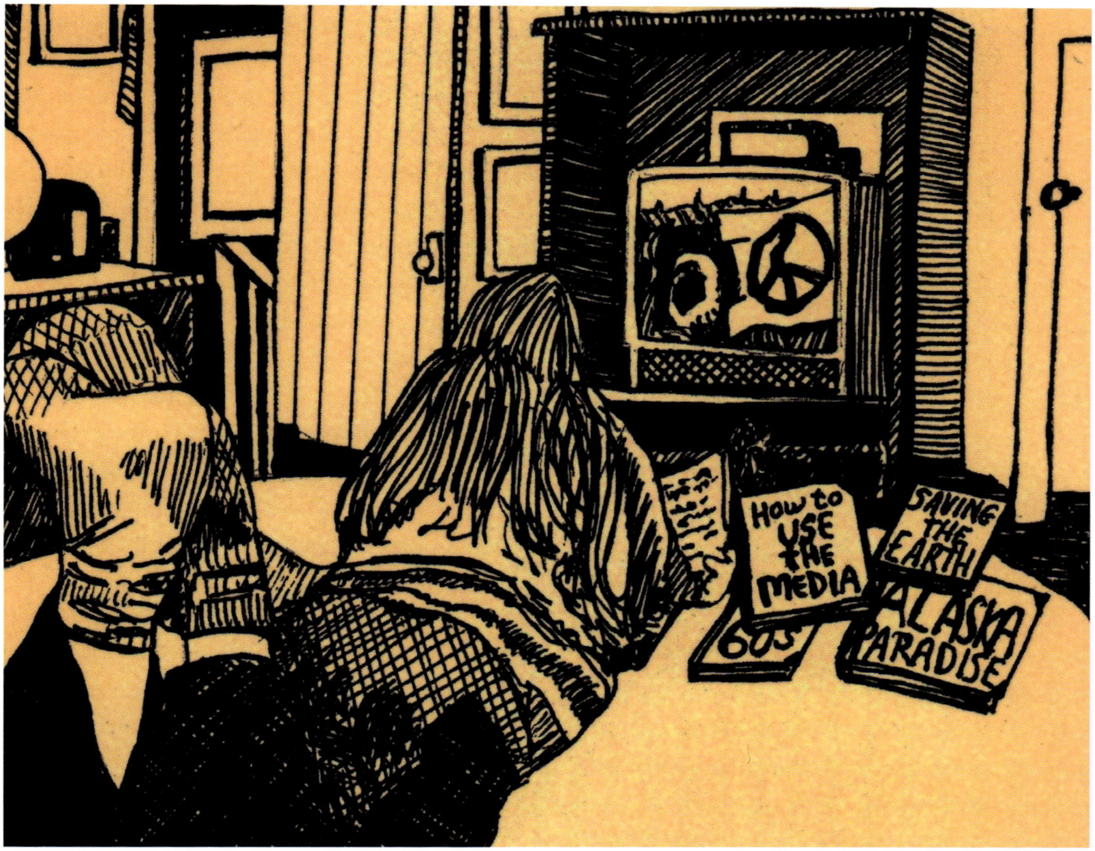

Sun Green: Use the Media. Neil Young, *Greendale* (London U.K.: Sanctuary Publishing, 2004). Courtesy of James Mazzeo.

images than digital video. The homemade quality of the image captured through Super 8 filming makes the mediation process much more visible than digital video. When asked if he considered using digital video to film *Greendale*, Young responded:

> Only as an effect. I mean, if you wanted something real clean that represented the establishment, that represented the news media, that represented government official proclamations and everything like that, I think video is a great tool for that.[18]

Young did use digital video to shoot scenes in the *Greendale* movie that involved reporting by the mainstream media, particularly the news. Like the other forms of media that construct the *Greendale* package, the *Greendale* film complicates divisions between constructions of reality and reflections of reality by using

18 Chris Fujiwara, "Neil on Film: A Rocker Takes His CD to the Screen", *ThePortlandPhoenix.com*, www.portlandphoenix.com/music/other_stories/documents/03702366.asp (accessed 17 January 2005), p. 4.

multi-mediated modes of representation, even through juxtaposed films. In addition to the thoughtful use of film effects in the *Greendale* movie, the limited use of color in most of the images on the web site and in the trade publication book aligns itself well with Young's desire to expose media while complicating the modes of production. As Bolter and Grusin note, "hypermedia and transparent media are opposite manifestations of the same desire: the desire to get past the limits of representation and to achieve the real".[19]

When asked about the overabundant use of media in the *Greendale* package, Young, in an interview with Greenwald, reflects on the character of Sun Green commenting that, "Sun has taught me how to use the media to do something positive... Then I'll be able to prostitute myself for something positive, instead of just selling a record".[20] Through her actions and the corresponding images that represent her character, Sun Green models what it means to "use media". In an audio recording taken during a live concert performance (also transcribed and published as a sound-file on the web site), Young identifies one of the diverse forms of media employed by Sun to communicate with audiences beyond the small town of Greendale:

> Sun wants to be an artist, maybe a performance artist. She's working on something out in the field she wants a lot of people to see someday. She's working in hay. She carries bales of hay on the back of a flatbed truck out into the middle of the field on a green hillside, and that's her canvas.[21]

By arranging bales of hay on a hillside in Greendale, Sun creates a large peace sign with the inscription "No War" that becomes an image for passengers flying over Greendale, as well as an image used during the rock-opera that shares the stage with Young during his live concert performance of the album. Other media events employed by Sun include, "chaining herself to a statue of an eagle/in the lobby of PowerCo" and announcing the company's dirty deeds through a megaphone during which "news cameras recorded the speech" creating "a golden moment/in the history of TV news/no one could explain it/it just got great reviews".[22] In another instance, Sun Green is charged for possessing marijuana, which again "made the headline news/but then the charges all got dropped/and the story got confused".[23]

On the Greendale web site, the DVD and in the trade publication book, visitors can view a flowchart image of the Green family tree, read biographies about each family member, and view their sketched portraits. Sun Green's location on the Green Family Tree is significant. The visual depiction of the Green

19 Bolter and Grusin, p. 53.

20 Ibid., p. 13.

21 Neil Young and Crazy Horse, "Telling the Story", *Greendale CD* (Reprise Records, 2003).

22 Neil Young and Crazy Horse, "Sun Green", *Greendale CD* (Reprise Records, 2003).

23 Ibid.

family shows how, in a time when most family trees are expanding to incrementally include more members, the Green family tree tiers are decreasing. Of the four lowest tiered members (those presumably of child bearing age), Jacob and Luna Green are deceased, Jed Green is in jail, and Sun Green has gone to Alaska to "be a goddess in the planet wars/tryin' to save the livin' things".[24] The image of the family tree and the earthly names it contains reveals that the Green family, as their name suggests, is a symbol of the environment and nature. As the chart of the diminishing family tree suggests, there is a shared relationship between the declining state of the environment and the decreasing size of the Green family. The family members on the tree – their images, names, and biographies – represent the challenges of contemporary life.

The *Greendale* album/project is a representation of how the visual genres of album covers are shifting alongside access to technologies/new media and articulates the possibilities when the flat-landscape of an album cover like Young's *Greendale* is brought to life, not only representing but becoming social history. In the intricate context of *Greendale*, the viewer is called upon to be media savvy – to process media and construct their own understandings of the events assembled through a diverse range of mediums. In a day and age when fans are more frequently positioned as consumers of media, the demands placed upon the reader in the context of the *Greendale* packages raises attention to how readers create symbolic realities. The participation that the *Greendale* package requires on behalf of the listener/reader establishes an interplay between the *Greendale* project and the larger socio-political context within which the work is being received. There is a certain level of irony to Neil Young's cautionary comment that "[t]oday entertainment and news are being blended together so you can't tell the difference".[25] By making visible the production of Greendale as a construction of reality, the Greendale package also, to borrow the words of Jean Baudrillard, "masks and perverts a basic reality".[26]

24 Ibid.

25 Greenwald, p. 12.

26 Baudrillard, *Simulations*, p. 11.

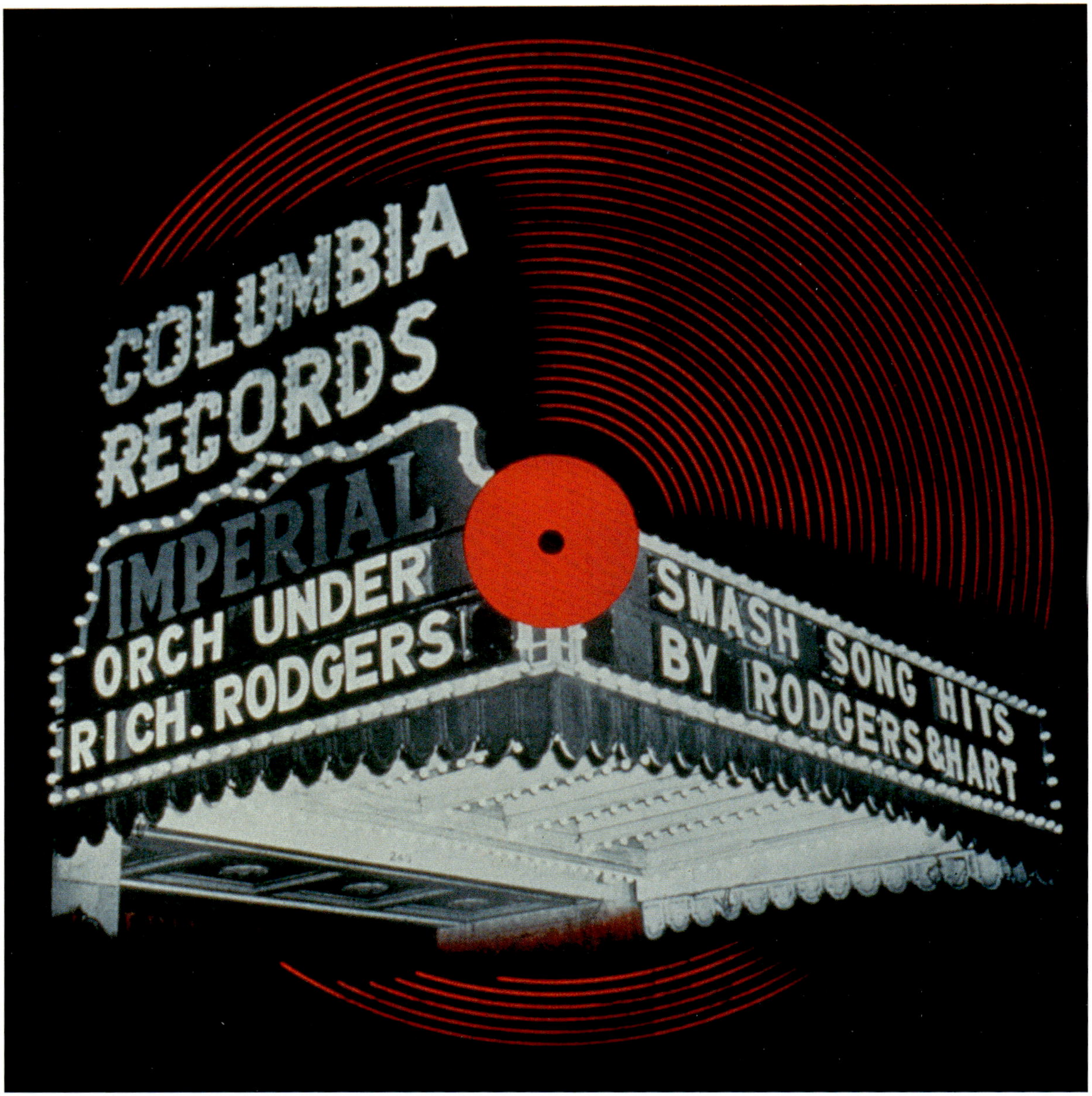

Smash Song Hits by Rodgers & Hart, album cover. Designed by Alex Steinweiss, 1939.

Envisioning Music in the Digital Environment

Anne Galperin

In 1939 Alex Steinweiss, a 23-year-old graphic designer at Columbia Records, created the first record album cover as we know it, replacing the previously unadorned cardboard sleeve with a new aesthetic interface and, in the process, established an irrevocable association between visual and musical identities. Some six decades later, album art, as defined by the 12-inch vinyl format, is mostly the subject of nostalgia. And while there is a growing trend to package CDs as fine art objects and artists' books, it is digital technologies and the increasing ubiquity of downloadable audio files that continue to transform commercial music's traditional, static, visual interface. In the age of iPods and iMusic, and particularly in the context of powerful laptop computers used by musicians and graphic designers alike, the visual aspect of contemporary music has clearly evolved. How have these representational changes come about, and what do they mean?

Because art directors and graphic designers (in varying degrees of collaboration with musicians) have traditionally created the visual imagery which describes and promotes music,[1] this essay engages questions which are part of critical graphic design practice, including: how does technology affect representation, design practice, and distribution/consumption? What is the relationship between the work and the audience?[2] To put the issue of design for music in a historical context, this genre of work tends to be marginalized within the profession because its "problem solving" aspects do not seem sufficiently serious. Despite Steinweiss' considerable talents as a designer, his significant contributions to visual culture, and a book showcasing his album cover work,[3] first-rank status in the field has historically been granted to more mainstream practitioners.[4]

Apple's Macintosh computer, launched in 1984, was a breakthrough in representational technology for graphic designers, because both letterforms and images were reduced to the same atomistic constituent part, the pixel, and

1 There are some notable exceptions in which musicians designed and produced their own album covers, including Joni Mitchell (who studied painting, fine and commercial art), Jerry Harrison, and Don Van Vliet/Captain Beefheart. Storm Thorgerson and Aubrey Powell, *100 Best Album Covers* (New York: Dorling Kindersley Publishing Inc., 1999), pp. 11–12, 52–53, 70–71.

2 I should state here that I am a graphic designer and not a musician, but my argument rests on an assumption that a parallel line of questioning also applies to contemporary music practice.

3 Jennifer McKnight-Trontz and Alex Steinweiss, *For the Record: The Life and Work of Alex Steinweiss* (New York: Princeton Architectural Press, 2000).

4 Rick Poyner, in "Mark Farrow: Knowing" (*Eye*, vol. 6, no. 24 (Spring 1997), p. 27), makes the point that talent being equal, designers outside mainstream practice are under-represented in design histories. Industry recognition of Alex Steinweiss came late in his career, with his 1998 induction into the Art Directors Club Hall of Fame, and the awarding of an American Institute of Graphic Arts medal in 2004.

in defiance of the usual time-space limitations of conventional paste-up, layers of these pixels could easily be organized and output in every imaginable relationship to each other. Although the early software was rudimentary and crude, there was no longer a production-based reason for separating text and image, and hybrid forms, including the work of graphic designer David Carson, which quite literally blurred the conventionally understood differences between the two emerged.[5] In the early 1990s Carson's designs for *Ray Gun* magazine, the self-proclaimed "bible of music and style", mainstreamed layered, chaotic, lush, and sometimes indecipherable magazine pages.

Likewise, over the past dozen or so years, advances in computer technology have increasingly led to musicians and designers employing the same hardware, and sometimes software, with the resultant merger of sound and vision extending the expressive language of both. Not only have the tools become digital, but the processes of creating (sampling, sequencing, multi-tracking, and programming) are parallel, and new works have emerged with aesthetic characteristics directly reflective of the tools.

These processes of creating may be categorized under the computer operations of selection and compositing that, according to the new media designer and theorist Lev Manovich, have resulted in a significant new aesthetic.[6] They certainly are very different from conditions that prevailed in the album era: at that point, music and design production were completely separate practices, both technologically and functionally. Making and recording music had little in common with designing its image. The advent of the (digital) compact disc marked the beginning of a radical shift in the way music is produced, represented, distributed and consumed, and was the first step toward shared media, tools and processes.

Digital technologies move us to combine multiple activities – entertainment, production, education, communication – enacted in the old days in different locations, on different appliances, at different times, not only driving new types of content but also new sites for its consumption. One used to go to the record store to buy an album and return home to play it on a turntable and stereo system. In contemporary scenarios one may listen to or procure music online. Audio files may be downloaded onto a personal computer (for listening while working) or portable player (for listening while mobile), burned to CD, or emailed to a friend.[7]

Because information, no matter whether text, audio, or visual, is treated similarly by a computer, digital technologies have also made music's visual component more portable and broadly available. While MTV's original music video

5 An earlier breakthrough with ramifications for representing text and images (and redefining the way meaning was conventionally assigned to them) was László Moholy-Nagy's experimental "typophoto" work of the 1920s. In his poster for Pneumatik tires, Moholy Nagy's drawn letterforms render a plausibly curvy road upon which a photo-collaged small car roars along.

6 "Together these two operations simultaneously reflect and enable the postmodern practice of pastiche and quotation. They work in tandem: one operation is used to select elements and styles from the 'database of culture;' another is used to assemble them into new objects. Thus, along with selection, compositing is the key operation of postmodern, or computer-based, authorship". Lev Manovich, *The Language of New Media* (New Haven, CN: The MIT Press, 2001), pp. 141–142.

7 According to results from the Pew Internet Project and American Life Project, as of March 2004, 23 million Americans had downloaded music from the internet. www.pewinternet.org/PPF /r/148/ report_display.asp (accessed 30 November 2005).

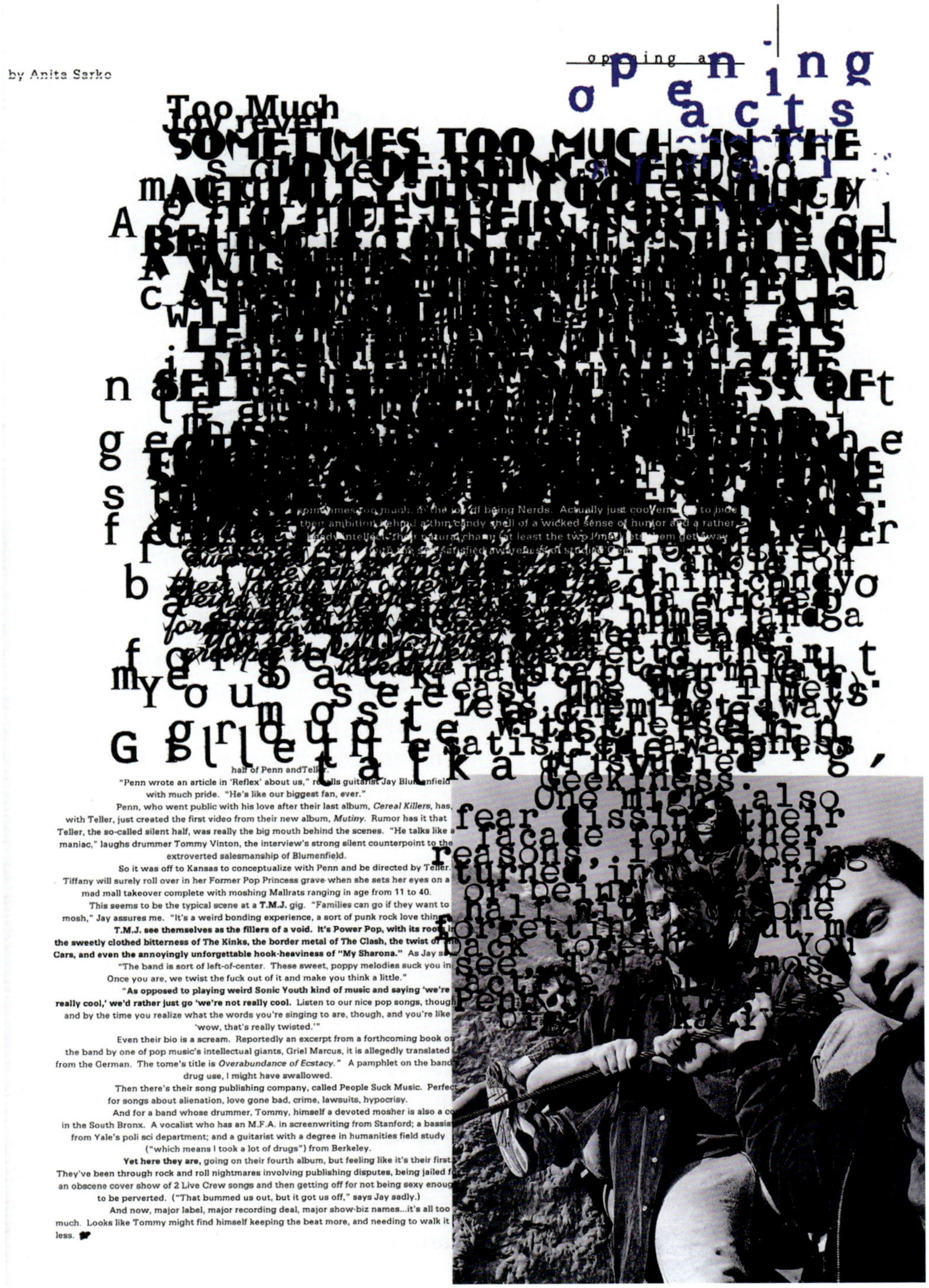

by Anita Sarko

opening acts

Too Much Joy revel

half of Penn and Teller.

"Penn wrote an article in 'Reflex' about us," recalls guitarist Jay Blumenfield with much pride. "He's like our biggest fan, ever."

Penn, who went public with his love after their last album, *Cereal Killers*, has, with Teller, just created the first video from their new album, *Mutiny*. Rumor has it that Teller, the so-called silent half, was really the big mouth behind the scenes. "He talks like a maniac," laughs drummer Tommy Vinton, the interview's strong silent counterpoint to the extroverted salesmanship of Blumenfield.

So it was off to Kansas to conceptualize with Penn and be directed by Teller. Tiffany will surely roll over in her Former Pop Princess grave when she sets her eyes on a mad mall takeover complete with moshing Mallrats ranging in age from 11 to 40.

This seems to be the typical scene at a **T.M.J.** gig. "Families can go if they want to mosh," Jay assures me. "It's a weird bonding experience, a sort of punk rock love thing."

T.M.J. see themselves as the fillers of a void. It's Power Pop, with its roots in the sweetly clothed bitterness of The Kinks, the border metal of The Clash, the twist of the Cars, and even the annoyingly unforgettable hook-heaviness of "My Sharona." As Jay says, "The band is sort of left-of-center. These sweet, poppy melodies suck you in. Once you are, we twist the fuck out of it and make you think a little."

"As opposed to playing weird Sonic Youth kind of music and saying 'we're really cool,' we'd rather just go 'we're not really cool. Listen to our nice pop songs, though, and by the time you realize what the words you're singing to are, though, and you're like 'wow, that's really twisted.'"

Even their bio is a scream. Reportedly an excerpt from a forthcoming book on the band by one of pop music's intellectual giants, Griel Marcus, it is allegedly translated from the German. The tome's title is *Overabundance of Ecstacy*." A pamphlet on the band's drug use, I might have swallowed.

Then there's their song publishing company, called People Suck Music. Perfect for songs about alienation, love gone bad, crime, lawsuits, hypocrisy.

And for a band whose drummer, Tommy, himself a devoted mosher is also a co... in the South Bronx. A vocalist who has an M.F.A. in screenwriting from Stanford; a bassist from Yale's poli sci department; and a guitarist with a degree in humanities field study ("which means I took a lot of drugs") from Berkeley.

Yet here they are, going on their fourth album, but feeling like it's their first. They've been through rock and roll nightmares involving publishing disputes, being jailed for an obscene cover show of 2 Live Crew songs and then getting off for not being sexy enough to be perverted. ("That bummed us out, but it got us off," says Jay sadly.)

And now, major label, major recording deal, major show-biz names...it's all too much. Looks like Tommy might find himself keeping the beat more, and needing to walk it less.

Ray Gun magazine, November 1992, "Opening Acts" review column about the band Too Much Joy (by Anita Sarko). Designed by David Carson.

format proved unsuccessful – taste in videos and music preferences proved too individualistic to keep viewers of all stripes from channel surfing[8] – and was rather quickly replaced by programming featuring sitcoms and reality TV, music-oriented content in contexts more under an individual's control, like the internet, has met with enthusiastic acceptance. As part of the same digital phenomenon, consider the advent of artist/fan/label websites, which go beyond album covers as a visual container for the music to create a comprehensive environment. In their ability to contain both sound and visuals – particularly motion, in the form of video and animation – websites can provide something closer to the immediacy and satisfaction of a concert experience, serve an archival/historical function, and create a communal space for fans. The web also serves to disseminate other sound/visual works, including interactive compositions and music videos.[9] By adding a wealth of visual content to the now-prosaic, sound-only CD, DVD and CD/DVD combinations motivate even devoted downloaders to buy the same music again and again. And lest you think that the iPod is just for music, one current incarnation features storage capacity of up to 25,000 color images, which can be synchronized to music, and output not only to the iPod's two-inch LCD screen, but to a projector.

Because digital tools and media have become ubiquitous at every stage in the processes of creation, dissemination and consumption, the album or CD, with a single visual created by a graphic designer at the behest of a record label's marketing department, has given way to music with a multiplicity of visual correlatives, created by everyone from musicians themselves to close collaborators and fans.

This essay showcases musicians and designers whose embrace of digital technologies to give visual identity to music traces the trajectory of this phenomenon in development. These artists may use computers both as an instrument/medium and a tool; they represent only a subset of current music practices, generally confined to techno, electronica or electronic dance music in which the music is digitally composed using sampled or synthesized sounds. But given the increasing ubiquity of the hardware – many university-based music programs now require laptops as a compositional tool – and the usual lag time during which people figure out how to make new things with them, more variations will emerge, and growing numbers of artists will create in this manner.[10] I have deliberately sought examples in which sound and visuals are either produced by the same person(s) or via longstanding collaborations between visual and musical artists in order to highlight the hybrid practices shared tools have resulted in.

8 Chuck Klosterman, "MTV: Giving the People What They Want", in Will Hermes and Sia Michel (eds.), *SPIN: 20 Years of Alternative Music* (New York: Crown Publishers, 2005), pp. 32–35.

9 Those curious about dj-ing should visit Anthony Flackett's self-described "Interactive Hip-Hop Site", and try out his visually and conceptually lucid music interfaces. http://babel.massart.edu/%7Eflackett/interactive.html (accessed 30 November 2005).

10 It is not uncommon for the first use of any new technology to mimic the incarnation it is meant to replace. For example, the dense lettering of the typeset Gutenberg Bible imitated scribes' handlettering; it took about twenty years for new (Roman) forms designed especially for metal type to develop.

Tomato: Pioneers of Digital Music + Design Collaboration

> We are all on a journey; all work is about experience and the mapping of that experience, and for us at tomato [it] is where we go to compare these maps. In effect we bring a map (or maps) from one territory and overlaying (sic) one upon another to see what happens. This is how our individual work evolves, and how we work together.
> *John Warwicker, Tomato*[11]

For graphic designers, a seminal example of interdisciplinary media practice is Tomato, founded in the UK in 1991. The original eight-man collective included four designers (John Warwicker, Graham Wood, Simon Taylor, and Dirk van Dooren), and two musicians, Karl Hyde and Richard Smith, two-thirds of the popular techno/electronic dance music group Underworld, founded in 1988 (Darren Emerson, Underworld's DJ, left the group in 2000 to pursue a solo career). At the time, Tomato were literate practitioners of a dense, multilayered, expressive design which emerged in the early '90s, fueled partly by what new design software could do, and partly out of an interest in subjective and process-oriented practice not limited to print design. Tomato's work also reflected the period's embrace of deconstructivist theory in design practice. The idea that meaning isn't fixed gave designers carte blanche to stop trying for Modernism's 'objective' clarity and move instead to a more subjective, emotionally expressive, open-to-interpretation mode of design. Some designers availed themselves of this opportunity, while others did not, and much heated debate in the design community about the nature of the profession's responsibility to the audience ensued.

Though many primarily print-based design studios during this period evolved to include motion work (those layers of image and text that the Macintosh helped one to create were piled up waiting for *something*), Tomato's designers had extensive experience in new media and video from the get go, and from the studio's inception were working collaboratively with the musicians in the studio on Underworld's material in both print and music video format. Design critic Rick Poyner attributes the success of the joint effort to both the shared computer platform [the Mac] and a common fascination with language.[12]

Tomato's early videos for Underworld looked unlike the standard MTV fare of the time: the musicians themselves were generally, and remarkably, absent. Dense layers of text and image composited from what appears to be an

11 Tomato, *Process: A Tomato Project* (London: Thames and Hudson, 1996), n.p.

12 Rick Poyner, "Information Sculpture", *Eye*, vol. 4, no. 13 (Summer 1994), p. 29.

“Cowgirl” video, Robert Shakleton and Graham Wood (of the U.K. design firm Tomato), 1993, sequence of 16 video images. ℗ & © 1993 Rick Smith, Karl Hyde & Darren Emerson t/a Underworld.

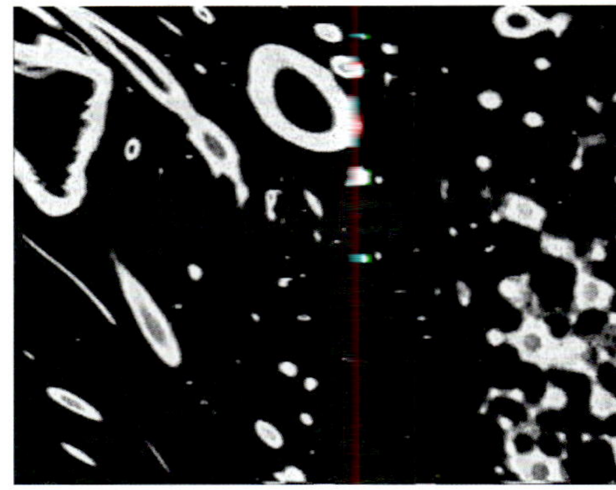

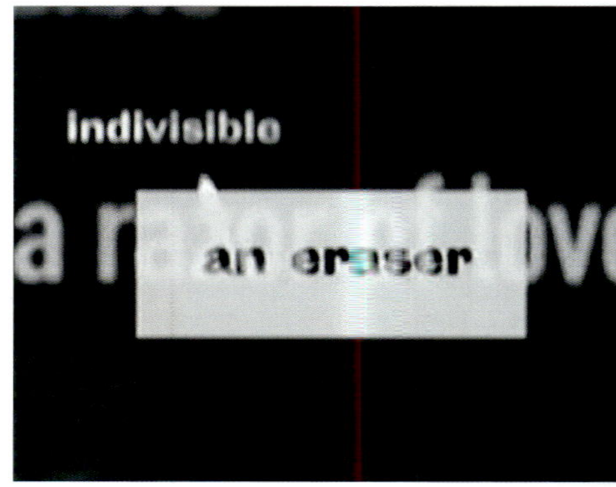

archive of Tomato’s projects and sketches frequently appear, often with no apparent connection to the lyrical content. Typical imagery includes graphically appealing abstract forms or rapidly changing environments seen from the vantage point of a moving train or car. The lyrics, which are generally personal and internal, are visually expressed through the seductions of motion and travel, disconnected textual ruminations, neutral forms like geometric shapes and bubbles. Images are closely synched to the music, and repeated both within and across videos. The reuse of images is both suggestive and functional: it calls attention to the music’s highly repetitive structure, creates a distinctive visual language identity for the band, and transparently reflects the ongoing construction and utilization of Tomato’s image archive.

A representative example is the music video for “Cowgirl” (1993, Robert Shakleton and Graham Wood), one of the best songs from Underworld’s album *Dubnobasswithmyheadman*. Its visual sources include analog video, photography, printed matter and sketches, and text and effects added and manipulated

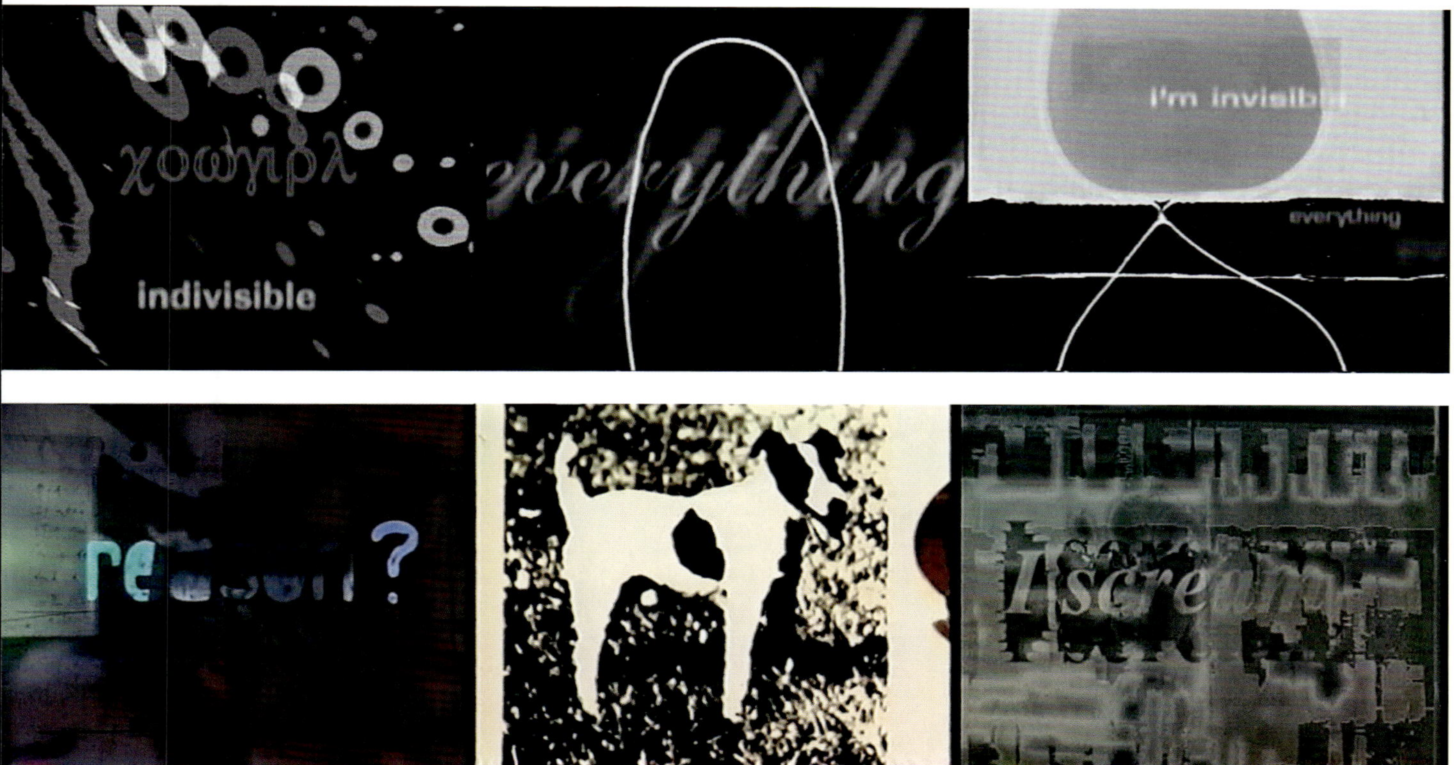

in digital processing. It's a flamboyant example of the phenomenon of digital technology used to visually represent music in the early 1990s.

The video begins in black and white (which places it in the visual past and, with its documentary look, suggests art or science) using footage of abstract bubbles previously seen in "Rez", another Underworld video (circa 1993). For a song about lost love, the visuals are rather dispassionate: the bubbles call to mind actively regenerating primordial forms, more like the objects of scientific study. Wordplay abounds within the lyrics ("I scream/ice cream") and in the on-screen texts ("reason/raisin/raison?"). Images flood in, resembling a wholesale download of the contents of one's memory: a walk in the park, a glimpse of the newspaper, a photo of the dog, napkin doodles, and a flash of television. Another layer of text, unrelated to the lyrics, appears on screen: "The facts all contribute to setting the problem, not to its solution", "The ear hears the silence that the eye sees", "What we cannot speak about we must pass over in silence".

As in many of the Underworld videos, there's an apparent tension be-

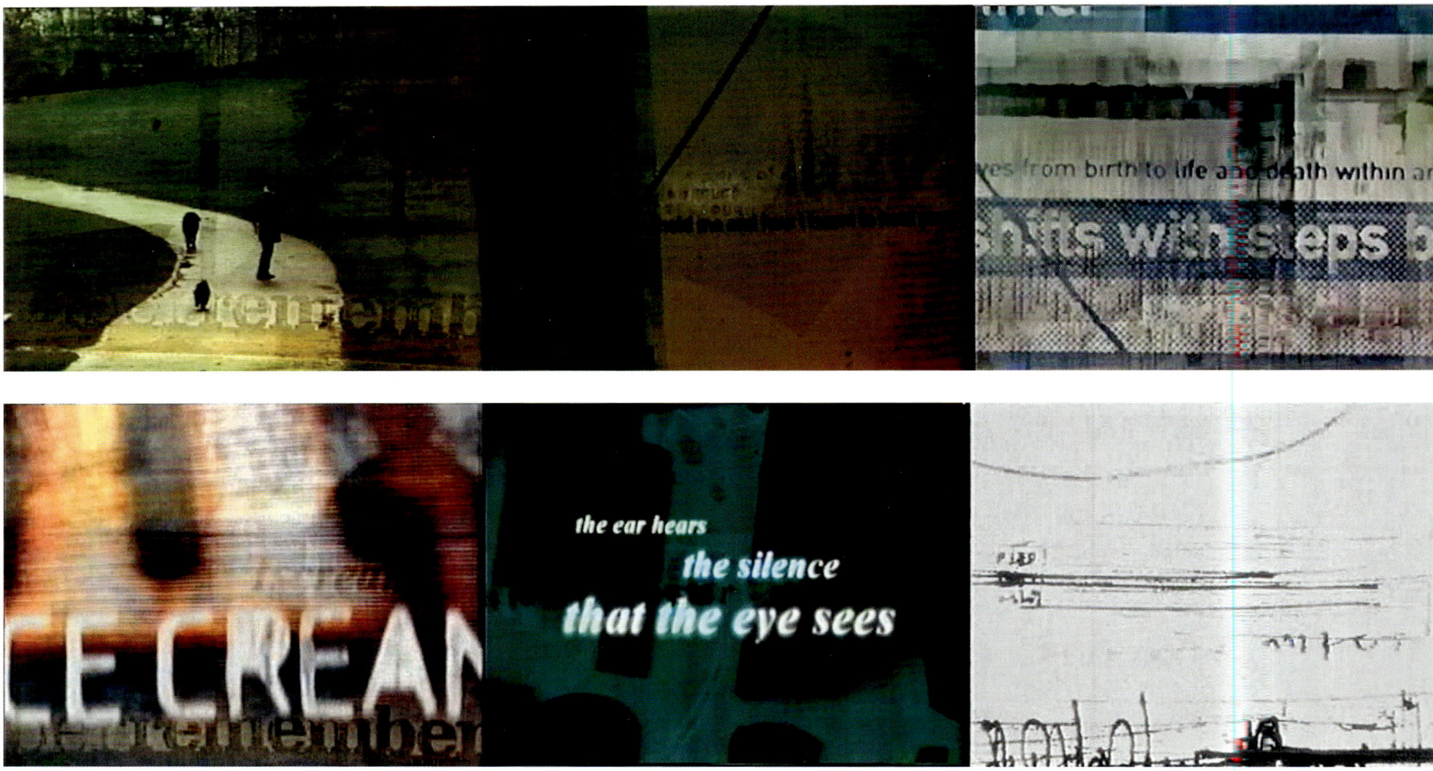

tween the abstract and the literal. “Cowgirl”’s first third is visually distinctive and closely related to the music: the black-and-white bubble footage is graphically engaging, the short snippets of text are well integrated into the images, and the whole is synchronized to the beat. The video’s remaining two-thirds are much more open, and more stream of consciousness in the use of images (obviously tapping into the aforementioned collection of Tomato material), with text and lyrics only indirectly related to each other. But it is the latter part of the video that refers more to the speed and complexity of everyday life. Its emotional communication of personal experience extends the lyric’s narrative. In emailed correspondence during February 2005 Graham Wood explained that “Cowgirl” was originally the duration of the bubble video segment. When Underworld extended the song’s length (extending and remixing tracks is a common practice in the dance music world), Wood went back to augment the video. In doing so he provided an object lesson in using new technology, old style, to make montage, a “visual, stylistic, semantic, and emotional dissonance between different

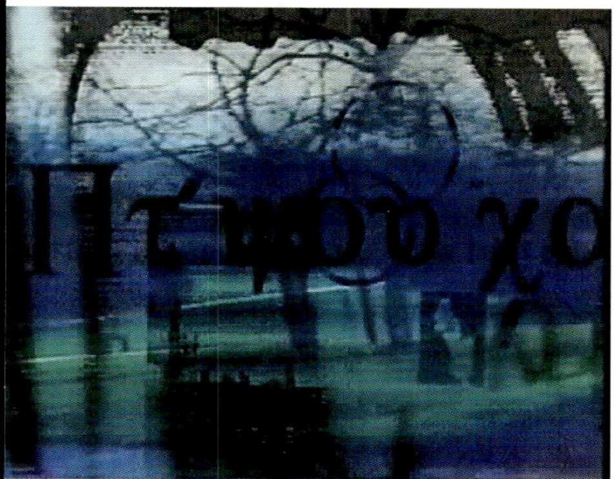

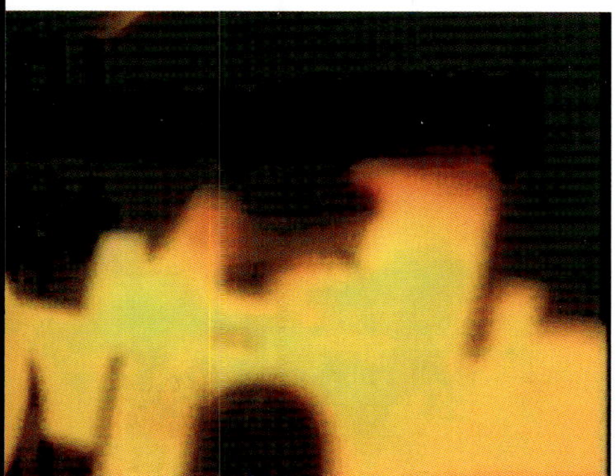

"Cowgirl" video, Robert Shakleton and Graham Wood (of the U.K. design firm Tomato), 1993, sequence of 16 video images. ℗ & © 1993 Rick Smith, Karl Hyde & Darren Emerson t/a Underworld.

elements".[13] The montage aspect of "Cowgirl" and some of Tomato's other early music videos is reminiscent of experimental film (particularly the non-narrative works of Maya Deren and Stan Brakhage). But the smoothly layered still images sourced from the studio's own print projects exemplify a newer, computer-driven aesthetics of continuity,[14] and provide a time-capsule-like glimpse of an era's expressive, idiosyncratic investigations in digitally produced *static* graphic design.

From the audience's point of view, notwithstanding the fact that Karl Hyde is a physically expressive live performer (the other performers are stuck behind keyboards and consoles, mixing tracks and basically pushing buttons), DJ-based electronic music is not generally that interesting to watch. It is much more compelling to dance to, in which case an immersive audiovisual environment is a plus. In the concert setting, the audience both enjoys the music and, with the common practice of splicing live video feeds into concert graphics, becomes part of it. On a concert DVD of the band's 1998–1999 world tour, one has

13 Lev Manovich, *The Language of New Media* (Cambridge, Mass.: The MIT Press, 2001), p. 144.

14 Ibid. "Digital compositing, in which different spaces are combined into a single seamless virtual space, is a good example of the alternative esthetics of continuity; moreover, compositing in general can be understood as a counterpart to montage esthetics. Montage aims to create visual, stylistic, semantic, and emotional dissonance between different elements. In contrast, compositing aims to blend them into a seamless whole; a single gestalt".

“Dowhile X” video, Sebastian Oschatz / Oval, 1995, sequence of 12 video images. Stills reproduced courtesy of Thrill Jockey.

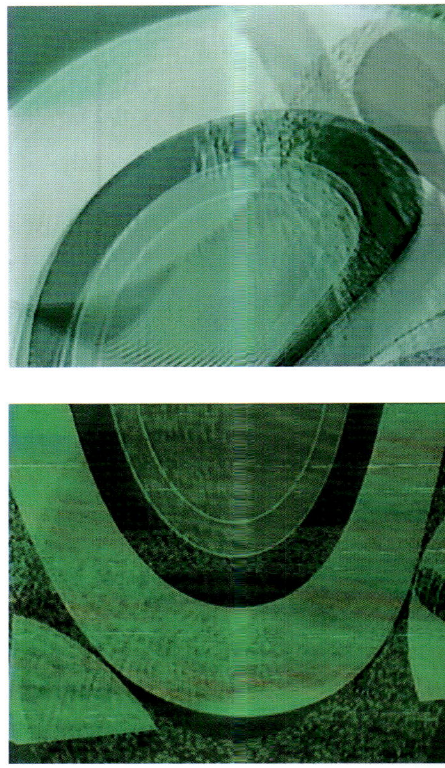

the option to view the music videos indirectly as part of the concert footage, as well as on their own as “video art” (the term used on the DVD package), indicating an awareness of the visual value and interest in the videos alone.

Oval: Theorizing Process/Music as Software

> In the simplest explanation, music is an effective compression technique for certain kinds of sound tracks.
>
> – *from the introduction to the Apple ComputerTM Quick TimeTM programmer’s manual, circa 1990*

Contemporaries of Tomato’s, but working in an entirely different digital vein, are Oval, the German trio originally comprised of Markus Popp, Sebastian Oschatz and Frank Metzger (Oval is now solely Popp). Oval came together around

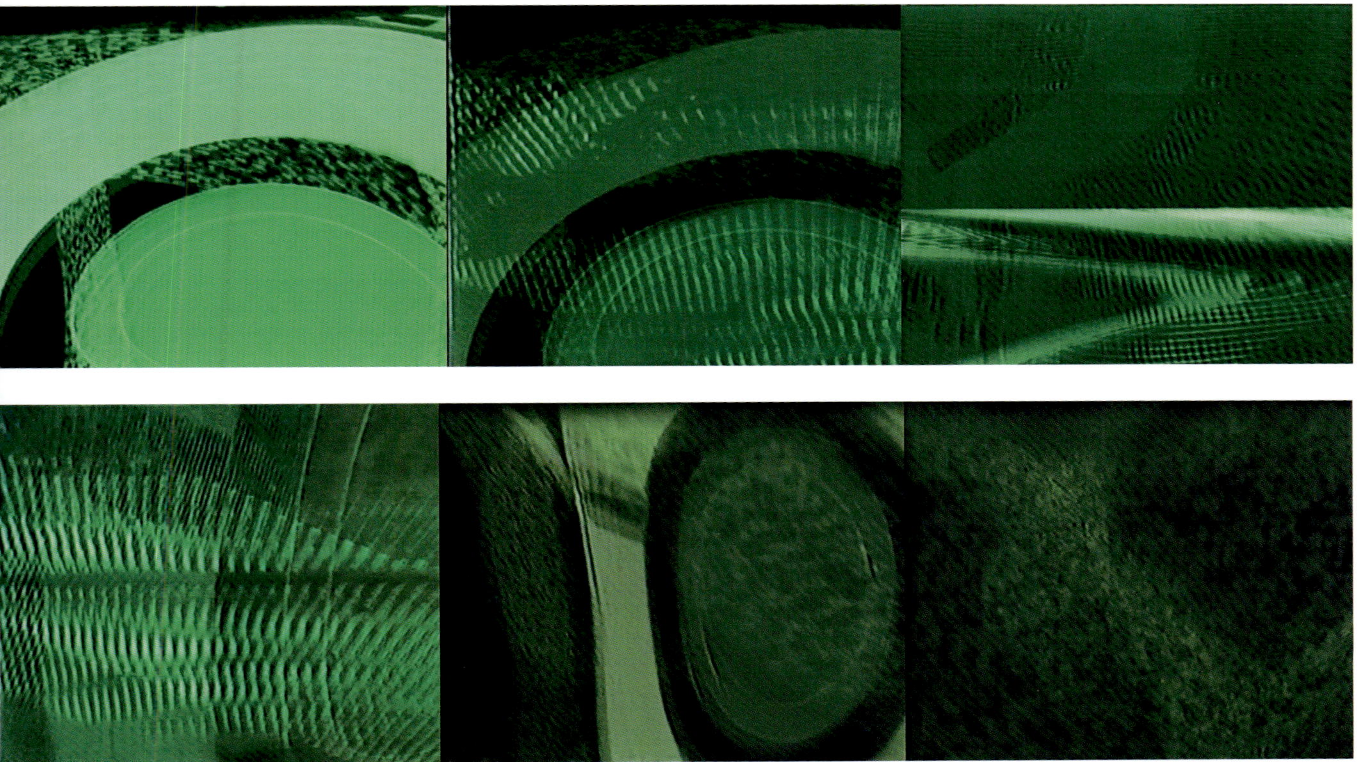

1990 as an outgrowth of informal jam sessions at Popp's home. Using analog instruments, mostly guitar and bass, they soon graduated to a computer and sampler, deliberately altering CDs and equipment to generate audio samples. Their music and visuals make much more direct reference to digitalia: every sound, regardless of its source, is processed down to the sonic equivalent of the pixel and becomes part of a vast archive of audio bits from which music is composed. Oval's two releases from 2000, *ovalprocess* and *ovalcommers*, were both produced on Apple laptop computers. Their music and visuals share aesthetic and creative strategies by design. As Sebastian Oschatz describes the process and its impact upon visual form: "the process of making the music for oval [sic] was so abstract ... I think a video should ideally reflect the condition in which the music was made".[15]

Imagery for the music video "Dowhile X" (1995, Sebastian Oschatz) from Oval's release *94 diskont* is taken from sections of the silk-screened art used to decorate the *94 diskont* music CD itself, but digitally manipulated and colored

15 Email interview with Peter Hall, circa 2000; www.meso.net/oschatz/oval/hall.html (accessed 30 November 2005).

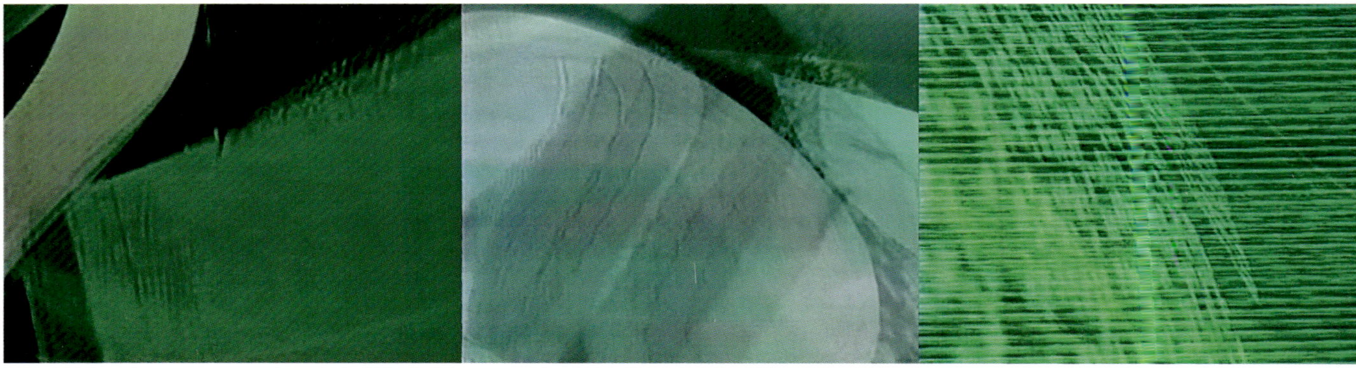

to give the feeling of moving in a fresh, green, textured space. In that they are non-representational but clearly address three-dimensional space, the images read as being digitally created, and match the music's ambient character. An absence of visual references to the everyday world combines with sound fragments to induce a comfortably disengaged state. If there is any tension in the work it is in the fluctuation between cool and warm, between artificiality and reality.

As an example of Oval's early digital manipulated video works, "Dowhile X" is the epitome of seamless compositing, and fits into popular conceptions of the digital world as an abstract, non-representational space. Though the visual language reflects identifiable aspects of technology and programming, whether actual or stereotypical (its precision and accuracy; dispassion and repetition; the creation of 3D spaces that do not actually exist), the video does not suffer from the visual clichés one would expect. It is not mechanical or cold: it is dreamily paced, beautifully colored, delicate, clean and Utopian. Where Underworld values the messiness, speed, and density of life and emotion, Oval values the meditative infinitude of manipulable digital space.

As with Tomato's early videos for Underworld, Oval's music videos are emphatically not centered around celebrity or the persona of the artist: design is the star. Whereas Tomato contributed a wordy and sometimes self-conscious intelligence to Underworld's music, Oval's sound is inherently cerebral. Oval, more so than Tomato/Underworld, embraced the essential anonymity of computer music. Eschewing conventional instrument-mimicking samples in their music, as well as rejecting text and photography as source material for their imagery, they create a virtual world. However abstract, "Dowhile X" has a reassuringly traditional sense of narrative: a beginning, middle and end.

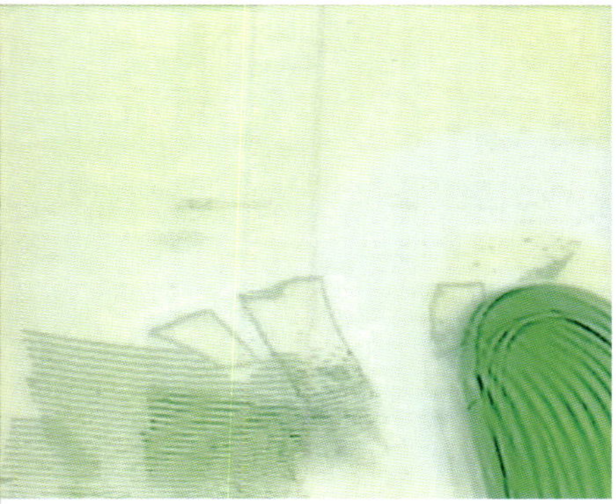

"Dowhile X" video, Sebastian Oschatz / Oval, 1995, sequence of 12 video images. Stills reproduced courtesy of Thrill Jockey.

With the release of *ovalprocess* in 2000, Markus Popp announced a conceptual shift from making music to music as software:

> [I]t seems meaningless to debate electronic music in the Powerbook era in terms of the capital 'M' Music that existed before. In my opinion, it was no longer interesting to just continue as a recording artist pretending I was composing this electronic music as if I was composing piano pieces. Even if the musical result is performed on a stage, or even if it's only distributed and sold and received as an audio CD, it's still not possible to isolate it from the productivity software that is used to create this music, because the electronic music that's existing today is to such a high degree depending on the possibilities that are implemented in the productivity software.[16]

Originally conceived of and promoted as software that one could use on their Mac for composing a la Oval, *ovalprocess*'s ultimate manifestation was as a standard music CD, with the software exclusively available as an interactive installation object, *skotodesk*, exhibited at various galleries and museums worldwide. Less a tool for actually making music, *skotodesk* is a visualization of Popp's process, and problematizes the effect of conventional music software tools on the act of composing. Former Oval member Frank Metzger considers Popp's current direction a natural outcome of using sampling as a dominant strategy. Because source melodies and rhythms exert a great deal of control over the structure of the finished piece, and the digital environment itself reinforces certain attitudes, it may have been inevitable that more theoretical concerns came to the forefront.[17]

16 Interview with Sam Ingles. www.soundonsound.com/soc/oct02/articles/oval.asp (accessed 4 February 2005).

17 www.meso.net/oschatz/oval/metzger.html (accessed 30 November 2005).

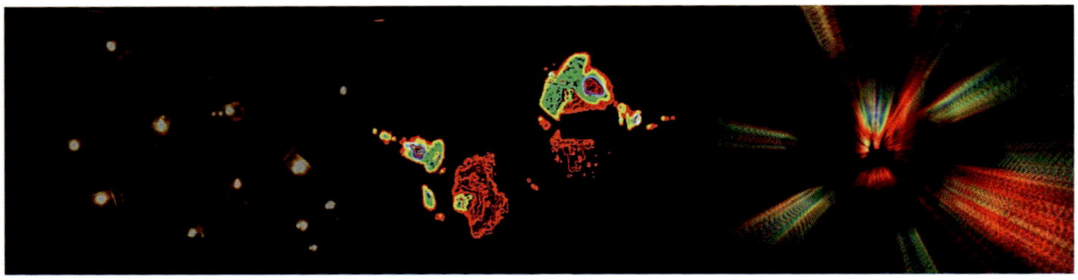

"Bruma" music video, Michael Schaeffer, 2004, sequence of 3 still video images. Artist Michael Schaeffer.

"Sultan" music video, Michael Schaeffer, 2004, sequence of 4 still video images. Artist Michael Schaeffer.

Laptop/DIY/VJ for Hire

A dozen years later, a plethora of sound and vision variations running the gamut from alternative to commercial have established themselves.

"Share", a weekly gathering at New York City's *Open Air* lounge, is an example of local laptop culture connected to an international network of digital musicians and artists. Every Sunday evening, aficionados gather at the venue with their laptop computers to plug in and play – output is both audio and video – and trade tips and software. An international roster of headlining acts arrives later. Unlike most music events in which the technology is concealed and attention is clearly centered on the performer, here the technology is so foregrounded that in a room full of people and laptops it is not immediately apparent who is playing. (This is not always the case: in other events laptop DJs make dance music from a DJ booth or platform, or square off against each other in competition.) Popular software, both commercially available and easily downloaded, can make a laptop mimic a synthesizer, and organize and sequence samples; more complex programs (Max/MSP, Reaktor) allow users to custom design their own instruments and to program music. Some software packages can manipulate both sound and visuals, and attract users from both practices.

The laptop scene is noticeably male-dominated. A rare exception is Japanese-born laptop artist Keiko Uenishi (aka o.blatt),[18] an internationally known artist affiliated with "Share". o.blatt's most recent work, "The Music of Living Beats", involves sound, light, and audience interaction in real-time performances. She explicitly seeks to de-emphasize her presence, and instead creates an environment in which the audience is encouraged to "scatter their [sic] attention in multiple directions".[19]

For many graphic designers, especially younger ones, it is a natural step to go from print to motion design, and then to sound. That the tool of choice, the computer, doubles as a music processor and instrument gives the designer interested in making music a great deal of control over the final product. For

18 Uenishi's unusual stage name is best explained by Nick Currie (the musician known as Momus) who describes it thus at www.demon.co.uk/momus/thought201201.html. (accessed 30 November 2005): "I came across a website about a Japanese laptop artist called o.blaat, a New York-based sound curator called Keiko Uenishi. Even the name o.blaat contains a reference to McLuhan's insight: in Japanese 'oblaat' means the colourless, tasteless, self-dissolving gel which surrounds pill capsules. You can't taste it, but it gives definition to the shape of the pill, helps you swallow it. It's a perfect symbol of making defining, invisible contexts visible". At http://home.iprimus.com.au/ltuttle/oblatt.html oblaat herself says, "Adding to the excellent comment, I should point out that the function of the material 'oblaat' is 'to melt & disappear'. The thing is made to melt and disappear. It is the raison d'etre for this product. 'Existing to disappear' is matching with my concept of creating situations (which includes audio factor)".

19 Email correspondence with o.blatt, January 2005.

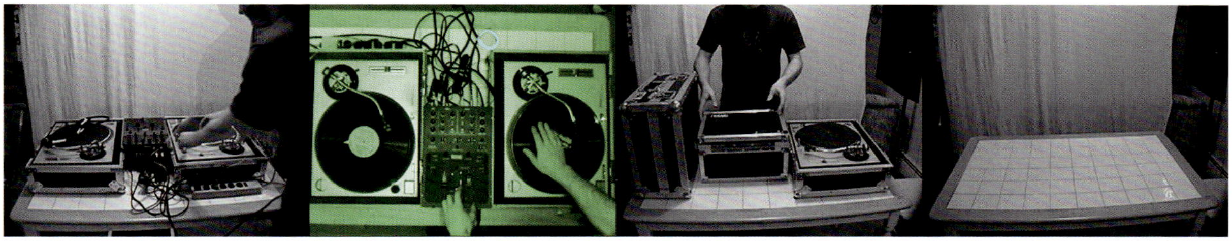

designers, for whom traditional practice involves giving visual form and meaning to someone else's content, the foray into composing is a provocative new direction in the profession's longstanding wrestling match with issues of authorship. There is some question as to whether or not graphic designers are "qualified" to take on sound design, much in the way the field's expansion to motion design was debated a decade ago, but this is an issue beyond the scope of this article.

Michael Schaeffer (aka DJ LaForge) is a graphic designer whose music videos "Bruma" and "Sultan" were created in 2004 as part of a BFA project at the State University of New York at New Paltz and conceived of as a set of experiments in audio-visual co-production. While the videos vary in style, both the visuals and the music are sample-based. "Bruma"'s cuts are meticulously synchronized to the number of beats per minute in the audio used to create the soundtrack. Though the process is restrictive and mechanical, the end result is by turns dreamy and percussive. By visually re-enacting it, "Sultan" pays respect to the venerable practice (which was not so long ago, but technology changed very rapidly) of "scratching" vinyl records on a turntable, yet "Sultan" itself is entirely digitally produced.

A DJ used to be the person at the radio station who chose and played songs live on their radio show (in the age of corporate radio and playlists, the job description has lost a lot of its personal initiative and discretion). The postmodern version refers to someone who mixes music, live, in performance venues, and whose raison d'être is to get people dancing. Mixing can be either analog (the aforementioned vinyl on multiple turntables) or digital (using both samples and soundbits). Similarly, the term "VJ" was coined by MTV in the early 1980s to describe their on-air commentators who showed music videos and talked shop in between. Now a VJ is a digital artist who makes visual mixes for second-wave DJs and other musicians in live concert settings and for music videos. In the context of showcasing their laptops' powerful functionality, the Apple Computer website recently ran an extensive advertorial featuring Vello Virkhaus, a VJ known as V2, who designs elaborate visual mixes for high-profile musician clients.[20] It is telling that the company chose someone who works at such a large scale, and whose clients are mainstream musicians; it gives both the tool and the practice credibility.

The familiar continuum pinned down by artistic/experimental practice at one end and commercial practice on the other is in evidence here. Though truly hybrid practices like oblaat's tend toward "art", while visuals-only practices like V2's cluster at "commerce", there is a great deal of common activity: collaboration with other artists and musicians; working with (musician) clients; creating and recording audio-visual works;[21] exhibiting the work in museum and gallery settings; and live performances at music and computer arts festivals of every scale.

The nature of the relationship between music and design continues to evolve as practitioners of both disciplines share digital tools and production strategies. A range of hybrid practices, new aesthetics, and technological methods move the creation and control of music and its image interfaces more toward musicians, their audiences and collaborators, and away from media conglomerates. Visualization of music, which began as a marketing tool some 65 years ago, might ultimately turn out to be as integral to the making and experience of music as the sound of music itself.

20 The 2,500-plus-word feature ran at www.apple.com/startpage on 4 February 2005.

21 Product distribution is also part of this artistic activity. No stepchild to the music industry, the London-based Addictive TV, a collaboration of television producers, DJs, VJs and artists, were quick to claim control of their product in the marketplace and pioneered the first DVD label entirely devoted to VJ works in 1999. www.4rfv.co.uk/outside.asp?id=10566&to=www.addictive.com&cat=216 (accessed 30 November 2005).

Self-made CD

Texture and Narrative in Small-Run DIY CD Production

Eve Klein

Small music communities like Australian hip-hop advocate a Do-It-Yourself (DIY) approach to music production and distribution, with the aim of empowering and personalizing music for both artist and audience. With the advent of affordable home studio set-ups artists have experimented in the creation of recorded music outside of commercial and industrial structures, often creating packaged musical products. Rather than detracting from the music, DIY packaging can form part of an operational philosophy for some alternative musical communities. The DIY creation of covers adds to the cultural value of the music, as the rough, 'hand-made' qualities of the package tie the music and the product as a whole into a narrative of its creation, which acts as a guarantee of authenticity.

Small production runs of CDs and the creation of unique one-off CDs for special events and library collections promote an economy of exchange which can fetishize rarity. In his case study of alternative modes of music production on the Far North Coast of New South Wales, Australia, Chris Gibson notes that music which was "unavailable" through conventional retail outlets conveyed "subcultural capital" on the owner.[1] While music may be re-released or additional pressings made, notions of 'original', first-edition record covers are prized by aficionados within many music subcultures. Similarly, burnt CDRs with the title scrawled in pen on the CD face exploit the coarseness of DIY aesthetics to generate intimacy – the artist uniquely marking the musical package. Limited release can also allow for experimentation with unusual or unconventional textures in packaging materials, adding a tactile element to a person's interactivity with the musical product. This kind of exchange in small music communities resembles and parodies the exclusivity that has been associated with aesthetic experience in fine art for centuries. Using case studies from Sydney, Australia, this article aims to analyze how the idea of a packaged musical product is both utilized and fragmented in self-produced and small-scale/independent music production, aiding narratives of alternative space and artistic independence.

1 Chris Gibson, "Appropriating the Means of Production: Dance Music Industries and Contested Digital Space", in Graham St John (ed.), *FreeNRG: Notes From the Edge of the Dancefloor* (Alton, Victoria: Common Ground Publishing, 2001), p. 252.

DIY as Opposition in Music Cultures

When the term DIY is applied to music communities or musical products, it commonly references a historical and contemporary linkage to subcultural movements seeking to delineate space outside and against 'mainstream' cultures.[2] While focusing on the use of DIY culture in 1990s Britain, George McKay's edited volume highlights a trajectory of DIY in music throughout the post-war period, including mid-fifties skiffle-jazz, 1970s punk culture, and 1980s acid house parties (also known as free parties and associated with British squat and traveler culture) which lead to the widespread utilization of DIY in a variety of dance music cultural movements during the 1990s.[3] Other writing on DIY similarly constructs a lineage of the cultural application of doing-it-yourself to music cultures. Enda Murray's history of Australian DIY focuses on traditions of mobile dance parties known as "sound systems" by drawing an arch between Australian sound system events of the 1990s, Jamaican open-air dancehalls of the 1950s, New York's 'block parties', and 'rent' or 'blues parties' across England in the 1960s and 1970s.[4] The writing of such histories serves to fix and legitimize a notion of DIY across vastly different cultural, political and historical landscapes.

The directive to 'do it yourself' and the term 'DIY job' both position DIY as a response, a solution to a perceived problem – the collapsed shelf, the missing shed – but it is an unprofessional, an amateur solution; a kind of kludge that 'you' could implement 'yourself'. So the idea of DIY becomes, itself, a call or drive for action made up of seemingly conflicting or discontiguous adaptations of technology and self-driven modes/vectors of production. McKay links the "Action!" implicit in DIY movements to political-cultural conceptions of non-violent direct action, noting that the two "feed each other".[5] Graham St John emphasizes McKay's musings on action within DIY communities, commenting that they "offered a more accurate designation – a 'Do it *Ourselves*' culture – a network consisting of micro-*communities* of dissent and their collective creative interventions".[6] So DIY cannot be understood simply as producing or fixing something yourself (without 'professional' intervention), as many cost-saving home-improvement product lines would suggest; rather, DIY needs to be understood as a literal and metaphorical opposition through alternative modes of creative conduct and production.

Punk of the mid-1970s, one of the earliest musical movements to actively define and narrate a DIY politics,[7] simplistically utilized available technologies to dissent political and social changes of Thatcherite Britain. Combining this punk aesthetic with an abrasive championing of technological acceleration

2 For more information about subcultural definition and the construction of 'mainstream', see Sarah Thornton, "Exploring the Meaning of the Mainstream (or Why Sharon and Tracy Dance around Their Handbags)", in *Club Cultures: Music, Media and Subcultural Capital* (Cambridge: Polity Press, 1995).

3 George McKay, "DIY Culture: Notes Toward an Intro", in George McKay (ed.), *DIY Culture: Party and Protest in Nineties Britain* (London: Verso, 1998), pp. 1–2.

4 Enda Murray, "Sound Systems and Australian DIY Culture: Folk Music for the Dot Com Generation", in Graham St John (ed.), *FreeNRG: Notes From the Edge of the Dancefloor* (Alton, Victoria: Common Ground Publishing, 2001), pp. 60–61.

5 George McKay, p. 4.

6 Graham St John "Techno Inferno", in Graham St John (ed.), *FreeNRG: Notes From the Edge of the Dancefloor* (Alton, Victoria: Common Ground Publishing, 2001), p. 4.

7 So intertwined is the contemporary notion of DIY to conceptions of punk origin, that it even has its own Wikipedia entry. See "DIY Punk Ethic", in *Wikipedia, The Free Encyclopedia*: http://en.wikipedia.org/wiki/DIY_punk_ethic (accessed 7 April 2005).

was the science fiction literary movement cyberpunk. Cyberpunk literature was drawn into a subcultural evolution of punk which, according to Richard Kadrey and Larry McCaffery, appropriated "punk's confrontational style, its anarchist energies, its crystal-meth pacings and its central motif of the alienated victim defiantly using technology to blow everyone's fuses".[8] Cyberpunk emphasized the manipulation and merging of human bodies and culture with technology. This is stated in some sources as a kind of belief system not just intended to 'blow everyone's fuses' but to sophisticatedly use technical knowledge of emerging computer and information systems to "fend off the tendencies of traditional institutions to use technology to control society".[9] Cyberpunk highlights the self-awareness and subversiveness present in the ethos of DIY as it is utilized by local and alternative musical movements. To have the knowledge and control of technology, in the case of musicians, to actively control the modes of production and distribution is to disrupt the power structures that prevent agency and to practice an approximate freedom. In this light, hosting an illegal rave or *bush-doof*[10] is not very different to an independent musician recording an album in a spare room, burning it to CD and printing out the cover. Both acknowledge that other economic and social power-structures prevent a desired creative exploration. Illegal raves or doofs operate outside of expensive venues without permits or insurance, which would prevent club-based dance events from being hosted. In doing so, doofs and raves construct part of their 'alternative' appeal and activist orientation from this sense of opposition: opposition to commercial dance/club-cultures and associated venues and aesthetics, and opposition from legal structures. Similarly, the increasingly common practice of self-recorded, produced and distributed albums can be seen to challenge traditional economic and career paths presented to musicians by the major record labels. While some self-produced albums are intended as a stepping stone to attract label involvement, they simultaneously declare that music can, when needed, be released outside of the systems and incentives offered by major labels. The key difference between these examples is that DIY CD production is a creative practice which can easily conform to legal convention. Doofs circumvent the law because they cannot partake in the systems and incentives which would make their creative practice legal and still produce the same spontaneous, inspirational engagements for their participants. To do so would institutionalize doofs, making them reliant on the structures of commerce and industry which they view as having decayed club-oriented dance cultures.[11]

8 Cited in Darren Tofts and Murray McKeich, *Memory Trade: A Prehistory of Cyberculture* (Sydney: Interface, 1997), p. 15.

9 This idea was promoted on a cyberpunk website being hosted out of China: http://iroi.seu.edu.cn/books/ee_dic/whatis/cyberpun.htm (accessed 21 May 2004). The site has subsequently been removed but the definition was reproduced from a *Whatis.com* definition located at: http://searchwebservices.techtarget.com/sDefinition/0,,sid26_gci211882,00.html (accessed 2 April 2005).

10 Doof is an Australian name for mostly outdoor dance-parties. They are strongly linked to environmental and social justice activism of the late 1990s and early 2000s and built upon the declining Australian rave scene. For more information see Graham St John, "Doof! Australian Post-Rave Culture", in Graham St John (ed.), *FreeNRG: Notes From the Edge of the Dancefloor* (Alton, Victoria: Common Ground Publishing, 2001), pp. 9–36.

11 See ibid., pp. 14–17.

Auditing the Economies of Decentralized Production

In the chapter "Music and Copyright in the Information Age", John Connell and Chris Gibson approach a section on digital technologies and home recording with the subheading "Digital decentralisation?"[12] Their use of a question mark underscores a general concern about the idealism present in the discourses of production within some alternative music communities. New technologies have increased the potential for access to modes of production but, as Connell and Gibson point out, these modes have only served to decentralize music production within particular "selective geographies" where access is possible.[13] Connell and Gibson place decentralized digital production within competitive economies of exchange where "[l]ocal artists engaging in DIY music production" compete "with thousands of similar artists, all seeking success as small-scale entrepreneurs... Unless musicians could generate significant links from other websites, or could mobilize audiences for self-produced material, their sounds were likely to be lost in a 'sea' of digital noise".[14] However, Connell and Gibson's claim that musicians are being "lost" within the digital noise calls up the notion that a culture requires a canon with clearly identifiable sets of geniuses to define the *zeitgeist*. This view constructs DIY practitioners as lost to their imagined audience, lost from being discovered because of additional 'competition' allowed by the opening of production modes and distribution vectors like the internet. The exception offered by Connell and Gibson is the "sub-cultural style" of dance music which they describe as "placeless" due to its "lack of lyrics", thus allowing "more people to contribute to successful distribution beyond domestic markets".[15] The entrepreneurial accent to both descriptions situates these considerations of decentralized production within conventional economic models, and as such Connell and Gibson seem to be reading alternative music economies as desiring or eventually having the same structures as mainstream ones, albeit without the 'middlemen' of record companies. This appraisal does not leave space to consider that alternative economies generated by DIY cultures are driving a shift in the goals of cultural production. Artists do not have to be (or want to be) these great individuals who stand like colossi invoking the essence of a period for a "mass faceless" audience; instead artists are involving their audience directly in the production of art. DIY art is no longer transcendent but directly contextualized by its community because it is never removed from it. This is something inferred, but not attributed value in Connell and Gibson's reading of music communities in Byron Bay (New South Wales, Australia).[16] The economies Connell and Gibson are talking about are, in DIY terms, already a kludge in

12 John Connell and Chris Gibson, *Sound Tracks: Popular Music, Identity and Place* (London: Routledge, 2003), p. 257.

13 Ibid., p. 263. Connell and Gibson use the term 'selective geography' to highlight that digital recording is still limited on a global level to those who have access to the internet, computers and associated technologies. This idea is explored more fully in Phillip Hayward, "Cultural Tectonics", *Convergence: The Journal of Research Into New Cultural Technologies* 6 (Spring 2000), pp. 39–47.

14 Connell and Gibson, p. 261.

15 Ibid., p. 260.

16 Ibid., pp. 261–262.

themselves. They are making music, sharing culture with their neighbors, and sometimes generating an income. Yet this is not to claim that the musicians themselves are 'properly' DIY as they may well have dreams of being the next Black Eyed Peas. Individually, artists may struggle within the currents of decentralized economies; however, the broader subcultural appropriation of production technologies generates a mythos of "DIY" which can mobilize audiences through the creation of communities.

Australian electronica group Clan Analogue, fuelled by a lack of music venues and music distribution channels, formed a collective in 1992 and have been producing their own CDs (many originally recorded on four-track recorders in people's homes or warehouse venues around Sydney) and releasing them under the collective's label.[17] CDs like Carrier's albums *Mrs E* and *The Foley Artists* were packaged in hand-made cases, with stickers used as decoration and track lists printed on inkjet printers and attached to the case.[18] Despite increasing international recognition for their releases, Clan Analogue continue to support DIY as a central aspect of their community, as highlighted on their website:

> Clan aims to allow artists to produce work free of the constraints of the commercial music industry by developing self funded, artist initiated recording and publishing projects. This 'do it yourself' philosophy encourages the direct transmission of the artist's works to the listener without filtering it via label mediation. Through its diverse and multi-talented membership, the collective allows for the pooling of resources and the cross-fertilisation of ideas. This co-operative nature of working together allows large, otherwise unattainable goals to be reached for the benefit of the larger collective.[19]

Arguably, for members and supporters of Clan Analogue, the community connections, workshops, meetings and performances are exchanges as important as any financial remuneration from the Clan Analogue label, and, as their above statement highlights, the label would not be possible without the community. In this way, decentralized production can shift economic currency beyond monetary remuneration towards an economics measured through successful community engagement.

17 Information sourced from Clan Analogue, "A Brief History of Clan Analogue", from Clan Analogue's website, www.clananalogue.org (accessed 15 April 2004).

18 Carrier, *Mrs E*, Carrier/Control, 2003; Carrier, *The Foley Artists*, 2004.

19 Clan Analogue, www.clananalogue.org.

In-scribing the Author: Elena Kats-Chernin's *Selfmade CD* and Symbolic Fantasm's *Foot in the Door*

Situated between the subcultural discourses of DIY and the dissemination of production economies is an anxiety that Walter Benjamin observed between the means of reproduction/access and the creation of a unique or individual presence. Benjamin argued that new reproducibilities of enshrined artistic forms push their limitations in a way that both points towards new expressive uses of technological mediums, but also "changes the reaction of the masses toward art".[20] Benjamin reasoned that the diminishment of unique presence and tradition, aura, in mechanically producible and reproducible art forms coincided with them becoming objects of public exhibition and enjoyment.[21] Conversely, we might look at album covers created by the musicians and composers, who are featured within, as being highly prized by fans *because* they generate a 'unique' aura via authorship and exclusivity.

Since the early 1990s, emerging artists in Australia's closely-knit hip hop communities have recorded and swapped self-made tapes as part of the process of learning the craft and building a reputation. Nick Lunzer, a participant in the Sydney scene, commented that in the mid-1990s recording to CD was a bold statement because convention and cost dictated that only seasoned performers attempt a CD production.[22] As home recording has become more affordable, tapes have been replaced by CDRs and, arguably, a studio-recorded CD might be considered as daring as its antecedent. Symbolic Fantasm are one Sydney-based hip hop crew that have utilized CDRs with DIY covers to involve audiences in their live shows and generate continued attention once the performance is over. So lasting was the impression left by this kind of exchange that a performance from 2000 was recalled and described to me in 2005 by an audience member:

> The gig was at the Hopetoun in Surry hills, which is a small venue on a Sunday night when they used to hold 'Frigid'. The place was crowded and it was difficult to move around inside of it. I'm not sure how many times Symbolic Fantasm had actually performed... I think they could have been tighter as a group but the performance was fairly good. It was the first I had heard of the group. They handed out a promotional CD and didn't go to too much trouble in the design and layout.[23]

The CD handed out at the gig was entitled *Foot In The Door*. Inside a thin case with a blue, semi-opaque tray were photocopied sleeve notes. They featured the

20 Walter Benjamin, "The Work of Art in the Age of Mechanical Reproduction", in Andrew Utterson (ed.), *Technology and Culture, The Film Reader* (New York: Routledge, 2005), p. 115.

21 Ibid., p. 110.

22 Nick Lunzer, interview with the author, 17 November 2004.

23 The audience member wrote a statement for inclusion in this article but wished to remain anonymous. Statement dated 4 April 2005.

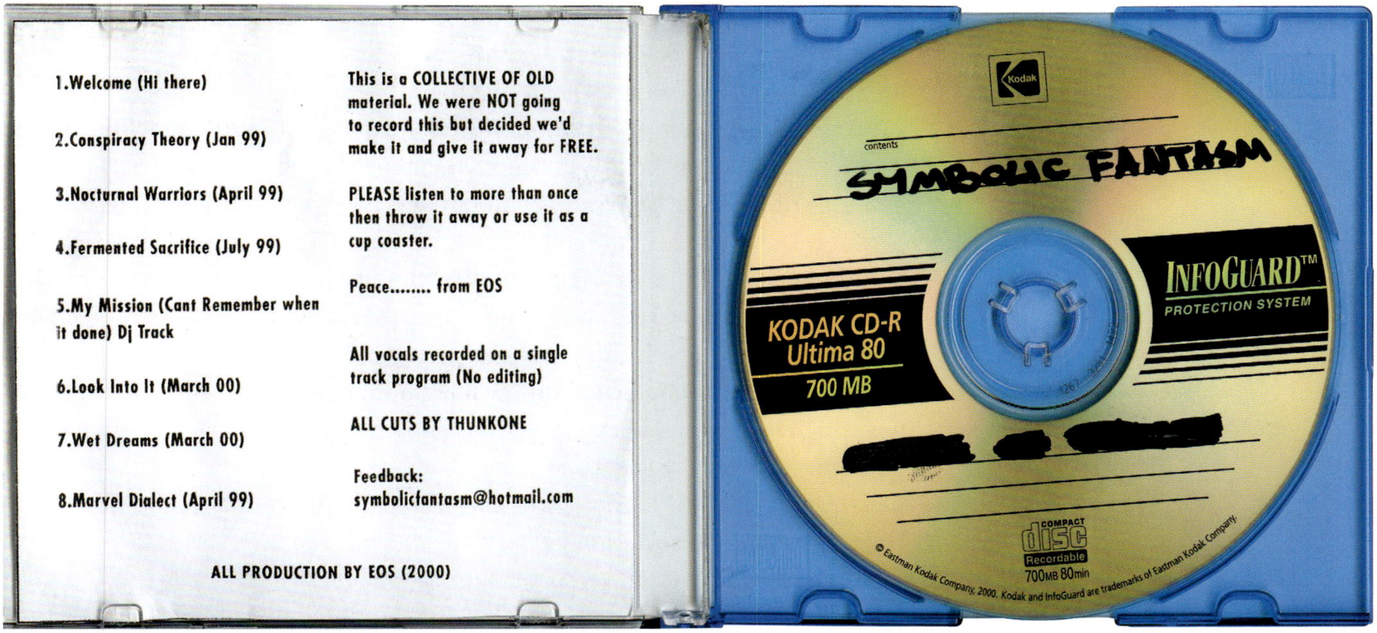

CD face and track-listing for Symbolic Fantasm's *Foot In The Door* EP (2000). Courtesy of Symbolic Fantasm.

band's name in stylized graffiti (presumably hand-written), but other details like track listings were presented in an unremarkable san serif. Upon opening the cover, the viewer's gaze is drawn to the shiny black and gold CDR face, contrasting with the blue tray it is sitting in. Scrawled on the CDR is the group's name, Symbolic Fantasm, but the CD title has been scribbled over. The scribble is messy and intriguing. Was there another title? Did they change the title? By leaving visible the scrawled marks of construction, the CD face draws its viewers into a narrative of their own imagining. As such, the viewer/listener becomes an active participant. The sleeve notes impress this role through the request:

> This is a COLLECTIVE OF OLD material. We were NOT going to record this but decided we'd make it and give it away for FREE.
> PLEASE listen to more than once then throw it away or use it as a cup coaster.[24]

By being an active participant, the person in possession of the CD becomes the means of documenting scarce material, carrying on its memory if they deem it worthwhile.

Contemporary copyright law dictates that there must be a single, defin-

24 Symbolic Fantasm, *Foot in the Door*, EOS, 2000.

able genesis to which a creative work can belong. Woodmansee and Jazi talk about this as a "regime of authorship" derived from the Western "Romantic belief that long and intense legal protection is the due of creative genius', thereby figuring authorship as an economic of "possessive individualism".[25] This regime positions creators as mythical donors of culture via the art they produce. Benjamin attributed the danger of reproduction to lie not within the mere act of copying, but rather in the relocation of art forms like painting away from the cultural space of their production.[26] Relocation damages or removes the aura of the artwork. Copyright law attempts to regulate how a creative work can be reconfigured, located and reproduced. By regulating ownership of a creative work the 'author' maintains a position of power over the culture and communities which receive and engage with it. However, conventional copyright law mistakes the aura of a work for a remunerable value which can be bought and sold, thereby splitting the 'author' from the 'aura' and the culture that produced it.[27] DIY CDs reference the author because they have a visible texture of inscription: either through the rough construction or, in the case of *Foot In The Door*, a literal marking in the handwriting of the creators. Handwriting directly links to authorship because the idea of an author only becomes necessary when you separate what is being said from the speaker. In writing the speaker is no longer present; hence a marker of presence, a recognizable trace to the physicality of the author, is needed. More broadly, artworks often feature the signature of their creator, inscribing onto the work a counterfeit of authenticity.[28] Being able to touch and hold something created personally by an artist, particularly something given directly to an audience member during a community event, generates an intimacy via contact and exchange. The inscribed handwriting perpetuates the exchange each time a recipient returns to the CD. In this way, DIY artworks circulate between artist and audience as a community artefact, closing distances associated with conventions of fine art cultures. But this relationship can be problematized when the artist is removed from direct exchange with the community which will receive the CD.

The library at Sydney's Conservatorium of Music has an extensive audiovisual collection containing many thousands of slickly packaged classical, jazz, and contemporary compositions. Amongst the shelves of twentieth-century composers is an oddity, a battered CDR case. Pulling it from the shelf, it is striking because of the handwritten inscription "Elena Kats-Chernin (*Selfmade CD* [1996])". Opening the case uncovers a shiny gold CD resting in a grubby white tray. A typed track-listing has been cut up and stuck to the CD's face along with a security strip and catalogue number. Pulling out the booklet reveals the text of a

25 Martha Woodmansee and Peter Jazi, "Introduction", in Martha Woodmansee and Peter Jazi (eds.), *The Construction of Authorship: Textual Appropriation in Law and Literature* (London: Duke University Press, 1994), pp. 2–3, 5–6.

26 Benjamin, pp. 107–108.

27 One striking example is the song "Waltzing Matilda", a surrogate national anthem of Australia, but whose copyright is heavily contested. Carl Fischer New York Inc. has registered copyright in the United States until 2011 and there have been attempts to both sell back or license the song to Australia, and according to Roger Clarke, the Australian Olympic organisers had to pay a licensing fee to play "Waltzing Matilda" at the closing ceremony of the Atlanta Olympic Games of 1996. See Roger Clarke, *Copyright in "Waltzing Matilda"*, www.anu.edu.au/people/Roger.Clarke/WM/Copyright.html (accessed 1 April 2005).

28 This recalls Derrida's response to Austin talking about the role of legal signatures affixing the presence of a person. Derrida notes that the iterability of a signature calls into question its singularity which thereby problematizes any possible link between author and writing. Yet, as Derrida notes, the signature performs for us its guarantee everyday. See Jacques Derrida, "Signature, Event, Context", in *Margins of Philosophy*, trans. Alan Bass (Brighton: Harvester Press 1982), pp. 307–330.

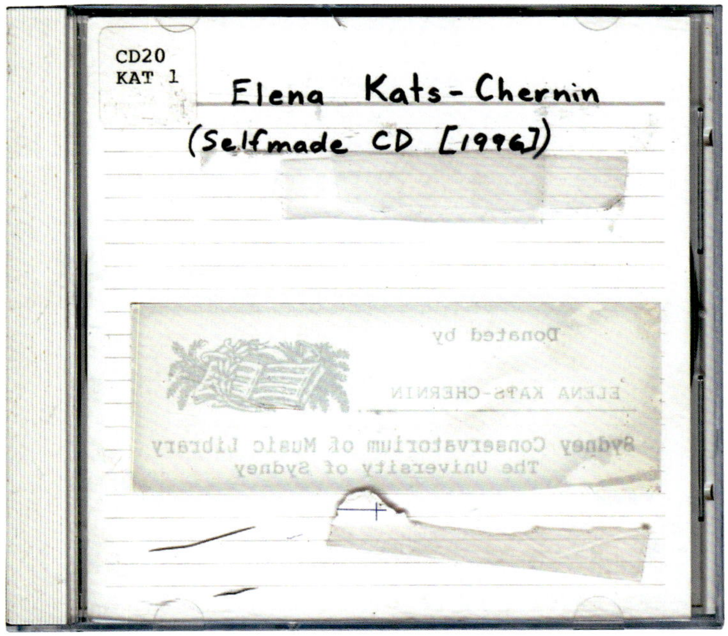

CD face and track-listing for Elena Kats-Chernin's *Selfmade CD* (1996).

Shiny gold CD resting in a grubby white tray.

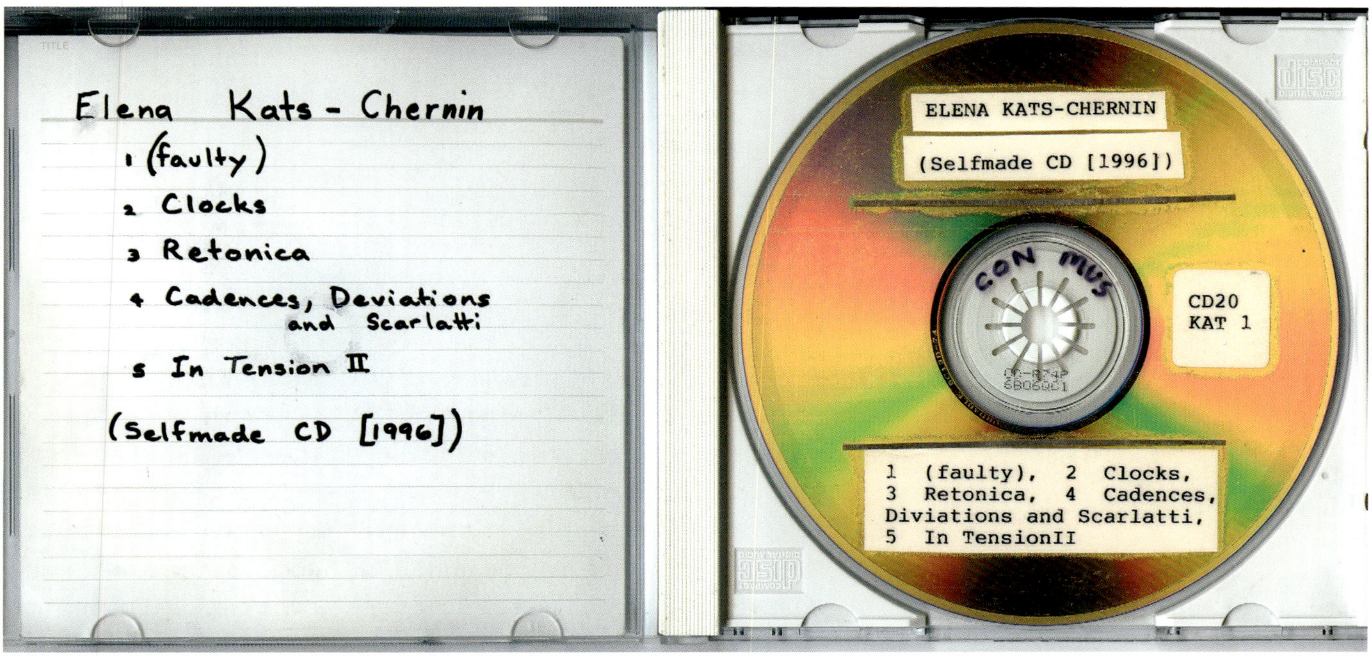

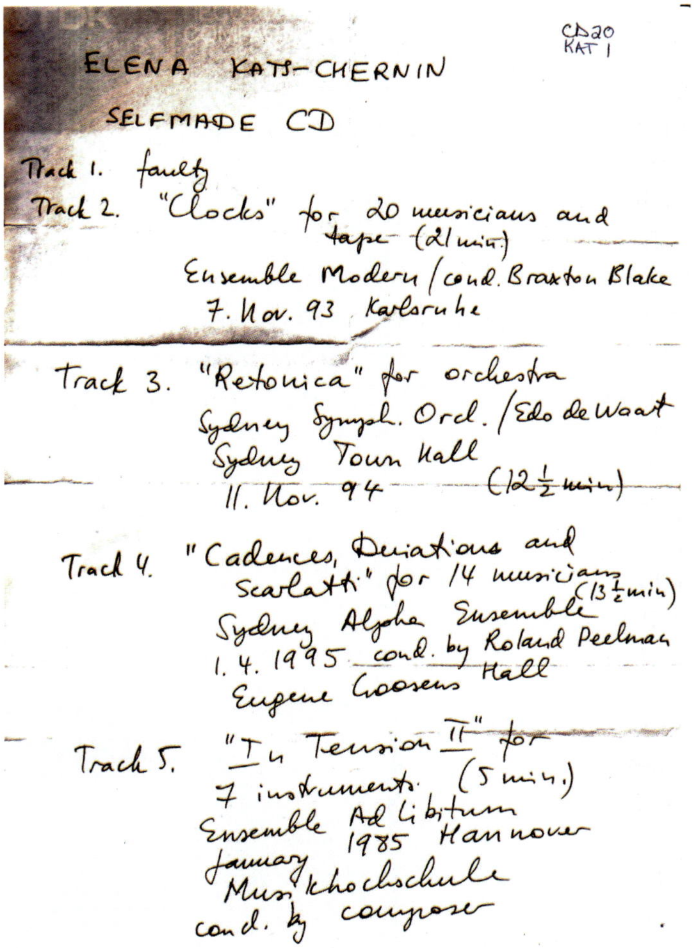

CD20
KAT 1

ELENA KATS-CHERNIN

SELFMADE CD

Track 1. faulty

Track 2. "Clocks" for 20 musicians and tape (21 min)
Ensemble Modern / cond. Braxton Blake
7. Nov. 93 Karlsruhe

Track 3. "Retonica" for orchestra
Sydney Symph. Orch. / Edo de Waart
Sydney Town Hall
11. Nov. 94 (12½ min)

Track 4. "Cadences, Deviations and Scarlatti" for 14 musicians (13½ min)
Sydney Alpha Ensemble
1. 4. 1995 cond. by Roland Peelman
Eugene Goossens Hall

Track 5. "In Tension II" for 7 instruments (5 min.)
Ensemble Ad Libitum 1985 Hannover
January
Musikhochschule
cond. by composer

A4 sheet of paper marked with black felt-tip ink.

sticker stuck inside the case: "Donated by ELENA KATS-CHERNIN/ Sydney Conservatorium of Music Library/ The University of Sydney",[29] making known that Kats-Chernin is both the composer *and* the donor. This information allows the title *Selfmade CD* to take on a new significance and places the rough construction of the CD as within a narrative of creation. Stuck opposite the warranty text of the insert card (declaring that the CDR, if "defective", is replaceable within a year of purchase) is an A4 sheet of paper marked with black felt-tip ink now yellowing against the page. Listed in a wide cursive hand are the details of each performance. Listening to the CD reveals that the writing has been deliberately misleading. While other tracks have a brief description, the first track is listed as

29 Elena Kats-Chernin, *Selfmade CD*, Elena Kats-Chernin, 1996.

"faulty". Like *Foot In The Door*, a story can be constructed from the packaging, questions forming in the mind of the holder like: "Why is the CD faulty?" What was on the track? When the sounds of the first composition begin, the ruse is revealed, which in turn illuminates the hand-crafting of the CD as deliberate: formative to the creation of the artwork itself.

The text on the booklet is written in two different hands; the folded page inside is cursive while the cover is plainly printed. It is difficult to discern whether these are crafted by one or two different people. This generates a mystery as to which hand (if any) belongs to the composer. The "Selfmade" aesthetic plays on notions of DIY to create something which will circulate outside of the 'grassroots' cultures of DIY and within the institutionalized space of fine-music education. While the CD as an object of self-made coarseness can poke fun at the other highly stylized CD casings which surround it, it serves to accentuate the gap between the composer and audience in several ways. Firstly, the audience is not present or involved in the process of receiving the CD. It is not intended to become part of an identity-building community interaction – nor is it intended as a personal artefact of an event or experience for an individual to remember and recall through engagement with the object. Secondly, being situated within the exclusive walls of the Sydney Conservatorium of Music as a special 'donation' from one of Australia's most regarded contemporary composers accentuates the perceived rarity and 'preciousness' of this CD as an art object. Thirdly, the positioning of the *Selfmade CD* as an art object within an elite institution *fetishizes* the interaction between CD and viewer; the CD may be 'borrowed', held and listened to, allowing a transitory adoration and glimpse of the author via its inscription and crafting. Yet this revered distance generated via the inscription of the composer onto *Selfmade CD*, or similarly, the intimacy generated through the exchange of *Foot InThe Door* is only possible because the audience/viewer/listener chooses to read the rough crafting of the CDs as meaningful. Both CDs require a consented and established relationship between performer/composer and listener/community.

Fashioning Authenticity via Exclusivity: Dappled Cities Fly

Selfmade CD creates itself as a work of art through the meshing of fine-art and DIY aesthetics. Some musicians working within local cultures of DIY reverse this process, referencing fine-art as a signifier of 'value' in their work. One such band is Sydney-based Dappled Cities Fly, who has associated their DIY constructed albums with fine art practices since their third release: an EP entitled

Dead Bodies Where Their Mouths Were. The album was partially recorded at the prestigious College of Fine Arts at the University of New South Wales (known as COFA) and the band produced sixty hand-made copies of the EP for a special Halloween performance which they crafted from the pages of a children's encyclopedia.[30] Oliver Heath describes the CDs:

> The discs were home burnt and the packaging was hand made by art-school friends. Not wanting to risk scratches from staples, the cd envelopes were constructed using glue. The finished product was like the old bootlegs distributed with zines in the days before the Internet, with the addition of just enough glitter to be reminiscent of a pre-pubescent fan mural. The catch was that while the glue did a good job of keeping the envelope together, it also managed to take the cd apart. The entire top surface of the meticulously packaged EPs adhered to the paper envelope and delaminated, leaving disappointed fans with nothing but a transparent plastic disc and sparkling hands.[31]

Though perhaps not the outcome the band may have intended, the DIY crafting of *Dead Bodies Where Their Mouths Were* effaced the musical content of the CD. The audience, by opening the CD, revealing its demise and engaging with its textures, become part of the encoding of the work. Benjamin argues that the "uniqueness" of an artwork is "inseparable from its being imbedded in the fabric of tradition" but that tradition itself "is thoroughly alive and extremely changeable".[32] Benjamin is drawing out the work of art as a kind of ceremonial "cult" locus, noting that the "unique value of the 'authentic' work of art has its basis in ritual, the location of its original use value".[33] Benjamin notes a difference between works of art intended to be received and valued on a mass scale, and works of art intended for small, restricted audiences in a specific location.[34] In this way, for Benjamin, there would be fundamental differences between, say, an album being pitched at the American Billboard charts or the latest Disney film soundtrack, and the Halloween gifting of *Dead Bodies Where Their Mouths Were* to the audience – differences beyond mere issues of scale. Value is polarized in works of art as either "cult value" or "exhibition value".[35] By associating *Dead Bodies Where Their Mouths Were* with fine art production, Dappled Cities Fly is arguably tapping into the ceremonial notions of the 'cult' to generate a value for their audience via its exclusivity. As such, the ruin of the musical content of the EP is not as important as the colloquial memory/recollection of the event for the audience, because, as Benjamin surmises, what matters in ritualis-

30 Dappled Cities Fly, www.dappledcitiesfly.com/musicdead.htm (accessed 16 April 2005).
31 Oliver Heath, email to author, 7 April 2004.
32 Benjamin, p. 109.
33 Ibid.
34 Ibid., pp. 109–110.
35 Ibid., p. 109.

tic artistic production is the idea of its existence, not its "being on view", or its being heard.[36]

Dappled Cities Fly highlights the interplay between DIY cultures and fine-art conceptions of exclusivity. *Dead Bodies Where Their Mouths Were* draws upon fine-art modes of production to generate a sense of authenticity and value, but, as Heath describes, the finished aesthetic more strongly resembles artifacts of DIY media. This mélange has continued in subsequent releases. Dead Cities Fly enlisted COFA student Tim Rogers to design the cover of *Peach*, a radio single which followed on from the *Dead Bodies* EP. Rogers has described the process of creating the CD for the COFA student magazine, *The College Voice*, saying:

Cover Artwork for Dappled Cities Fly's single *Peach* (2004). Courtesy of Dave Rennick.

> They didn't have any money and my scanner was broken. Black and white photocopying is cheap. Text can be generated without a scanner.... The cover could be printed and folded without any glue, or too much difficulty, although the band may disagree. It ended up being a bit of a burden and I don't know whether they were very happy with the final outcome. It looked quite ugly, but that was incidental to what it was about... I guess the underlying concept was inspired by fluxus thoughts. The whole colouring-in exercise was meant to create a conceptual bond (distance collaboration) between the Band and radio (since it was mainly just for radio): that the Band would colour in the sleeve partially, and then the pencil would be attached to the sleeve for the radio announcers to finish colouring. Maybe they would comment on it; say something more about the Band than the Band's name and what a strange name it is. (They may even pronounce it correctly). I think a coloured pencil says a lot about Dappled Cities Fly.[37]

Two hundred copies of *Peach* were made for distribution, and each copy was individually numbered, emphasizing its limited circulation. The stated Fluxus inspirations, and more broadly Rogers' role as conceptual artist on this project, suggests that the band was trying to conceal the limited budget and DIY production methods by fashioning an aura redolent of art traditions. In doing so they also exposed DIY aesthetics, using its textures and inbuilt call to 'action' to attract involvement from radio announcers. This attempt at bonding via "distance collaboration" acknowledges a relationship resembling that of art critic/curator and artist, rather than that of local artist within a local community, with the announcer assuming the dominant subject position. This play on distance draws into Benjamin's definition of aura which he describes as a "unique phenomenon of a distance however close it may be", saying that it "represents nothing

36 Ibid.

37 Tim Rogers, cited in Ben Maher, "Art & Music: The Colour of Sound", in *The College Voice*, Sydney: COFA, 17 October 2004: www.cofasa.unsw.edu.au/voice/archive/issue4.php?id=67 (accessed 14 April 2005).

but the formulation of the cult value of the work of art in categories of space and time perception".[38] For Benjamin, distance opposes closeness and "the essentially distant" object becomes "unapproachable", a quality he considers central to the creation of the "cult image".[39] So distance is integral to the cult-produced aura, and Benjamin characterizes this relationship thus: "True to its nature, it remains 'distant, however close it may be'. The closeness which one may gain from its subject matter does not impair the distance which it retains in its appearance".[40] The brash assemblage of a fine-art cult value through fine-art rhetoric and DIY aesthetics in *Peach* is only problematic if trying to read the album as definitively embodying either fine-art or DIY traditions. The subversiveness of DIY lies in its ability to usurp both the exclusive distance inherent in the art-object and the modes of production aligned with mass reproduction and exhibition. In doing so, DIY practitioners create their own economies of exchange which celebrate *ritual through community*. DIY culture is fluid, inconsistent, and oppositional in its appropriation of means towards creative solutions

Conclusion, or DIY CDs Tell Stories

DIY albums tell simple narratives of seeing, feeling and hearing. They create intimacy or a fetishized cult value via a complex process of inscription and authorship. More broadly, DIY plays with distance simultaneously assembling communities and/or deliberately limiting access to increase distances and enhance value. DIY narratives flow and are exchanged 'glocally' because they usurp the spaces, vectors, modes and boundaries to which they are denied access.

The success of DIY can be measured by its continual resurgence in subcultural communities, which in turn has led to an appropriation of DIY aesthetics and textures outside of its socio-political sphere. The coarse scrawls, smudged printing, and rough collage-juxtapositions have been mimicked in professionally designed and printed releases like Mugison's *Niceland*[41] and openly exploited in System Of A Down's *Steal This Album!*[42] When these techniques are used in environments of mass production, the roughness does not signify, it only cites. DIY's appropriation into an aesthetic commerce constructs a perverse feedback loop between the subcultures that produce its textures and technologies, and the mass reproduction of these aesthetics removed from their cultures and communities. The artefacts of mass reproduction may appear and be consumed within these same subcultures, but they only serve to diminish the aura and opposition of the subculture. However, because DIY culture is decentralized, this feedback shifts and marshals itself to reappear as another call for 'action',

38 Benjamin, p. 121.
39 Ibid.
40 Ibid.
41 Mugison, *Niceland*, Accidental, 2004.
42 System Of A Down, *Steal This Album!*, American Recordings, 2002.

reforming communities where a need is exposed and configuring itself into new DIY cultural artefacts with new formations of aura. DIY culture is always in narcissistic motion, usurping technologies and modes of production to tell the stories of *its* production.

Re-Presenting Mixed Tapes and CDs

Gavin Steingo

To B, who will receive this as I have his mixes.

A "mix", briefly stated, is a tape or CD created by copying songs from various sources one after another to create a customized compilation. In contrast with a mass-produced compilation, a "mix" is usually made as a single unit. Although there are various types, in most cases mixes are created for a specific occasion, and therefore multiple duplications of an original mix are uncommon. To further distinguish these single-copy mixes from commercial compilations and mass-produced mixes, the term "home mix" is sometimes used. Much of the time, mixes are created as gifts for others, and recently there has been a serious attempt to theorize "mixing" as courtship.[1] Although there are obvious differences between mixed tapes and mixed CDs, for the purposes of this essay I argue, with Kamal Fox, that "the 'concept' of mixing is not medium-specific".[2] As a digital mixer and former "tape-head" told Fox: "What makes a mix 'work' is the consideration put into the content, not the medium it is recorded on. As long as there is obvious love and time put into the final result, that's what's going to have an impact".[3]

While in the past five years or so a small but substantial body of literature on mixes has emerged, almost nothing has been written on the mix as physical object. From narrative theory and politico-legal approaches, to "mixing" as a discursive construction of masculine identity, scholars invariably have written about what's "on" the mix.[4] Considering the emphasis on mixes as gifts and courting "devices" (Fox even suggests that the flower bouquet is a predecessor of the mixed tape), it is surprising that there has not been any effort to interrogate the physical characteristics and presentation of mixed tapes and CDs. Important questions like: "What do mixes look like?" and "How are mixes presented?" have, thus far, been neglected. In fact, usually when people write about mixes,

1 See Kamal Fox, "Mixed Feelings: Notes on the Romance of the Mixed Tape", *Rhizomes* 5 (2002). www.rhizomes.net/issue5/fox.html (hereafter cited as Fox, "MF").

2 "MF", section 6. Fox uses the word "tracks" for the various sections in his article.

3 However, Fox does note: "This is not to say that mixers don't have medium-specific preferences. Some mixers feel that tapes allow far more personalization than CDs. One author, advancing this point-of-view, confirms his nostalgic fetishism: 'Computerized mix CDs suck all the creativity and charm out of the process. [...] A neatly stacked pile of small plastic boxes [CDs] just doesn't have the same warm feeling as a heavy stack of big vinyl albums'". The quote in Fox's quote can be found in A.J. Michael, "Tapehead", *The UTNE Reader*, May/June 2001, p. 45, in Fox, "Mixed Feelings", section 6.

4 For narrative theory, see Fox, "MF"; for a politico-legal approach see Rob Drew, "The Space Between: Copyright, Consumer Rights, and Home Audio Mixing" (unpublished manuscript, 2004, hereafter cited as "SB"), and idem, "Mixed Blessings: The Commercial Mix and the Future of Music Aggregation", *Popular Music and Society* 28, no. 4 (2005), pp. 533–555; for mixing as a masculine construct see Philip Bagust, "'... The Making of a Good Compilation Tape is a Subtle Art ...': Selling the 'Real Me' with the Music Compilation or 'Mix' Tape" (paper presented at the conference Sonics. Synergies: Creative Cultures, The Hawke Institute, University of South Australia, Adelaide, 17–20 July 2003, hereafter cited as "MGCT").

the physical tape or CD is completely ignored to the point of becoming invisible. For example, when Rob Drew describes the mixed tape as "an art of the segue" ("SB") he is obviously alluding to the songs "on" the tape and not the tape itself or its encasement and cover. In fact, Drew does not even mention the "look" of mixed tapes, and it seems that the tape and its cover are thought of as nothing more than the container "of" songs. Kamal Fox and Philip Bagust similarly fail to mention the presentation of mixed tapes and CDs in their writing. I am not criticizing these writers. Rather, I am trying to illustrate the pervasive focus on *music* in discussions of mixing.

That the word "mix" often automatically excludes physicality and refers only to the invisible (to the human eye) information stored on a tape or CD risks constructing a skewed understanding of what a mix actually is. In my research I have found that the presentation of the mix is as important as what is "on" it. When lovers exchange tapes, for example, the drawing, photograph, or poem on the cover is as important as the songs. It is important not to neglect this crucial aspect of mixes. Further, the fact that some people choose *not* to make a cover for a mix is significant. Although I will discuss this aspect later in detail, now I want to point out only that a blank piece of white paper accompanying a tape or CD in the box is, in a way, a type of cover. In a certain sense, the pure white jumps out at the receiver and conveys the very absence of creativity that went into making (or rather, not making) the cover. Thus, not making a cover is an act, insofar as it is a decision on the part of the mixer.

As Drew points out, the practice of mixing began in the 1960s with the commercialization of cassette tapes and recorders. In the 1970s mixing increased in popularity, largely because of technological advancements. The '70s saw the invention of the boombox and Walkman – two devices that would forever change music consumption.[5] The tape mix has been translated into the digital age in the form of the mixed CD.[6] Of course, the above historical sketch is very limited. For, while it is easy enough to trace the development of these "home" mixes, the mix's relationship to contemporary creative processes is more complex. There is, of course, a connection between mixing and the creative processes involved in many contemporary music genres, especially hip-hop. Moreover, the creative process involved in mixing bears a strong resemblance to contemporary DJing. The important point to note here is that while "deejay mixes are a one-to-many medium aimed at a wide audience, home mixes are most often exchanged one-to-one".[7] The fact that mixes are very often given as gifts to others and are thus personal cannot be over emphasized. Still, in terms of what is "on" the mix, there are important points of comparison between mixes and DJing.

5 See especially Drew, "SB", and see also Drew's 2005 article cited above.

6 As I pointed out earlier, for the purposes of this essay it is sufficient to state that the "the 'concept' of mixing is not medium-specific".

7 Drew, "SB".

For example, it could be argued that both DJs and mixed tape and CD creators need to master the skill of "flow". As DJ Amy Kellner describes it: "Have you ever made a mixtape for someone you had a crush on? Then you already know what flow is – the ability to maintain a mood".[8]

The above historical sketch is a fairly standard example of how mixes are theorized. In every piece of extant literature I have read on mixes, technological advances are discussed and then there is a discussion on the creative processes involved in mixing and how these processes relate to broader transformations in creativity evidenced by practices like DJing and by genres like hip-hop. Something is clear from these discourses: this history again foregrounds what is "on" the tape, and says little about the actual presentation of the tape. That many writers compare DJing to creating mixes further illustrates the persistent and consistent focus on the music "line-up" – the "chronology of songs" – or, what is "on" the mix. Because DJs use computers and various CDs as well as mixing desks and PA systems, it seems obvious that the physicality of a mixed tape or CD contrasts sharply with that of a DJ set-up. Comparing mixes to DJs (in)conspicuously "hides" the fact that the physicality of mixes is important, and the comparison discursively constructs the *mix itself* as something non-physical.

In this essay I will shift the terrain from "inside" (or what is "on" the tape or CD) to "outside". It is significant that an obvious ambiguity arises here. That is to say, the common meaning of the word "on" a tape or CD actually refers to the non-visible data stored on the magnetic tape of a cassette tape or the readable (under-)surface of the CD. If the word "on" refers to what is "on" the magnetic tape strip or under-surface of a tape or CD respectively, what word can be used to refer to what is on the outside of a plastic tape "cassette" (that is, its *casing*), or on the non-readable side of a CD? One would have to say something like, "*On* the actual, physical tape or CD, itself", if one wanted to specifically designate the "outer" surface of the tape or CD. If a reply to the question, "where is my Velvet Underground CD?" was: "On one of my tapes", this response could (here, ironically) be interpreted as saying that the Velvet Underground CD has been recorded "onto" the (magnetic) tape. If the physical CD was lying on top of a physical cassette tape, in order to avoid ambiguity, one would have to say something like: "Your Velvet Underground CD is literally on top of one of my tape cassettes". From this it can be seen that the very emphasis in both theoretical and colloquial discourses on the "data" stored "on" the mix creates confusion and ambiguity right down to the level of language and signification itself. Language is, in fact, prioritized towards tape and CD "data", and the fact that spatial designations like "on" relate to the songs on a tape or CD means that

8 Amy Kellner, "Hey DJ, Fuck You! (Anyone Can Rock the Party)", *Vice* 11 (2002), pp. 81–82.

talking about a physical tape or CD is difficult because common prepositions that one may want to use are hence unavailable. From now on, I will usually use the term "inside" the mix to refer to what is "on" the mix (in terms of "data" or "information"), and I will refer to the "outside" of the tape as its physical presence and presentation, including the tape cover. By renaming what is usually referred to as "on" a mix (and calling it instead) "in" or "inside" a mix, I literally turn the discourse inside-out.

However, instead of focusing on the actual tape or CD, I will look at how mixes are adorned, decorated, and presented – I will look particularly at mix covers. The relationship between mix cover and the music "in" the mix can be further theorized in terms of paratextuality. It is plausible to think of the cover as a paratext of the musical text (i.e., the music that is "in" the mix). Yet, here again it is clear that the analysis of paratexts always contains a certain amount of ambiguity with regards to borders of inside and outside, and permeability. Gérard Genette writes that the paratext is "neither on the interior nor on the exterior: it is both; it is on the threshold".[9] Moreover, the paratext may be defined as precisely that "undefined zone",[10] somewhere between inside and outside: and yet this boundary is porous, it is a "fringe"[11] (a threshold, a limit) of the main "text". The "immanent" text is always transcended, it always overflows in a fluid intertextuality.[12] The cover of a mix is certainly a paratext in that it surrounds and extends the (musical) text, "precisely in order to present it, in the usual sense of this verb but also in the strongest sense: to make present, to ensure the text's presence in the world".[13] Yet, I would be hesitant to view the mix cover as a paratext in the sense that a paratext is "always subordinate to 'its' text".[14] Rather, I think it is more helpful to see the mix cover and the music on the mix as two texts of equal importance which are somehow thresholds of each other. The "inside" and "outside" of a tape or CD, then, can be thought of as different, but related texts. Moreover, even though there are obvious differences between the cover of a mix, and what is in (or on) the mix, certainly the "outside" and "inside" of a mix need to be compared. I contend that the form rather than the content of "inside" and "outside" are similar.

I use the existing literature on mixes as a point of departure for this essay. Even though I have pointed out that problems arise when the word "mix" refers exclusively to what is (now) inside the mix, at times I will use the term as it has been used by other authors and will later problematize the term once more, and also draw connections between "their" mix and the mix viewed from both "outside" and "inside".

9 Translated and quoted in Richard Macksey's foreword to Gérard Genette, *Paratexts: Thresholds of Interpretation* (Cambridge: Cambridge University Press, 1997), p. xvii (hereafter cited as *PT*).

10 Genette, *PT*, p. 2. See also C. Duchet, "Pour une socio-critique, ou Variations sur un incipit", *Littérature* 1 (1971), p. 6.

11 See Macksey's foreword to Genette, p. xvii; and see also Philippe Lejeune, *Le Pacte autobiographique* (Paris: Seuil, 1975), p. 45.

12 Macksey, in *PT*, p. xvi.

13 Genette, *PT*, p. 1.

14 Ibid., *PT*, p. 12.

On Mixed Tapes and CDs

As I have already noted, Rob Drew has called home mixing "an art of the segue; an art, as Sergei Eisenstein defined film editing, of making one plus one equal three".[15] By creating a new connection between songs, a mixer is able to give new meanings to songs, and infer a unity between songs which otherwise may have seemed completely different. While musicians create and "own" the "property" of songs, mixers, on the other hand, "create, and own, the space between".[16] Stated in another way, the experience of listening to a mixed tape can be described as the "willful suspension of discontinuity",[17] where the creator "glues" or "sutures" the songs together into one whole. In summarizing the work of Mary Douglas and Baron Isherwood, John Storey reminds us that:

> The symbolic value of objects in the "information system" is not inherent in the objects themselves. Value is something "conferred by human judgements". [...] To understand the value of one object, it is necessary to locate it in the information system as a whole.[18]

In *Distinction: A Social Critique of the Judgement of Taste,* Pierre Bourdieu argues "that what people consume does not simply reflect distinctions and differences embedded elsewhere, that cultural consumption makes visible". Instead, "cultural consumption is the means by which they are produced, maintained and reproduced".[19] De Certeau suggests that "[e]veryday life invents itself by *poaching* in countless ways on the property of others".[20] In this context, Henry Jenkins' writing on fandom can be easily transposed to mixers, who "raid mass culture, claiming its materials for their own use, reworking creations and social interactions".[21] By borrowing and inflecting mass culture, mixers (for Jenkins, it is fans) become active creators of meaning.

Regarding this appropriation of existing property, Kamal Fox has drawn our attention to Barry Truax's concept of "schizophonia" which he describes as "the challenge that faces listeners in the age of the mechanical reproduction of sound; it is the sensation that results when a sound is heard, via mechanical means, in a context other than its original one". Truax claims that "the use of the Greek 'schizo', meaning split or separation, emphasizes the difference in context which characterizes electroacoustic manipulation". Truax argues that "[t]he challenge of the schizophonic situation for the listener is to make sense out of the juxtaposition of two different contexts".[22] While I think that Truax has made an interesting point, I believe that his approach does not take into

15 Sergei M. Eisenstein, *The Film Sense*, trans. Jay Leyda (New York: Harcourt Brace, 1957), p. 14, quoted in Drew, "SB".

16 Drew, "SB".

17 Fox, "MF", section 1.

18 John Storey, *Cultural Consumption and Everyday Life* (London, Sydney, Aukland: Arnold and New York: Oxford University Press, 1999), p. 43, quoted in Fox, "MF", section 1. Fox provides a page number for this citation, but for some reason does not list any book by Storey in his bibliography. Even though he did not provide a reference, his quotation can be found in the book by Storey cited in this footnote. The phrases in quotation marks in this quote can be found in Mary Douglas and Brian Isherwood, *The World of Goods: Towards an Anthropology of Consumption* (London: Routledge, 1996), p. xxii.

19 Storey, *Cultural Consumption and Everyday Life*, p. 43, quoted in Fox, "MF", section 1.

20 Michel de Certeau, *The Practice of Everyday Life* (Berkeley: University of California Press, 1984), pp. xi-xii, quoted in Fox, section 1. Again, Fox provides a page number for this quote, but does not provide reference information for this book in his bibliography. I located his quotation in the de Certeau book cited in this footnote.

21 Henry Jenkins, *Textual Poachers: Television Fans & Participatory Culture* (New York and London: Routledge, 1992), p. 18.

22 Quoted in Fox, "MF", section 1. While Fox (again) provides a page number for this quote but does not include any books by Truax in his bibliography, I have located the exact quote in Barry Truax, *Acoustic Communication* (Norwood, NJ.: Ablex, 1984), p. 120.

account the fact that today music often lacks an "origin" and that the space of music listening is usually very decentralized.[23] Today, rather than having a specific origin, a song may be recognized merely as "that song that I heard on the radio last week". Even canonical works such as Beethoven's *5th Symphony* are known to many only in the simulacral form of the "fate motive" used as a cell phone ring, for example.[24]

Rather than Truax's simplistic model of the "juxtaposition of two different contexts", "schizophrenia" or "schizophonia" may be considered a far more traumatic transformation of the soundscape and the experience of listening on the whole. Paul Virilio's conception of a complete "loss of orientation" seems more accurate: "The specific negative aspect of these information superhighways is precisely this loss of orientation regarding alterity (the other), this disturbance in the relationship with the other and with the world".[25] Truax's theory necessitates a referent, or master signifier, but it may be more useful to read mixes in terms of the hyperreal, the endless profusion of signs and of free-floating simulacra. The death of the Baudrillardian "real" results in a frenzied and almost desperate creation of countless images where politics and history are simulated in the form of depthless signs. The "age of the mix" therefore signals a new kind of subjectivity: the death of the author and the birth of the mixer.

But what of "schizo-optica"? Briefly, in the above, songs are described as "objects", and indeed "mix" discourses often regard songs as identifiable and in some way tangible "things". Insofar as songs can be thought of as "objects" in the current context, covers are created in the same way. The magnetic tape of a cassette tape and the printable and readable surface of a CD are essentially – that is to say, are *in essence* – parallel to the "canvas" of the cover. Like songs recorded on a tape or CD, people often use photographs, magazine or book cutouts, draw pictures, or type or write out lines of an existing poem, on the tape or CD cover. In almost all cases, these "images" or "objects" are pre-existing cultural products and are used to mediate relationships, memories, and feelings. I will speak more about this process later.

Decentralizing the Subject

I suggest that mixing is a type of writing. Following Roland Barthes, I believe that "the text is not a line of words releasing a single 'theological' meaning (the 'message' of the Author-God)...". Rather, the text is "a multi-dimensional space in which a variety of writings, none of them original, blend and clash. The text is a tissue of quotations drawn from innumerable centers of culture..." The au-

23 In actual fact, Truax's position is more complex than what I have suggested here. Truax does actually acknowledge that music in the contemporary soundscape does not have a centred origin, yet he seems to find such a situation bewildering. "In many cases", he writes, "the 'sense' becomes conventional acceptance. We come to expect that voices should appear from the walls and ceilings in public places such as airports and train stations to give us information". His is an analysis based on the comparison of contemporary simulacra and earlier notions of the auratic body in terms of presence. For example, he says in astonishment: "We think nothing of hearing music (even of a 100-piece orchestra!) emanating from the smallest places". It is interesting to compare Truax's position to that of Paul Virilio (see below).

24 See for example, Mina Yang, "Für Elise Circa 2000: Postmodern Readings of Beethoven in Popular Contexts", *Popular Music and Society* 29.1 (2006), pp. 1–15.

25 Paul Virilio, "Speed and Information: Cyberspace Alarm", *Ctheory*, 27 August 1995. www.ctheory.net/articles.aspx?id=72.

thor's "only power is to mix writings, to counter the ones with the others, in such a way as never to rest on any one of them... To give the text an Author is to impose a limit on that text, to furnish it with a final signified, to close the writing...".[26] Thus, the "author" is only the instance of writing. In a similar way, Claude Lévi-Strauss has stated that "I appear to myself as the place where something is going on, but there is no 'I', no 'me'. Each of us is a kind of crossroads where things happen. The crossroads is purely passing; something happens there".[27]

Drew claims that others' "words and music, even those borrowed from mass culture, can carry as much interpersonal resonance as our own words". He goes so far as to say that a "home mix is the sort of secondhand text that aspires to the status of liturgy".[28] Similarly to songs, images (magazine cut-outs, drawings "of" something known, etc.) on a self-made cover form a "secondhand text". Again, in this regard, the form of the "inside" and "outside" of mixes are similar. Mixers merely arrange the text (whether it be the "inside" with songs, or the "outside" with graphic images); mixers mix various texts, and are inscribed into the new text as the expression of the unity of the text itself. As pointed out earlier, perhaps the "I" of the mix can be read as the space between the songs – or, now, the space "between" the images, those "borderlines", where one image melts into another – as the glue, or as the crossroads where the songs or images meet. Thus, the cassette does not "describe" the mixer, but rather "represents" the mixer, as the mixer re-presents the mix. Mixing is dialectical: on the one hand, it is a way of speaking through the Other (i.e., an already existing, "found" object), and, on the other hand, allowing the Other to speak through you. By the latter, I mean that tracks are given voice through their inclusion inside the mix. Thus mixing accepts the "death of the author" and encourages "expressing oneself without pretending that there is some honest, unmediated 'self' to express".[29] Mixed tapes, then, "are not about the disclosure of the 'self'" but are rather "about creating a sense of availability".[30] For example, Rob, the protagonist in Nick Hornby's novel *High Fidelity* (1995), uses mixes to "pour out his essential Rob Gordon-ness".[31] Seen this way, mixes represent a distillation of the "essential but (perversely) contingent you of the moment". Like many others, Rob's mixes say: "Here is a worthy individual, can you read the text closely enough to establish the attributes of the individual that compiled it?"[32]

It is important to re-iterate that covers, like the "inside" of mixes, are almost always made up of images available to the general public. From cartoon and comic characters to magazine cut-outs and quotes from famous writers, these "public" fragments (like "public" songs) mediate relationships in unique

26 Roland Barthes, "Death of the Author", in *Image, Music, Text* (Glasgow: Fontana/Collins, 1977), pp. 142–148, here pp. 146–147.

27 Claude Lévi-Strauss, *Myth and Meaning* (London and New York: Routledge, 2002), pp. 1–2.

28 Drew, "SB".

29 Fox, "MF", section 5.

30 Ibid.

31 Bagust, "MGCT".

32 Ibid.

ways when used in mixed tapes. Even a drawing on a mix is almost always a drawing of something (known "publicly") – of a person, or of a place. The crucial point here is that mix-fragments are, in a fundamental way, impersonal. Frederic Jameson has pointed out that the end of the autonomous subject or bourgeois ego does not only "bring with it the end of the psychopathologies of that ego" – it means much more. For one thing, it means the end of style (in the sense of the unique and the personal, the "subjective"): "the end of the distinctive individual brush stroke (as symbolized by the emergent primacy of mechanical reproduction)". With regard to expression, feelings, or emotions, the "liberation, in contemporary society, from the older anomie of the centered subject may also mean not merely a liberation from anxiety but a liberation from every other kind of feeling as well, since there is no longer a self present to do the feeling". However, this does not suggest that "cultural products of the postmodern era are utterly devoid of feeling, but rather that such feelings – which it may be better and more accurate, following Jean-François Lyotard, to call 'intensities' – are now free-floating and impersonal and tend to be dominated by a peculiar kind of euphoria...".[33] The job of a mixer, then, is to use impersonal cultural products personally. The crucial point here is that, although cultural products have the ability to become personal, they never lose their impersonal qualities. This dialectical movement parallels the emergence of a "postmodern, 'performative' self".[34]

As I have demonstrated, mixes defy the Romantic conception of subjectivity where writing is seen "as a medium in which a singular personality heroically exposes itself"[35] and at the same time provide a way of "saying 'I think you are really neat' without being cliché or falling into the whole trap of sincerity".[36] Contrary to the conception of the Author "as a tormented self raping its own unique subjectivity",[37] the performance of "decentralized subjectivity" relies on "externalising the 'essential me' through display of our 'style sets'".[38] Thus, cultural products are "drawn in" to relationships (are poached, as de Certeau put it) at the same time as a person's characteristics are projected *outwards* on those cultural products.

However, here Fox adds a cautionary note: this 'letting the Other speak' and the multivocality and openness to multiple interpretations involved can also act as an escape route for the mixer. If the mixer is seen only as "an instance" and not as a responsible ego-subject who creates, it is also possible to say, in tricky situations, "They're just songs [one could substitute: images, or pictures], I didn't mean anything by it".[39] This new kind of subjectivity then can alternatively and negatively be read as a "persona [which] reveals without be-

33 Fredric Jameson, *Postmodernism, or, the Cultural Logic of Late Capitalism* (Durham, NC: Duke University Press, 1991), p. 72.
34 Bagust's abstract for "MGCT".
35 Susan Sontag, "Introduction" in *Selected Writings*, by Antonin Artaud (Berkeley: University of California Press, 1988), p. xviii (hereafter cited as *SW*).
36 Fox, "MF", section 5.
37 Sontag, *SW*, pp. xviii-xix.
38 Bagust, "MGCT".
39 Fox, "MF", section 5.

ing personal" or "a buffer that protects the narrator's ego".[40] For many mixed tape and CD creators it is "much safer to quote from cultural products than to speak for oneself...".[41] Fox's warning about the lack of responsibility involved in conceptions of "postmodern" subjectivity brings to our attention the subtleties involved in the mix as an object mediating relationships. In the following section I turn more explicitly to the aspect of relationships and mixes.

It may be worth pointing out first, however, that there are certainly many other types of mixes than "romantic" (courting) mixes, or even "gift" mixes more generally. One taxonomy[42] describes the following types of mixes (among others): the house party mix, the road trip mix, the workout mix, and the hangover mix. Although it may seem at first that these mixes have nothing to do with the "gift" mixes mentioned earlier in this essay, it is important to note that almost all types of mixes are at one or another point *performative*, and almost all mixes mediate relationships in some way. The road trip mix, for example, is often given to a traveler as a gift before s/he departs. The road trip mix may also be made as a mix to be shared by the various parties traveling in the vehicle. The workout mix, like the hangover, on the other hand, may be made for the mixer him/herself. The crucial point to note is that there almost always comes a point when a mixer says: "Check out this mix I made", or "You should borrow my workout mix". Like songwriters, mixers think of themselves as creators and often want to share their work with others. Moreover, people often perform for themselves (see the next section). While not all mixes are "gifts", the vast majority of mixes are, at some point, either given, lent, or shown to others. In all of these cases, the cover is important because it is the first thing seen; and the cover, like the "inside" of the mix, is both a performance and a kind of writing.

Relationships and Mixes

I have mentioned how mixers commonly use pre-existing cultural products. Mixing, like the process of consumption, has the ability to "extract items from the market and make them personal".[43] By collecting and putting together songs and later giving a mixed tape to someone as a gift, home mixers "sacralize" songs, "transforming them into inalienable expressions of love and devotion".[44] Using Miller's description of gift shopping as "the construction of the other as a desiring subject", Drew suggests that in the process of mixing, the mixer hears familiar songs as though for the first time, repositioning him/herself as the recipient. In other words, the mixer must include what Prince calls "signs of the 'You'".[45] And, in fact, "Some of us, in our heart of hearts, are always thinking in

40 Ibid.

41 Ibid.

42 See www.artofthemix.org. artofthemix.org is a great resource for anyone interested in mixing.

43 David Miller, *A Theory of Shopping* (Ithaca, NY: Cornell University Press, 1999), p. 131; quoted in Drew, "SB".

44 See Drew, "SB".

45 Gerald Prince, *Narratology: The Form and Functioning of Narrative* (Berlin, New York, Amsterdam: Mouton Publishers, 1982), p. 17; quoted in Fox, section 5.

terms of mixes when we listen to music – always thinking, 'Kate would love this song', or, *'This one would be good for Bill'*".[46]

Pursuing the idea that the gift of a mixed tape is often a kind of courting, Fox notes that the words "mix" and "promiscuous" are both derived from the Latin verb *miscere*. He suggests that – as systems of signs – calling cards, bouquets and LPs are, in fact, predecessors of the mixed tape.[47] The mix, then, falls "between" relationships. The receiver of a mix becomes as much an author as the mixer him/herself. Alternatively, Drew suggests, a home mix is often more like a scrapbook than a love letter. However, perhaps we could read this rather as a love letter addressed to oneself, where a scrapbook might be defined as "a commemorative text ... designed for self-consumption, with the maker's projected 'self' serving as the primary future audience".[48]

Moreover, both (1) songs or images and (2) collected and mixed songs or images are texts. However, the two texts are different and form different "levels". The two "levels" of texts can be read through Roland Barthes' "second-order semiological system": "That which is a sign (namely the associative total of a concept and its image) in the first system, becomes a mere signifier in the second".[49] Hence, in mixes, each song or cover-image (S_1 or denotation: first system) is transformed from sign to signifier as it becomes one element in the mix (S_2 or connotation: second system). A mixer is she or he who understands that a sign in a first level text (either song or image) becomes a signifier as it enters the mix. Hence, the mixer builds a second order semiological system which may also be called, following Barthes, a *mythology*. The form of a DJ's creation is exactly the same as that of a mixer (of either songs or of images). That is to say, DJs also create second order semiological systems. Although the mixer or DJ succeeds the Author (or Composer, in the traditional sense), mixing involves a kind of post-Author authorship that can only be called mixing. Stated in another way: DJs also mix. Hence, this act of "authorship" does not signal the absolute death of the author-subject, but rather its complete transformation. DJ Amy Kellner jibes that one of the best things about being a DJ is getting complimented on playing a song. She recounts that sometimes when playing a "kickass" song people will run up to her and shout "I love this song!" Kellner sarcastically states that: 'You get all proud and pretend you wrote it. You're like, 'Thanks!' Yeah, I downloaded 'Youth Gone Wild', I rule'".[50] Sarcasm aside, Kellner cannot, of course, be credited with writing "Youth Gone Wild", but she can be credited with creating a second order semiological system by transforming "Youth Gone Wild" from sign into signifier and thus driving the youth wild (which is, of course, the function of a DJ).

46 Drew, "SB" (my italics).
47 Fox, "MF", sections 2 and 3.
48 Tamar Katriel and Thomas Farrell, "Scrapbooks as Cultural Texts: An American Art of Memory", *Text and Performance Quarterly*, 11.2 (1991), pp. 1–17; quoted in Drew, "SB".
49 Roland Barthes, *Mythologies* (London: Vintage, 2000), p. 114; quoted in Fox, "MF", section 4.
50 Kellner, "Hey DJ, Fuck You! (Anyone Can Rock the Party)", p. 82.

Two Kinds of Mix(ed) Covers

In my research I found that there were two main kinds of mix covers. The first kind of cover is characterized by the very lack of a cover, or at least the lack of any visible effort to create an attractive cover.[51] This observation is not without significance. Many mixers spend hours or even days on the "inside" of the mix, but spend little or no time at all on the mix's presentation. Often, mixers either do not use a cover, or simply write the names of the songs on the mix in print. While this description may sound peculiar, there is an easily formulated explanation for this phenomenon. Bagust observes that "most commonly the production of a tape (as was the case in 'High Fidelity') has become associated with attempts, mainly but not exclusively by men, to 'break the ice' with members of the opposite sex".[52] Further, Drew's preliminary research suggests that mixers are more often men than women. During my research I found that mixing is often thought of as a "cool" and "masculine" kind of creativity, and discourses on mixing are often embedded in (middle-class, white) masculinist or phallogocentric ideology.[53] While many other forms of creative expression – for example painting and poetry – are traditionally considered feminine, mixing has become the preferred (perhaps even the quintessential) creative outlet for middle-class white males. Further, the era of the amateur "performing" musician is over,[54] and mixing thus provides an easily accessible and enjoyable alternative creative outlet in the contemporary cultural milieu. As one example, in my research I spoke with a 32-year-old male, an ex-vice president of JP Morgan in Chicago, who spent hours making mixed tapes. He was very proud of his mixes, and believed that they were especially effective in helping to create favorable atmospheres at parties. For him, creating mixes was perfectly consistent with his corporate position and cool bachelor image.

Significantly, conventionally "masculine mixers" only work on the "inside" of the tape. It appears that the reason for this is that making a collage for a cover, for example, is seen as either "girly" or "gay".[55] One 30-year-old female respondent showed me a collage that her boyfriend had made for her and called it "the naffest [i.e., "girly" or "pathetic"] thing ever". The same boyfriend had made her mixed tapes, and these were accepted gratefully and were thought of as "cool". Thus, while the "inside" of mixes relate to masculine constructions of "coolness", the "outside" of mixes relate to femininity.

Here it is important to point out that Roy Shuker observed that in the related, but of course different practice of record collecting, critical discussion is sparse, and the most famous representation of record collectors is (arguably)

51 Still, this non-cover is a type of cover. As I will illustrate below, the lack of effort that sometimes goes into (not) making a cover is often a particular form of performativity. In *Paratexts*, Genette writes that "one may doubtless assert that a text without a paratext does not exist and never has existed" (p. 3).

52 Bagust, "MGCT".

53 Drew, "SB".

54 See, for example, Roland Barthes, "Musica Practica", in *Image, Music, Text*, pp. 149–154.

55 See Example 1.

that provided by Nick Hornby's best-selling novel, *High Fidelity*, and the subsequent film released in 2000 (directed by Stephen Freers).[56] Shuker contends that the portrayal of record collectors – both in the book and film – as obsessive males represents only a small portion of record collectors on the whole. While the stereotype (which in this context is already a pun) of record collectors as obsessive males has attracted much interest both in popular and academic literature, this should not obscure the fact that record collectors are far more varied in terms of class, gender, and race than such a narrow stereotype might have us believe. Will Straw, for example, identifies several characteristics of record collecting "which are more easily recuperable": hipness, connoisseurship, bohemianism, and the adventurous hunter.[57] These characteristics are related to the record collector's "obscurantist interest in the marginal",[58] a position inherent in rock music's emphasis on oppositionality. Shuker points out that "the valorising of the obscure is linked to trash fandoms generally, and the consequent discourse surrounding these is a feature of the homosocial world of young men".[59] However, in actuality, collecting is not a male-dominated practice, and in fact there is evidence that the majority of collectors are women.[60] While Shuker's discussion on collecting cannot be directly translated to mixing, it does sound a warning against assuming that all mixes are created as "lekking [mating] devices"[61] by obsessive males. And while, contrary to collecting, Drew's preliminary research suggests that mixers are more often men than women, there are certainly millions of female mixers in the world.

This brings me to the second kind of mix cover. These mixes are created by people of various classes and racial backgrounds and have only one thing in common: they do not subscribe to the (usually white and middle-class) masculine construction that belies many mixes. In this second type of mix, the distinction between the "inside" of a mix as masculine and the "outside" of a mix as feminine is eclipsed, and the form of the creative process involved "inside" and "outside" the mix is almost exactly the same. Or, one could argue, both "inside" and "outside" are feminized. As has been noted, in a similar way to songs – "mixed" to create the "inside" of a mix – images are "mixed" to create the "outside" of a mixed cover.

There are no "rules" to mixing (if we define "rules" as syntactic features, the *sine qua non* made of the various formal syntagmata), but there are "conventions" (defined here as "the presentation of preferred readings)".[62] Certain "conventions" of mixing – both inside and out – have been described throughout the course of this essay. Usually, mix cover artists use pictures from the popular press, photographs (of themselves or others), small sketches, and words.

56 Roy Shuker, "Beyond the 'High Fidelity' Stereotype: Defining the (Contemporary) Record Collector", *Popular Music* 23.3 (2004), pp. 311–330 (hereafter cited as "BD"); see also Nick Hornby, *High Fidelity* (New York: Riverhead Books, 1995).

57 Will Straw, "Sizing Up Record Collections. Gender and Connoisseurship in Rock Music Culture", in Sheila Whiteley (ed.), *Sexing the Groove: Popular Music and Gender* (London: Routledge, 1997), pp. 3–16, here p. 10 (hereafter cited as "SURC"); in Shuker, "BD", 313.

58 Straw, "SURC", p. 11, in Shuker, "BD", p. 313.

59 Shuker, "BD", p. 313.

60 See Shuker, "BD". See also Russell W. Belk, *Collecting in a Consumer Society* (London: Routledge, 2001); Susan Pearce, *Collecting in Contemporary Practice* (London: Sage, 1998).

61 Fox, "MF", section 3.

62 Fox, "MF", section 5; after Vladimir Propp.

Some mixers (like the fans described by Jenkins earlier in this essay) appropriate cultural products in such a way that those products constitute a particular (personal) signature. In most instances, mixers use and adapt well-known icons, images, words, or patterns in a very personal way. But essentially, mixing is an unrestricted creative act, and individual mixes are therefore as creative as their individual mixers. I therefore end this essay with a few varied examples.

Example 1: Tape cover given with tape from male 20-year-old to male 20-year-old friend. The songs on this tape have been extremely important in mediating the relationship between the sender and receiver of this tape. The first song "in" the tape was, in fact, written and performed (on guitar and vocals) by the maker of the tape for the recipient of the tape. Considering this lovely and sentimental gesture, it is striking that the tape cover is so completely bare.

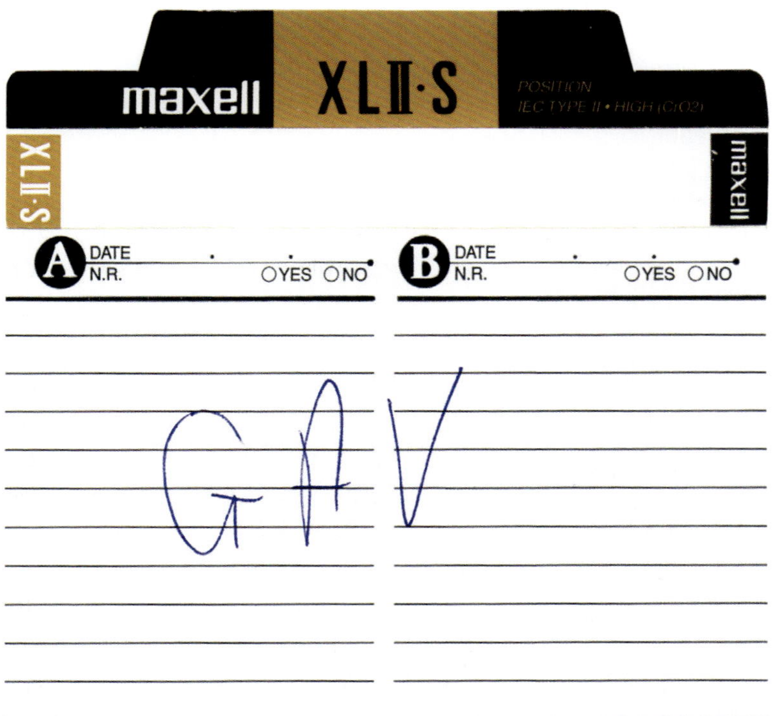

Tape cover given with tape from a young adult male to male friend. Courtesy of Dan Linden.

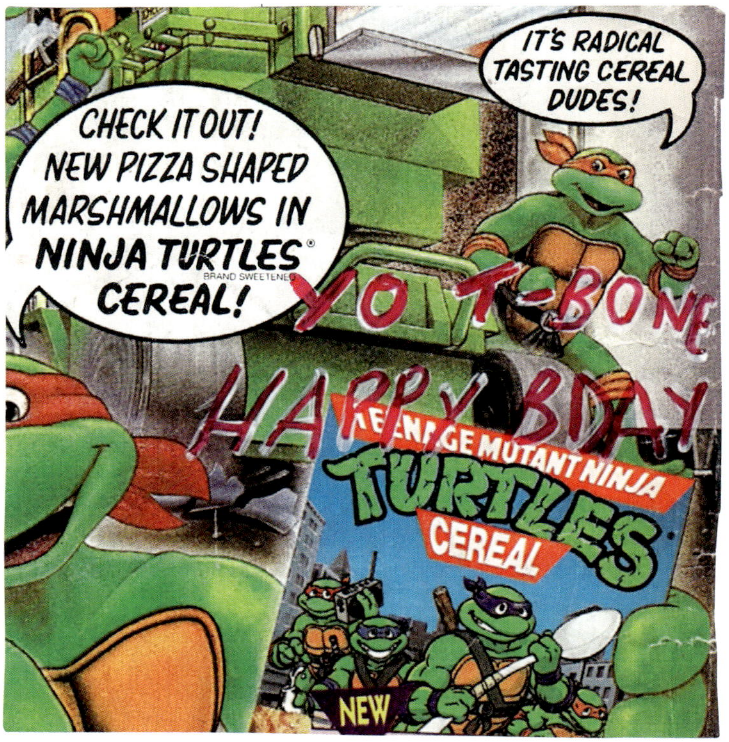

Ninja Turtles cereal comic. Courtesy of Shachar ben Zeev.

Examples ("2nd kind" of cover):

2. *Cover for friend*. Ninja Turtles cereal comic, used as cover for mixed CD given to a friend for her birthday. Here, the humorous Ninja Turtles comic gains special meaning as it enters into the m(atr)ix of the mix-gift.

3. *Cover from a man* (no image provided). A tape cover was given by a man to a woman he was courting at the time of her 21st birthday. A 20 cent and a 1 cent coin (South African currency, the receiver was South African) are glued onto the cover. Also, two keys were glued to the cover. Under the coins and keys, the cover is painted in blue and red. These are apparently (although the receiver did not understand what it means, or why) the "signature" colors of the mixer. The mixer sent an accompanying mixed CD with cover painted in the same colors and in the same style as the tape cover.

4. *Cover from companion* (2001). Pretty abstract paper cut up and stuck back together as collage. The cleverness of this cover is that the "created" or "mixed"

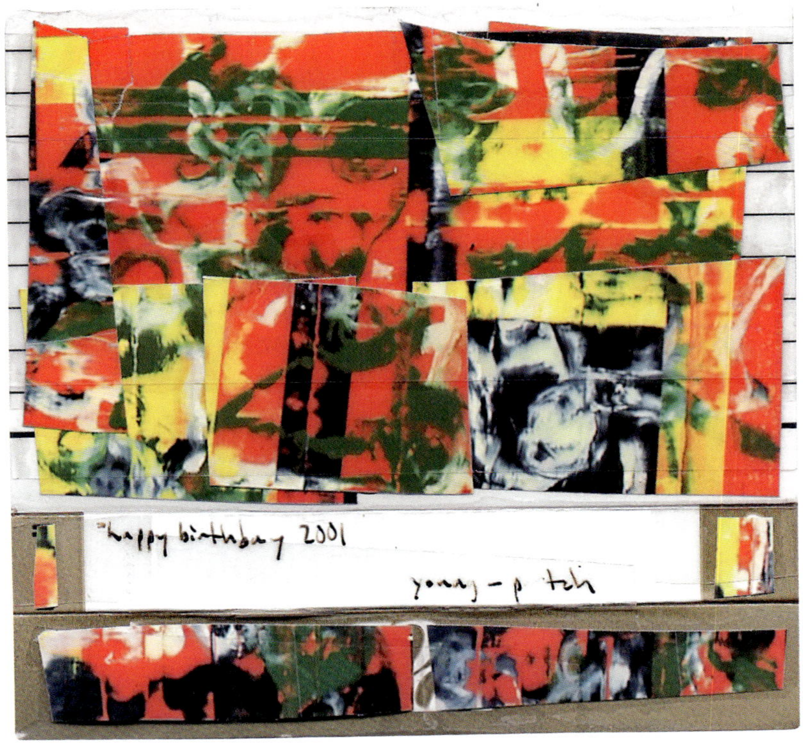

Pretty abstract paper cut up and stuck back together as collage.

second order semiological system is almost exactly the same – is a cut and then sutured version of – the (untouched) first order semiological system. “Inside”: Pieces by Partch, Young, Feldman, etc.

5. *Collage from companion* (2003). This collage was not made as a cover for a CD, but rather accompanied a CD in a package as a birthday present. In this sense, the collage is the “visual equivalent” of the audio CD. Aside from the piece of fabric torn from the mixer’s underwear, the collage shows a distorted collage-version of the mixer, with arrows pointing to the neck-collar region of his body. A cut-out from a photograph of the *receiver’s* neck-collar region lies to the viewer’s left of the (collaged) mixer’s body. There are matches at the top of the picture, and a folded till slip at the bottom. On opening the till slip, the receiver tore it and was never able to find out what it said. The receiver could make out only one word on the slip: *Avenue*. The receiver has speculated that this “Avenue” is part of Avenue Victor Hugo, a second-hand bookstore in Boston which he, at one point, frequented with the sender. “Inside”: Pieces (among others) by a) Velvet Underground, “I’ll Be Your Mirror” (lyric: “I’ll Be Your Mir-

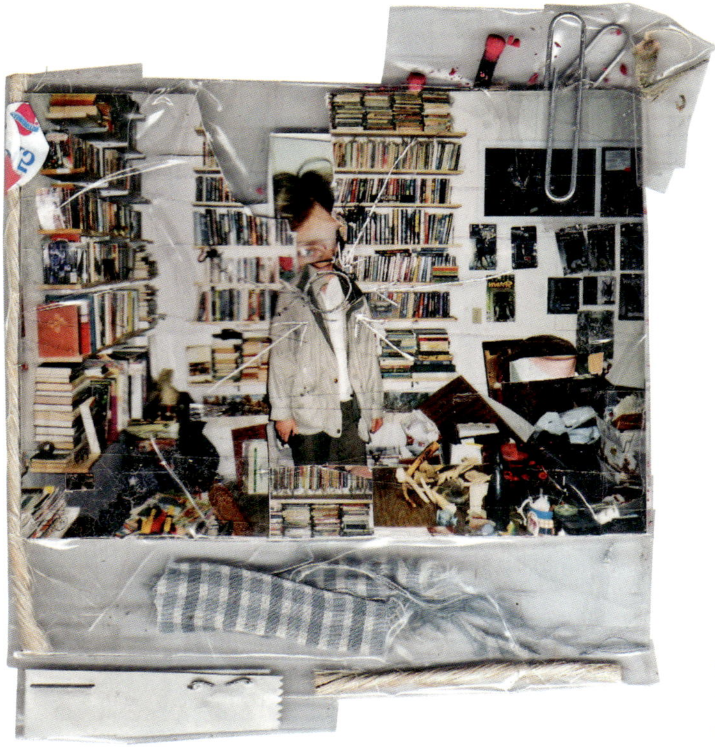

This collage was not made as a cover for a CD, but rather accompanied a CD in a package as a birthday present.

ror, reflect what you are, in case you don't know... I find it hard to believe that you don't know the beauty you are. But if you don't, let me be your eyes ... I'll be your mirror"); b) Franz Schubert. Song from *Dichterliebe* (lyric: "Ich grolle nicht, und wenn das Herz auch bricht, ewig verlor'nes lieb! ...". Translation: "I bear no grudge, even when my heart is breaking. Love lost forever! I bear no grudge. Although you shine in diamond splendor, No beam falls into the night of your heart. I will know that for a long time").[63]

I would like to thank Roger Grant for commenting on and editing an earlier version of this essay.

63 Translated by Paul Hindemith. See www.recmusic.org/lieder/get_text.html?TextId=7545.

"How Near you Stand to Me"

The Blues, Blacks and Whites of The Smiths' Record Sleeves*

Andrew Warnes

In early 1984, as their fingers danced through the piles of newly released LPs, British record buyers would have come across one whose cover was quite unlike those stacked before and after it. An indie release that had somehow crept into the mainstream charts, the cover of the eponymous *The Smiths* belied its alternative origins, violating many of the conventions then obtaining in record sleeve design. Almost all of the successful albums in Britain that year – from Lionel Richie's *Can't Slow Down* to Wham!'s *Make it Big*, and from Michael Jackson's *Thriller* to Sade's *Diamond Life* – presented their subjects in various states of repose, gazing smilingly or coquettishly into the camera lens from the kinds of well-appointed apartments associated with the era's growing bands of yuppies. Yet these record buyers, as they flicked from one pair of 'come-hither' eyes to another, scanning the metropolitan panoply of Thatcherite success, could well have been surprised to encounter an image at once less seductive and more sexual. Culled from the Andy Warhol film *Flesh* (1968), directed by Paul Morrissey, the black-and-white still on the cover of *The Smiths* features a young Joe Dallesandro gazing downwards, his dark, lank fringe cascading over his eyes and making him seem suspicious, and even disdainful, of the commercial enterprise – the selling of music – into which he has been pressed. More pornographic than erotic, and neither as tanned nor as nourished as the average pop idol of the post-postpunk scene, Dallesandro's frozen portrait contrasted markedly with the record covers around it; an open subject of homosexual desire.

Each of The Smiths' subsequent single and album covers reinforced this initial impression, confirming the suspicion that the band's lead singer Stephen Patrick Morrissey (no relation) would be more likely to lose his fabled virginity to a man than a woman. These designs sampled freely from a familiar paradigm of homoeroticism, their iconographic compass ranging from male nudes – such

* An earlier version of this essay appeared as "Black, white and blue: the racial antagonism of The Smiths' record sleeves," *Popular Music* 27:1 (2007), 135–149.

as that which the band lifted from Margaret Walter's book *The Nude Male* (1978) for their debut single "Hand in Glove" (1983) – to filmic images like the 1965 still of Terence Stamp on the cover of "What Difference does it Make?" (1984). Even Morrissey's love of the willful, independent, northern woman, which helped to place the *Coronation Street* actress Pat Phoenix on the cover of "Shakespeare's Sister" (1985) and Avril Angers from *The Family Way* (1966) on the cover of "I Started Something I Couldn't Finish" (1987), bears comparison with what Susan Sontag has characterized as camp's interest in the dramatic, ironic, exaggeration of normative gender roles.[1]

And yet, as The Smiths' career progressed – and as Morrissey's virginity was somehow transformed into the less anticipatory state of celibacy – many came to feel skeptical about the band's apparent decision to present a perfectly gay face to the world. Fans, fellow musicians, and journalists came to feel that this homoerotic aura was perhaps a little too perfect – a little too knowing, calculated, and strategic. Morrissey's reluctance to answer questions about his sexual preferences only deepened such doubts. Between the mid to late 1980s, the letter pages of music weeklies like *Sounds*, *Melody Maker* and *NME* duly speculated on the issue *ad nauseam*.

The following pages attempt to think beyond such gossip, to spirit attention away from Morrissey's individual sexuality and back towards the more properly critical issues that arise from The Smiths' iconographic preoccupation with the homoerotic and the camp. They suggest that this preoccupation can only be understood if it is related to The Smiths' *racial* politics, the debate about which has long burned as ferociously as that concerning the band's sexual representations, even as both have maintained a curious discursive distance from each other. By trying to depersonalize these issues, and by ending this curious discursive isolation, I hope to work towards a new approach that acknowledges the aforementioned knowingness of The Smiths' gay iconography but, rather than attributing it to the overdetermined story of Morrissey's sexual diffidence, associates it instead with the band's deft mythologization of a postindustrial, postsocialist, white proletarian identity. At the root of this essay thus stands a simple contention: that The Smiths' strategic use of gay iconography not only shrouds Morrissey's sexual preferences in mystery, but also banishes key figures – figures crucial to the development of The Smiths' aesthetic – from view.

Two reasons in particular make it hard not to find significance in The Smiths' failure to incorporate black faces on their record sleeves. One is that – as Joe Dallesandro's appearance on *The Smiths*' cover suggests, and as later tributes to Candy Darling and The New York Dolls confirm – the band was steeped

1 Susan Sontag, "Notes on 'Camp'", in *Against Interpretation* (London: Vintage, 1994), pp. 275–292.

in the recent New York *avant-garde* tradition, a tradition that, largely thanks to Robert Mapplethorpe's photography, had recently grown transfixed by the physicality and beauty of black men. Moreover, the incorporation of such classic homoerotic images on the covers of The Smiths' releases would have been entirely in keeping with the powerful Black Atlantic echoes that one cannot fail to hear in the music and lyrical temperament of the band, which – by resurrecting the classic marriage of the harmonica and guitar, and by finding succor and much humor in the reminiscing of misery – clearly owed a heavy debt to early blues innovators like Robert Johnson, Bessie Smith, Howlin' Wolf, and Leadbelly. Mere familiarity with the pronounced Englishness of The Smiths' creative output has prevented us from remarking that by far the closest historical precedents for Morrissey's belief in the cathartic opportunities of the song stem from such past blues masters.

But clues remain. The Smiths' reformulation of a blues aesthetic may have generated a paradoxical nostalgia for a prelapsarian, pre-immigrant North into which no black or nonwhite subject could easily be allowed to enter. Likewise, Morrissey's understandable longing for a fading proletarian phase of productivity, creativity and dignity – for an era when, in the terms of Tony Harrison's *v.* (1987), trades could still be engraved on the headstones of men – may have left precious little scope to reflect the many black and Asian fans whom his band nonetheless attracted. But the marginalization of the nonwhite figure that these imaginative circumstances entailed created a new anxiety, and came to haunt the cover art of the band, generating parodic, buried tributes to Mapplethorpe's photography, intercessory allusions to Shelagh Delaney's play of cross racial love *A Taste of Honey* (1959), and a general atmosphere of excessive, overburdened whiteness. Beneath the dazzling facade of The Smiths' homoerotic dilemmas, I argue, thus lies a yet more unspeakable love: for the blues, blacks and whites, for the inadmissible hybridity, whose novel combinations spawned the genius of The Smiths.

> Vulgarization
> Teenage dole-wallah piss-up, then tattoos.
> *Brown Ale* and boys' bravado numbs their fright –
> MOTHER in ivy, blood reds and true blues
> against that North East skin so sunless white.
> *Tony Harrison, "Divisions I, II" (c. 1978)*

far noh mattah wat dey say,
come wat may,
we are here to stay
inna Inglan
Linton Kwesi Johnson, "It Dread Inna Inglan" (1978)[2]

Both at the beginning and the end of the 1980s, the British pop scene inclined toward the restatement of an old and long deferred promise: that the interracial influences of the music would promote antiracist thinking in the fans. The decade began with the mammoth festivals of "Rock against Racism", the leading organizers of which, such as Jerry Dammers of the Coventry ska outfit The Specials, were determined to exploit the music's political opportunities – to release the freedom suggested by the "hybrid black-and-white" styles that (as an impressed *Newsweek* reporter told US readers) swung freely from "a flawless reggae rhythm ... to a fiery rock gutbuster".[3] At the other end of the decade, the Acid House phenomenon repeated many such mobilizations. Held in other people's fields rather than local councils' parks, this was perhaps a more ramshackle, and certainly a more dissolute, affair. Indeed, many may feel that Ecstasy's chemical stimulation of contact between Britain's different racial and class groups cannot rival Rock against Racism's signal accomplishments, which after all dealt a blow to the National Front and, internationally, contributed to the dawning of the February morning in 1990 when Soweto schoolchildren could sing "Free Nelson Mandela", Dammers' most famous song, for the final time.[4] But others would perhaps recall that Acid House not only revived Rock against Racism's attempt to harness pop's diverse influences toward interracial mixture but did so in a far more adventurous, far less didactic, fashion, exchanging the streetwise politicking of a Dammers or Joe Strummer for the liberating, blissful liminality of a dance floor thrown open to all.

For Paul Gilroy, Acid House and Rock against Racism belong to a single line: both exert profound influence on the formation of the automatically antiracist 'conviviality' that distinguishes today's British pop scene.[5] Gilroy suggests that at their

> insubordinate and carnivalesque best, ... [both] project an immediacy, a rebel solidarity, and a fragile, universal humanity powerful enough to make race and ethnicity suddenly meaningless. This worthwhile message was signaled long ago by Rock against Racism and the mongrel social movement that created its surrogates in various countries ... [T]hat move-

2 See Tony Harrison, "Divisions I, II", in *Tony Harrison: Selected Poems* (London: Penguin, 1987), p. 173; and Linton Kwesi Johnson, "It Dread inna Inglan", in *Mi Revalueshanary Fren: Selected Poems* (London: Penguin, 2002), p. 25.

3 Allan Tannembaum, "Britain's 'Ska' Kings", *Newsweek*, 7 April 1980, p. 74.

4 Seamus Milne, "Mandela Free: People worldwide celebrate Mandela's release", *The Guardian*, 12 February 1990, p. 1.

5 Paul Gilroy, *After Empire: Melancholia or Convivial Culture?* (Abingdon, Oxfordshire: Routledge, 2004), p. 104.

ment still moves, but more quietly and in de-centered, less formal patterns. Its effects are still conveyed in the underground club and rave scenes, in illegal radio broadcasting, and in the alternative public spheres that surround these initiatives.[6]

And yet it is possible that, like the waves that keep rolling in even when the tide is going out, these high points in pop's sense of antiracist possibility – these moments when what Gilroy characterizes as the idyllic state of racial *meaninglessness* apparently drew within reach – mask a current that pulled more powerfully in the opposite direction. That is to say, as Rock against Racism's festivals drew to a close, and as Acid House's initial euphoric outbursts faded, so race tended to regain its lost meaning, recovering power from the resurfacing society as well as from a commercial record industry that spent the 1980s discovering how lucrative demographics could be. Motored by the industry's realization that race let you organize music by genre and people by taste, this counteractive process, which some would call *segmentation* and others *ghettoization*, is, of course, responsible for some of the tawdrier features of the new pop landscape: it leads to the cultural apartheid of the twenty-first century radio industry, for example, in which AOR stations target white listeners, soul stations target black listeners, and skin can duly seem to determine all.[7]

These essentializing entanglements of race and culture can be glimpsed in the eyes I mentioned earlier – in the seductive eyes of Sade and Lionel Richie, the complex racial heritages of whom were effaced by a record industry that, in the mid 1980s, sought to dissolve the liberating racial chaos of the postpunk era, associate genre with color once more, and market on this basis. And as this increasingly genre-bound industry awoke to African-American popular culture's potential profitability, brokering new sponsorship deals, advertising contracts, and product placements, so it came to assume that such commerce would always run one way, and to do much to appeal to soul's white followers while ignoring altogether Britain's legions of black and Asian rock fans.

The independent music scene of the mid 1980s often emitted a strange, surprising ambivalence towards this rampant commercialization. Working within the only pop genre whose name derived from an economic condition, Indie music practitioners of the period largely extended the disdain they felt for the major record labels into an automatic and predictable contempt for any new commercial venture that these labels undertook. Rather as the businessmen in Sinclair Lewis' *Babbitt* (1922) publicly deride the exclusive "Union Club" but privately long to join it, a good proportion of these successful Indie bands would

6 Paul Gilroy, *Between Camps: Nations, Cultures and the Allure of Race* (London: Penguin, 2001), p. 249.

7 See Richard Barbrook, "Melodies or rhythms?: the competition for the Greater London FM radio licence", *Popular Music* 9:2 (1990), pp. 203–219; and Keith Negus, "Plugging and programming: pop radio and record promotion in Britain and the United States", *Popular Music* 12:1 (1993), pp. 57–68.

prove surprisingly happy to contract themselves to the erstwhile object of their scorn, separating the cherished economic autonomy of their chosen genre from its dazzling surface rebellion – from its subversive postpunk sheen – and carrying these latter into the industry's corporate heartlands.[8]

Even the most diehard and politicized Indie fan could not accuse The Smiths of such heresy. The band numbered among the very few Indie acts who eschewed the commercial overtures UK Top Ten success attracted and remained loyal to their original label, Rough Trade. Morrissey and Marr's impressive sidestepping of the economic contradictions in the behavior of their less socialistic peers is nowhere more evident than in their jaundiced swansong "Paint a Vulgar Picture" (1987) and the gruesome manner by which, from its opening line onward, the corporate meeting goes cannibalistic:

> At the record company meeting
> On their hands – a dead star
> And oh, the plans they weave
> And oh, the sickening greed...
> Re-issue! Re-package! Re-package!
> Re-evaluate the songs
> Double-pack with a photograph
> Extra track (and a tacky badge)[9]

The jeremiad is reminiscent of the vitriolic leftist anthems of The Clash, presenting another example of a rabidly anti-commercialistic song by a band who attracted considerable commercial success. "Paint a Vulgar Picture" strongly recalls The Clash's contempt for those decadent metropoles who get their "advice from the advertising world" or wish the band would "wear suits", reprising the recurring lyrical conceit whereby Strummer would follow the marketing men into their committee rooms and then watch in appalled indignation as the project of his impending commodification unfolded.[10] The vulgar picture that The Smiths paint of 1980s corporate capitalism enacts a similarly renegade system of surveillance. Here, the appalled star helplessly watches as birth once more turns into death – as the true vocation of those for whom such projects are *babies* to be *launched* is tentatively revealed, and as they are in time unmasked as plasticizing butchers, determined to convert the flesh of the fallen star into CD packaging, "tacky badge[s]", re-releases, and other sellable "cuts".

But the forceful clarity of these punk echoes does far more than prove that The Smiths were fully committed to the anticapitalist ethos other Indie acts

8 Sinclair Lewis, *Babbitt* (Harmondsworth, Middlesex: Penguin, 1980), p. 47.
9 The Smiths, "Paint a Vulgar Picture", *Strangeways Here We Come* (Rough Trade, 1987).
10 See The Clash, "Koka Kola", *London Calling* (Epic, 1979); and The Clash, "Garageland", *The Clash* (CBS, 1977).

forgot. It also propels us towards the more troubled territory of the band's racial representations. The anticapitalist, anti-American bravado of the frenetic Clash anthem "Koka Kola" cradled the needle about halfway through *London Calling* (1979), occupying grooves in a vinyl soundscape that was altogether as chaotic and heterogeneous as the postcolonial city that inspired it. *London Calling* could indeed be compared to a proletarian Inner London street, and the reggae basslines of Aswad and Burning Spear, the flourishes of white Cockney rockabilly, and the dub distortions that the band's bassist Mick Jones had imbibed from Caribbean innovators like Lee Scratch Perry and King Tubby were all raucous multiracial neighbors to the album's belligerent, leftist punk anthems. And this riotous, anarchic, 1970s concoction – which does dare to conceive of a racial *meaninglessness* wherein no particular significance accords to the playing of white reggae or black punk – could not be less like the album on which "Paint a Vulgar Picture" appears, *Strangeways Here We Come* (1987). *Strangeways Here We Come* contrariwise presents the last and most complete installment in The Smiths' lyrical dramatization of a sunless North and its albino unemployed. And it maintains, seemingly as a result of this preoccupation, an awkward silence on the question of race – a silence that indicates that punk's promise of racial *meaninglessness* has been, not fulfilled, but abandoned.

The doomed disco dancer, the comatose girlfriend, and the other wretched characters who inhabit this album – all of whom, to invoke Toni Morrison, we know are white "because nobody says so" – speak to a kind of lyrical adoration of prior northern pop culture that comes dangerously close to lapsing into the logic of repatriation, and to expressing a Powellite yearning to teleport oneself back to the idyllic pre-immigrant era.[11] The fact that The Smiths' final album cover, like that of their debut, is of an actor who is American (in this case, *East of Eden*'s Richard Davalos) but nonetheless so pale as to qualify as an honorary "northerner" merely strengthens our suspicion that this sign constitutes a racial as much as a regional category. Race now seems the stranger at the table, the awkward presence who the band would fain forget, displace, and remember, perhaps, only in the fraught neurotic riot heard – as though in angry flashback to the fiery summer of 1985 – before the opening chords of "Last Night I Dreamt that Somebody Loved Me".

The wall of whiteness that The Smiths erect between themselves and multiracial British reality, and their ensuing marginalization or displacement of the nonwhite figure, contrast sharply not only with The Clash's jubilant hybrid experimentation but also with the Manic Street Preachers' anthemic demand to see "more black in the Union Jack".[12] Alone among these leading British alter-

11 Toni Morrison, *Playing in the Dark: Whiteness and the Literary Imagination* (New York: Vintage, 1992), p. 72.

12 Manic Street Preachers, "ifwhiteamericatoldthetruthforonedayitsworldwouldfallapart", *The Holy Bible* (Epic, 1996).

native bands, The Smiths confirm Holly Kruse's suggestion that even the most leftist Indie bands can maintain a startling cultural conservatism; they alone fall easily in line with the contemporary segmentation of music, producing an apparently uncomplicated white body of work that, with uncharacteristic conformity, succumbed to the external demographic demand to nurture all links between race and genre.[13] Indeed, one might even venture that if *London Calling* mirrors what John McLeod sees as the "[p]erpetually restless, inevitably pluralized and endlessly transforming" character of the postcolonial metropolis itself, then *Strangeways Here We Come* more closely resembles one of those embattled northern white neighborhoods, bedecked with St. George flags long after England's early exit from the World Cup, into which all outsiders tread nervously.[14] It is true that, on one level, the album's opening chorus ("a rush and a push and the land/that we stand on is ours/it has been before/so it shall be again") mourns the passing of national particularity, presciently condemning Americanization as vulgarization at best, and McDonaldization at worst. But it is also true that, on another level, this chorus carries obvious echoes of the rhetorical tropes of British fascism, repeating its neurotic appropriation of victimage, its premature claim to dispossession, and its over-defensive attitude to England's so-called "heritage". And it is even truer that these troubling echoes suggest that some shift – some epochal, ruinous disruption – has heralded the disintegration of the promise that Rock against Racism once dared to restate: that nobody can now maintain that the multiracial basis of *all* pop may yet lead its followers beyond race itself. But how had this lamentable turn of events come to pass? How do we explain it?

Paint it White

> 'The idea is to open each bucket and put in ten drops of this stuff', he said. 'Then you stir it 'til it disappears ...'.
> 'Yes, sir'. But when I looked into the white graduate I hesitated; the liquid inside was dead black. Was he trying to kid me? ...
> I filled it ...
> 'How's it coming?' he said, standing with hands on hips.
> 'All right, sir'.
> 'Let's see', he said, selecting a sample and running his thumb across the board. 'That's it, as white as George Washington's Sunday-go-to-meetin' wig and as sound as the all-mighty dollar! ... It's the purest white that can be found. Nobody makes a paint any whiter. This batch right here is head-

13 Holly Kruse, "Subcultural identity in alternative music culture", *Popular Music* 12:1 (1993), p. 40.

14 John McLeod, *Postcolonial London: Rewriting the Metropolis* (London: Routledge, 2004), p. 194.

ing for a national monument'.
'I see', I said, quite impressed.[15]
Ralph Ellison, Invisible Man *(1952)*

Even the lands surrounding that long neglected and unfinished monument, erected to the memory of George Washington, have been, in the last year or two, greatly improved and beautified, while the monument itself, in its desolate incompleteness, is a standing reproach to the gratitude of the Republic.
I look forward to the day when this reproach shall be removed [.]
Frederick Douglass, "Our National Capital" (1877)[16]

One need not look far to find some simple answers to these simple questions. Politicized British TV productions like *Boys from the Blackstuff* (1982) and *A Very British Coup* (1988), and more recent popular films like *Brassed Off* (1996) and *Billy Elliot* (2000) all agree that, in the period spanning The Smiths' career, the white northern working class fell under unprecedented attack. Unemployment rose exponentially, attracting little to no governmental action. Industry commenced its continuing exodus to the developing world. Englishmen were forced to leave their homes and families behind and seek work in Europe, and especially in West Germany. Police officers on horseback attacked unarmed miners at Orgreave. Many strikers went hungry so that their children could eat. The Labour Party seemed powerless to protect them, its most loyal supporters. Some among its London members seemed preoccupied by the new Equal Opportunities agenda. And in these years, Black Atlantic popular music flourished, and kept beaming onto those TVs not yet repossessed a tantalizing, idyllic, alternative, world – a Sesame Street world of "neighborhoods" and brownstones, populated by those the sun had not forsook.

These simple answers, however, mask more complicated matters. No evidence exists to suggest that the combined effect of the factors enumerated above led to an increase in racist attitudes among white northerners. Their usefulness lies rather in the light they cast upon the increasing tone of embattlement and victimage that existing racist politics acquired during the Thatcher premiership. Even here, though, we must still tread carefully, and remain alert to the distinction between society, which this prime minister of course did not believe in, and culture, which more simply she did not *believe*. That is to say, the Conservative government's strategic humiliation of the northern working-classes – its leader's famous inflammatory and divisive description of the striking miners,

15 Ralph Ellison, *Invisible Man* (Harmondsworth, Middlesex: Penguin, 1965), pp. 163–164.
16 Frederick Douglass, "Our National Capital: An Address Delivered in Baltimore, Maryland, on 8 May 1877", in John W. Blassingame and John R. McKivigan (eds.), *The Frederick Douglass Papers: Series One: Speeches, Debates, and Interviews*, vol. 4 (New Haven and London: Yale University Press, 1991), p. 448.

in the aftermath of the Falklands War, as the "enemy within" – is one thing; the studied English parochialism of The Smiths is quite another. In order to develop a more critical response to the latter, we must recast our simple questions. We must consider, for example, how postcolonial theory would currently understand the cultural transition apparent in the contrast between the joyous hybridity of *London Calling* and the unapologetic parochialism of *Strangeways Here We Come*.

It is certainly not difficult to predict which of the two albums postcolonialists would prefer. Today, *The Location of Culture*'s political enthusiasts seem determined to turn the hybrid domain that Homi K. Bhabha calls the "third space" – and from which *London Calling*'s organized chaos so obviously radiates – into a cure for all manner of social ills, and especially for racism.[17] Indeed, postcolonialism now seems close to abandoning *hybridity*'s received definitions, and to approaching it neither as a universal cultural phenomenon (as it was to Boasian anthropologists) nor a sometimes welcome and sometimes unwelcome natural occurrence (as it remains so in horticulture), but as a *de facto* force for the good, which can imagine worlds beyond race and drag them into the present.

The danger of this politicization of hybridity is that it effectively dilutes Bhabha's ideas into a crude binary opposition, and on this basis comes to vaunt those cultures considered intermixed over those deemed to be pure.[18] The ironic intrusion of such logocentrism into a field indebted to Derridean philosophy certainly underpins the fiendish delight many take when reciting the racist's supposedly shameful love of fusion – when pointing out, for example, that British fascists today frequently prefer curry to fish and chips. Such critics are typically so eager to expose the schizophrenic vacillation of the fascist tongue, and thus to confirm the alchemy of fusion, they rarely pause to consider that this accusation can only work if they are prepared to insist that such a thing as "pure" culture exists, and that the racist could have chosen to eat it instead of the "heterogeneous, hybrid sign" Bhabha finds in the English chapatti.[19] Even those postcolonialists who refuse to recognize that this bipolarization of culture remains marked by the bloody residue of racialism must apprehend that, like *all* artefacts said to emblematize national or racial homogeneity, fish and chips itself results from hybridization, being popularized by Britain's Jewish immigrants during the 1860s.[20]

This logocentrism marks *Out of Whiteness* (2002), Vron Ware and Les Back's otherwise timely manifesto of the New Abolitionism: the end of the so-called White Race. It surfaces as *Out of Whiteness* deems the popularity of jazz in wartime Germany to be an epitome of hybridity's ability to disturb racial

17 Homi K. Bhabha, *The Location of Culture* (London: Routledge, 1994), p. 36.

18 One among many examples of this theoretical simplification is Ana María Fraile-Marcos' recent interpretation of Toni Morrison's *Love* (2004), which rightly notes that all of the novel's milieus possess an "underlying racial and cultural hybridity" before contradictorily suggesting that the diverse women at the Convent are what make this "cultural hybridity possible" – as though something else might make it *impossible*. See Ana María Fraile-Marcos, "Hybridizing the 'City Upon a Hill' in Toni Morrison's *Paradise*", *MELUS* 28:4 (2003), p. 4.

19 Bhabha, p. 207.

20 In 1968 the National Federation of Fish Friers declared that Malin's in the East End of London, which had been established in 1860 by an East European Jewish immigrant, was the oldest fish and chip shop still in business in Britain. This history of intercultural exchange will be explored in forthcoming research by the food historian Panikos Panayi.

classification. Ware and Back cite a "Luftwaffe pilot who switched on the BBC, hoping to catch a few bars of Glenn Miller before bombing the antennae", to demonstrate that, even amid a totalitarian program of racial purification, hybridity's ability to ferment interracial understanding remained intact.[21] And this Luftwaffe pilot's behavior is indeed startlingly paradoxical; it indeed exemplifies the illogic of Nazi ideology. But *Out of Whiteness*'s attempt to present this paradoxical episode as a sign of hybridity's potency rather than its limitations testifies to the current tendency of such cultural or postcolonial studies to accelerate far beyond the evidence they present. After all, like the Indian restaurants that British fascists at other times frequent, the BBC still got attacked. Hybridity, on this as on other occasions, was bankrupt.

Out of Whiteness elsewhere mines more nuanced territory. It orients us back to Ralph Ellison's lifelong meditations on what Shelly Fisher Fishkin has characterized as the interdependence of blackness and whiteness in American life.[22] In particular, it reminds us of uncanny moments like that of this section's epigraph, in which *Invisible Man*'s protagonist, plunged into the dismal Fordian realm of an American paint factory, witnesses another kind of fusion: a fusion that obliterates, a fusion that kills. Here, Ellison's narrator watches numbly as the invisibility he has considered his own is replicated by the black droplets that, mixed by his own hand, vanish into the cauldron of white emulsion, perfecting it peculiarly. Destined to restore the immaculacy of the towers and domes that line the Washington Mall – to glorify the memory of those presidents who alternately held or freed America's slaves – the whiteness of the paint is appropriately contingent upon the blackness that it annihilates; it is a symbolic product of Ellison's belief that black cultural style had had a say and left a mark on even the whitest corner of the American nation-state. Surging into the fantastical realm of *Invisible Man*'s New York, such perceptions thus discredit hybridity's magic powers; they remind those enthusiasts for whom fusion has become a panacea of another kind of exchange, in which whiteness is optimized by its encounter with its black opposite.

On the cover of The Smiths' debut single "Hand in Glove" we encounter another brilliantly white prospect, in the form of Lou Thomas' photograph of the 1960s bodybuilder George O'Mara. This deliberate, highly posed, black-and-white study effectively takes Robert Mapplethorpe's contemporary fascination with the black male nude – a fascination popularized in Britain, in the months leading up to the release of "Hand in Glove", by a touring exhibition and the publication of *Black Men* – and turns it on its head. That is to say, the image that The Smiths selected for this their debut single suggests that their determination

21 Vron Ware and Les Back, *Out of Whiteness: Color, Politics and Culture* (Chicago and London: University of Chicago Press, 2001), p. 187.

22 Shelley Fisher Fishkin, "Interrogating 'Whiteness', Complicating 'Blackness:' Remapping American Culture", *American Quarterly* 47:3 (1995), pp. 428–466.

was not to reject Mapplethorpe altogether so much as to signify on him – to repeat his preoccupation with the appealing aestheticism of the male nude, but then to reverse it by making this nude as white as he possibly could be.

The portrait of O'Mara is certainly evocatively proximate to what Richard Dyer characterizes as the "strongly white representational tradition" of Greek and Roman Classicism. Its use of shadow and contrast, filtered by the record sleeve's reflecting lamination, optimizes not only O'Mara's muscles but also the uncanny featurelessness of his skin, its alabaster immaculacy, its angelic whiteness.[23] Reinforcing the classical connection, O'Mara's magical transportation from a photographed subject into a kind of statuesque inhumanity is hastened by the way he turns his back to the camera, hiding his face from us, fixing our attention further upon his unreal skin. In the record sleeve's bottom left corner – in a font as bare and unadorned as those that BBC realist dramas of the late 1950s typically used – the song title "Hand in Glove" draws the eyes toward O'Mara's adjacent fingers, which hang suspended, teasingly brushing his backside, as though in solicitation of another.

The record sleeve design in this way harnesses the potential racial invisibility of Dyer's 'strongly white representational traditions' even as it flaunts a pornographic homoeroticism that is not merely visible, but impossible to ignore. That is to say, although the use of black-and-white film and the maximization of color contrast create a photographic texture on which O'Mara's skin could not conceivably be lighter – and although this record cover image, on the level of its technological production, is thus clearly marked by race – the invisibility resulting from whiteness' normativity smoothly banishes such racial connotations beneath the overwhelming, obsessive, *is-he-isn't-he* gossip surrounding Morrissey's sexuality. The cover design thus proves instrumental to the critical process whereby, ever since its release, "Hand in Glove" has been lauded as a kind of covert gay anthem – as a lyric that, as the MSN Internet Music Guide today observes, contains "veiled references to homosexuality".[24]

Doubts duly arise. It becomes hard to understand why The Smiths would go to such lengths to ensure that their song's references to homosexuality would all be so euphemistic and "veiled" before then proceeding to release it in one of the most candidly homoerotic record covers in the entire pop tradition. It also becomes hard to understand why, if "Hand in Glove" is exclusively concerned with gay love, Morrissey still concludes the song by repeatedly singing a line ("I'll probably never see you again") lifted from *A Taste of Honey* (1959), Shelagh Delaney's powerful play about interracial, heterosexual, love. And it becomes harder still to shake off the suspicion that if the Washington Monument's surface

23 Richard Dyer, *White* (London and New York: Routledge, 1997), p. 150.

24 MSN Music Guide. http://music.msn.com/artist/default.aspx?artist=16074863 (accessed 6 January 2005).

can seem *too* white, and if it can seem somehow to orient attention back to the hackneyed and harmless myths about the first president – to stories about apple trees and wooden teeth – then O'Mara's skin dazzles to similar effect, paralyzing all inquiry into The Smiths' African-American influences.

Once the record buyer had rolled "Hand in Glove" out of its sleeve and laid it upon the turntable, these African-American influences should by right have become palpable. At the levels of its musical arrangement, vocal performance, and lyrical composition, the song is steeped in the blues. Musically, the song opens with Johnny Marr's wailing harmonica lines, which Robert Palmer suggests echo a train rhythm – a classic blues trope – and which certainly call to mind the urgent, baleful solos of Little Walter or Sonny Boy Williamson.[25] Similarly, the fact that the song never changes key and is organized around what Julian Stringer characterizes as "Johnny Marr's cruelly indifferent sheet-chords" suggests that the latter was at this early point already negotiating the influence of Bo Diddley – a negotiation that would later result in the swirling, marching guitar rhythms of "Rusholme Ruffians" on *Meat is Murder* (1985) and of the title track on *The Queen is Dead* (1986).[26]

These interconnections proliferate. For example, if Marr's compositions for "Hand in Glove" single-handedly revived the blues harmonica solo, importing it into the Indie paradigm for the first time, then Morrissey's vocals on cathartic songs like "Miserable Lie" did much the same for the male falsetto style that, in his brief itinerant life in and around the Mississippi Delta, Robert Johnson pioneered. Love in the lyrics of Morrissey as much as of Johnson similarly proves to be a consuming, engulfing, strangely dissatisfying sensation; in the songs of both, wherever it arises, violence is near at hand. And indeed, each of the most noteworthy aspects of Morrissey's lyrical sensibility – his confrontation of misery, his humor, his radical refusal to adopt a political affiliation – corresponds closely with Ralph Ellison's renowned definition of the blues:

> The Blues is an impulse to keep the painful detail and episodes of a brutal experience alive in one's aching consciousness, to finger its jagged grain, and to transcend it, not by the consolation of philosophy but by squeezing from it a near-tragic, near-comic lyricism. As a form, the blues is an autobiographical chronicle of personal catastrophe expressed lyrically.[27]

The critical failure – the critical *refusal* – to remark upon the tangible debt that The Smiths owe to the blues casts an incriminating light upon the cover of "Hand in Glove"; it suggests that this image of George O'Mara, like those of Joe Dalle-

25 Robert Palmer, "The Pop Life; New Disk by Smiths is a Hit", *New York Times*, 6 March 1985, p. 19.

26 Julian Stringer, "The Smiths: repressed (but remarkably dressed)", *Popular Music* 11:1 (1992), p. 23.

27 Ralph Ellison, "Richard Wright's Blues", in Henry Louis Gates, Jr. and Nellie Y. McKay (eds.), *The Norton Anthology of African-American Literature* (New York and London: Norton, 2004), p. 1539.

sandro and Richard Davalos which the band would later use, are strategically distracting attention from Marr and Morrissey's African-American debts and directing it instead towards an eclipsing, domineering set of sexual dilemmas. Such diversionary tactics, indeed, make it tempting to relate the band to the 1960s phenomenon, speculatively raised by Mike Daley, whereby British rhythm and blues players' "immersion in black music paradoxically energize[d] ... the whiteness" of their skin, transforming them into "paradigm[s] of hyperwhiteness". Admittedly, The Smiths, unlike some of the earlier British connoisseurs of Black Atlantic music style to whom Daley refers, neither invested their money in Apartheid South Africa nor played Sun City; nor did they ever get drunk, take the stage, and announce their support for Enoch Powell.[28]

Vital as these provisos are, however, once we have made them we are still left with a band that owed a large debt to the Blues but which proved remarkably backwards in coming forwards to declare it. Their aim was instead to present a white edifice to the world – an edifice fit to prove the resurgent humanity of the brutalized North, to redeem the humiliation of those whom the multiracial metropolis had seemingly forgotten and whom Thatcher had certainly demonized. The lingering traces of black expressive culture sat uneasily within the class-bound parameters of this project.

The cessation of the Washington Monument's construction during the national crisis of the Civil War is today commemorated by the subtle and unavoidable change in tone, just over halfway up the obelisk, of the stone used. Scrutinized more closely, a reproach yet deeper than that articulated by Frederick Douglass – a reproach touching on the purpose of that war, and on the displacement of slavery within American mythology – thus grows intelligible in the merest irregularity of the memorializing stone's whiteness.

The very whiteness of George O'Mara's skin, his virtual metamorphosis into a classical statue, can be read similarly. It is an errant sign of the lengths to which the production of "Hand in Glove" has gone to smuggle its Blues influence past us unseen. The excess of this whiteness, in other words, parades before us the sheer force of this determined displacement, of this neurotic attempt to curtail a narrative of racial alterity and turn it into one of sexual difference. And it is an excess which correspondingly suggests that critics of The Smiths have been led astray – have been encouraged to look in the wrong closet. The real secret about The Smiths – the real taboo – is that their powerful lyrical accounts of a sunless England owe so much to the culture of the American plantation.

28 Mike Daley, "'Why Do Whites Sing Black?': The Blues, Whiteness, and Early Histories of Rock", *Popular Music and Society* 26:2 (2003), p. 166. Eric Clapton's infamous *faux pas* is today largely forgotten and remembered only by those on the left with long memories. It is recalled in a fanzine website history of the Rock Against Racism movement: www.repeatfanzine.co.uk/Political/Rockin%20vs%20Racism.htm. It is also recalled in a *Socialist Review* article posted in 2004: www.socialistreview.org.uk/article.php?articlenumber=8931 (both accessed 5 January 2005).

Frame or Be Framed
This is Not De La Soul

Jonathan Silverman

Whether we like it or not, we often make our first judgments about an album based on its cover. Designers spend untold money and time in order to attract an audience, making each album as attractive as possible. Accordingly, it's no surprise that book and graphic design have become a source of academic study. Combined with the notion, expressed by James Whistler and more recently Jacques Derrida,[1] that artwork extends its boundaries beyond the work itself, the old admonition of not judging a book by its cover seems hopelessly out of date.[2] In fact, document design has, increasingly, become not simply a signifier of a band's album but also of its coolness, an emblem of its vision and message. Album covers are not just advertisements but windows into what a band – or its label – believes they represent.

No one knows this better than De La Soul. The cover of *De La Soul Is Dead*, the group's second album, seems to celebrate the reconstruction of the group while simultaneously declaring its demise: it pictures a broken flowerpot, foregrounding a dislodged daisy, and thus comments on the reshaping of an identity of "peace-loving hippies" critics and audiences attached to them based on their first album *Three Feet High and Rising*, an identity not completely undeserved. Though a cover literally frames the narrative on the album, its purpose and that of the album itself is often in conflict. Indeed, *De La Soul Is Dead* is about re-constructing identity but not only by use of its cover.

Within the album, the rappers take special care in constructing their own identities with a conscious structure in order to shape and engage audience expectation. De La Soul seeks to reconstruct its identity as African-American artists within the context of a genre (hip-hop music) that often pigeonholes its members. The album features a "sing-along storybook" (both visually and verbally) as a way of commenting on the band's reputation as a hippie rap group, demonstrating that loving peace does not mean being weak. Rather, the cover prepares viewers and listeners to place the group's work in its own context. The

1 Jacques Derrida, *The Truth in Painting*, trans. Geoff Bennington and Ian McLeod (Chicago: University of Chicago Press, 1987).

2 Adam Parkes, "A Sense of Justice: Whistler, Ruskin, James, Impressionism", *Victorian Studies* 42:4 (2000), pp. 593–630.

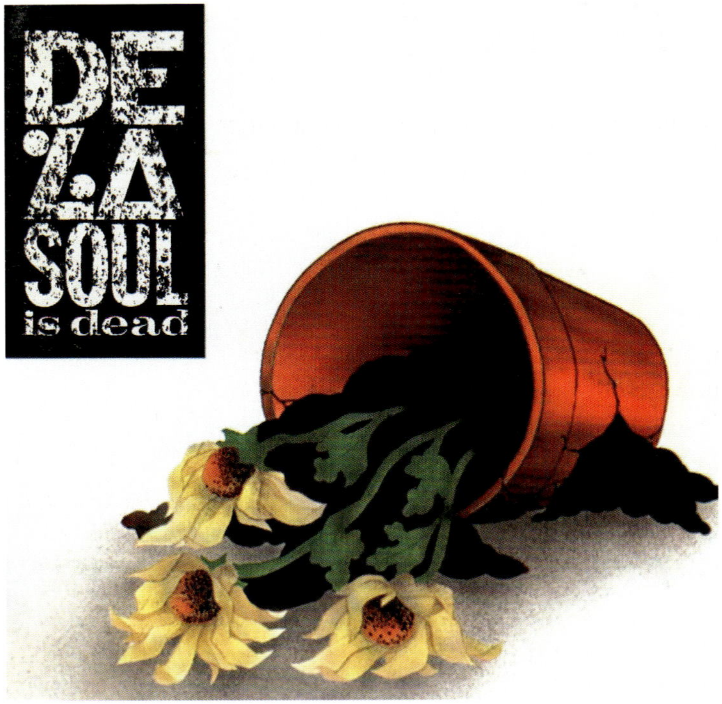

De La Soul, *De La Soul is Dead*, album cover. Courtesy of Tommy Boy Records/Warner Music.

irony of *De La Soul Is Dead*'s cover – instead of unifying form and content as album designers often aim to do – becomes part of the narrative against which the music itself responds. In other words, the album forces the potential listener to focus on the literal and biographical – is De La Soul dead? – before turning to the metaphoric and complicated nature of the work the album engages in. It is also a commentary on the intersections and differences of how visual material frames orality and literal presentations. In short, the album is a case study on why record covers matter.

De La Soul's initial success was also built on their visual appeal – on their first album, *Three Feet High and Rising*, the three rappers, Posdnous, Trugoy the Dove and Pasemaster Mase featured prominently on a day-glo cover. The cover features the heads of the three rappers, with flowers interspersed, over a yellow background; a peace sign appears in the "o" of "Soul" in De La Soul. The overall effect, truth be told, is rather "hippie-ish", and clever. This cover may have cemented the album's status as "hippie" rap and given the group a reputation that they felt undermined its place in the hip-hop community. The group, Posdnous

(Kelvin Mercer), Trugoy [yogurt spelled backwards] the Dove (David Jolicoeu) as well as P.A. System Mase (Vincent Mason Jr.), grew up in the suburbs of New York City, in Amityville, Long Island.[3] They put out their first album while two of them were teenagers and hit it big with a sound that was new and clever – and much friendlier to mainstream (read white) ears than earlier rap had been. Because of its cover, often (but not exclusively) lighthearted lyrics, and interesting samples (including some from Steely Dan, Johnny Cash, and The Turtles), the group earned a reputation for being hippie rappers. As the Dove said in an interview around the time *De La Soul Is Dead* came out, "100 percent of the people listening to De La Soul were really attached to the image and not to what we were trying to say".[4] According to Alan Light, De La Soul was "determined to shake the familiar De La image".[5] Posdnous himself takes it one step further: "We didn't want to be pinned down to a visual look, and so we thought, 'This whole daisy thing has to just die'".[6] And so, in constructing a follow up, the group wanted to find a way to both engage their audience and disengage their expectations: they turned to the postmodern conceit of a narrative that frames the album. In this narrative, three thugs beat up a young man who has found *De La Soul Is Dead* in a garbage can, and proceed to comment on the album while they play the album; the listeners hear both. By engaging in self-criticism and self-parody, De La Soul turns the tables on their ostensible critics, anticipating their reaction and showing to a more general audience their cleverness. De La Soul had the burden of producing a second work after a stunning debut; they needed to write a work that acknowledged the audience and its expectation, while remaining artistically vibrant. *De La Soul Is Dead* did both.

De La Soul's work is marked by a strain of pragmatic and perhaps organic postmodernism, one that develops from the problems it tries to anticipate, rather than an esoteric postmodernism that they try to falsely impose on their music. The multi-vocal approach that De La Soul took is similar to the one many writers and modern musicians adopt, coming in response to the difficulty of controlling audience response.

The problem of imagining and understanding audiences lies both in the way artists construct them and the way we as scholars interpret this interaction. While artists may claim that they are writing without a specific audience in mind, the idea of an audience is almost mandatory to complete the transaction of production an artist begins. And as scholars, we are increasingly interested in the ways artists imagine audiences and the way audiences receive what artists do. Through their works, it's clear that De La Soul wrote with a particular audi-

3 Stephen Thomas Erlewine, "De La Soul", *VH1*. www.vh1.com/artists/az/de_la_soul/bio.jhtml (accessed 21 March 2005).

4 Alan Light, "De La Soul", *Rolling Stone*, 18 April 1991, p. 57.

5 Ibid.

6 Ibid.

ence in mind. It assumed that whoever would be listening to *De La Soul Is Dead* would be familiar with *Three Feet High and Rising*. *De La Soul Is Dead* stands on its own, but the listening experience differs depending on whether one is familiar with *Three Feet High and Rising* or not. De La Soul intended this conception. *De La Soul Is Dead*'s central text literally begins where the other ended – with the mock-game show that framed *Three Feet High and Rising*. Other artists have extended stories or themes over multiple volumes – John Updike's Rabbit novels come to mind, as does Peter Gabriel's series of self-titled albums or even records like Led Zeppelin I, II, and III. Perhaps what is different between these works and *De La Soul Is Dead* is, however, the tension between a continuum of purpose that at the same time pulls away from previous work. In other words, De La Soul was clearly not abandoning its previous work as much as it was commenting on it and indeed building on it.

The engagement of a knowledgeable audience by De La Soul, especially through the media of the album cover and an internal frame, raises questions about the nature of any number of relationships – between audience and author, audience and text, author and text, and, crucially, the means of production and these groups. One way to look at audience is to construct an "implied reader" (in Wolfgang Iser's words), one who will presumably get what the artist is trying to do; another way is to assume a hostile or skeptical one. Or one could imagine both, as De La Soul was likely doing with *De La Soul Is Dead*. Rap music is a prime postmodern location because of the "pre-writing" audiences always do: they bring expectations to the text, and in effect begin writing a work before they read it. This pre-writing involves the construction of an artist. Michel Foucault reminded us that readers create authors as much as authors imagine readers. Determining as well as constructing and imagining authorship in musical groups presents a whole set of issues. The well worn and problematic distinctions between the "singer-songwriter" (Bob Dylan, Joni Mitchell, and more lately, Ani DiFranco for example) and the "performer" (Frank Sinatra) can easily underplay the role performing has on perceived authorship. Sinatra's performances of songs like "New York, New York" undoubtedly made those songs his.[7] Johnny Cash's cover versions of Beck, Soundgarden, and Nine Inch Nails songs confuse the nature of song authorship, placing performance on the same plane as songwriting, so much so that the term "cover" seems inadequate to describe what he did. Indeed, it seems impossible that someone else did "Hurt" before Cash did it, and even more unlikely that Neil Diamond was the source for the title of Cash's final studio album *Solitary Man*.

Rap authorship raises the questions of performance and authorship

7 John Kander and Fred Ebb wrote "New York, New York".

even more adamantly. Rap or hip-hop (or any of its offshoots like House music, Go-Go, or Trip-Hop) is largely a technologically driven medium, relying on the mixing (or re-mixing) of other artists' work along with the rap group or artist's own verbal participation. In fact, this relationship of one author to another accounts for the widespread classification of rap music as postmodern. As Richard Shusterman points out, critics and rappers themselves often refer to rap as postmodern for both textual and contextual reasons, as rap displays "transfigurative appropriation of older materials, eclectic mixing, an embracing of new media technology and mass culture, an emphasis on the local and temporal rather than the universal and eternal, and a challenging of modernity's notions of aesthetic autonomy and artistic purity".[8] But rap's postmodern label also comes from postmodernity's ubiquity in popular culture, which has led to a postmodernism that differs from the high artistic and academic version: "[P]ostmodernism has long been a concept with currency outside academia. Broadcasted by the popular mass media, it readily reached the streets".[9] Shusterman in a sense argues for an organic idea of the postmodern when he describes its affects in culture: "[P]ostmodernism has a positive side in the creative energy and new forms (of art and politics) unleashed through emancipation from modernity's constraints".[10]

Clearly, *De La Soul Is Dead* shows this emancipatory influence: *Dead* continues the artistic levity of *Three Feet High and Rising*, while taking on another level of self-referentiality and commentary. It uses the artistic self as a text that can be manipulated and enhanced with self-referentiality, in the hopes of preempting audience prewriting. By building audience reaction into its works, it situates itself in both locales, necessarily framing the critical and listener response. And yet, to attribute De La Soul's postmodern moves to anticipating the reader is not to deny the impulse to simply mark artistic distance from one work to another. De La Soul incorporating the old-school television storybook is a way of demonstrating savvy: the title is savvy, the counter-narrative is savvy and the effect is to show "hey, we're way ahead of you. Follow us".

Only two years separated De La Soul's first and second albums, but the pressure facing them was likely intense with *Three Feet High and Rising* on any number of top ten lists, including number five on *Rolling Stone*'s critics poll in 1989. *Three Feet High and Rising*, taken from a lyric from Johnny Cash's "Five Feet High and Rising", was a clever mix of rap songs, occasionally "peace loving", such as "Three Is the Magic Number", a captivating reworking of a Schoolhouse Rock song, as well as songs about sex, "Buddy" and "Jenny", urban problems,

8 Richard Shusterman, "Critical Response: Rap Remix: Pragmatism, Postmodernism, and Other Issues in the House", *Critical Inquiry* 22 (Autumn 1995), p. 154.

9 Ibid.

10 Ibid.

"Ghetto Thang", and goofy songs, including one about body odor, "A Little Bit of Soap". The group was also well known for its creative use of sampling, including the use of a Steely Dan song, and the use of other materials, including the minimal re-working of a French language instructional tape. The sampling of a Turtles song landed them in a lawsuit, which they eventually settled out of court.[11] In short, what they did prepared the listeners for future albums that would likely continue along the same path, perhaps with even more of a nod to popular culture.

Where the cheery, optimistic, wholly non-Gangster cover gave them a reputation as hippies, the music on *Three Feet* was more difficult to pin down – "Jenny" and "Buddy", for example, were only slightly subtle in their explicit discussion of sex, and "Ghetto Thang" certainly hits some moments of urban grit. What linked it to the cover was an eclectic musical approach. The diverse and funny use of samples – no rap group at the time and few since would think of using Steely Dan and the Turtles – was unprecedented at the time. Few would cite Johnny Cash in their album title. This approach, better experienced than described, was a critical and college radio favorite. However, judging from their reaction to *De La Soul Is Dead* and in interviews, the group did not like the image of weakness that they seemed to believe the cover suggested.

The problem was that listeners read De La Soul too simplistically. The big difference between groups like De La Soul, A Tribe Called Quest, and P.M. Dawn and other rappers was not only a softer, more layered sound but also a deeper subtlety of thought and humor. There's no question that rappers of all kinds have value as storytellers and social critics and most turn a good phrase here and there. But it's clear that De La Soul was after something more than sentiments about peace. *De La Soul Is Dead* is a remarkable mediation on everything from drug overdoses to one-night stands to the price of fame to the state of music – it's much closer to a book of short stories than a traditional album, in the vein of Willie Nelson's revolutionary *The Red-Headed Stranger*, which has a grouping of songs that overlap in content, and yet tell a story. I would argue that *De La Soul Is Dead* is even more interesting than Nelson's complex reworking of cowboy myth. But the internal complexity of the songs needs the external decoding of the album cover to help prepare listeners for what awaits them.

Indeed, any conversation about *Dead* must begin with the cover. Even at first glance, one has to notice that the package of the album cover and its title is unusually clever at making the reader/potential listener consider what the group might have intended. Obviously, the semiotic subject, a crumbling flowerpot

11 Light, "De La Soul", *Rolling Stone.*

full of daisies, is relatively straightforward. The daisies represent the group itself, which declared on its last album that it's part of a "D.A.I.S.Y. age" (meaning "DA inner sound y'all"),[12] and the flowerpot part of the notion of a dying daisy (though the daisies are very much alive on the cover). It also recalls the day-glo flowers on the cover of *Three Feet High and Rising*, but indicates the demise of what those hopeful flowers might have signified. "De La Soul Is Dead" is a title and a statement: as a title it certainly is true; as a statement, it is seemingly false. It recalls earlier negations and wordplay, most prominently René Magritte's "This is not" series, first with the pipe in *The Treachery of Images*, and then in *This is Not an Apple*. As Foucault articulates so clearly in his short book about the painting, the simple phrase part of the *calligram* of which the painting consists could mean any number of things, including the literal truth of the title. Some 75 years later, we know that De La Soul is not dead: it does continue to exist, even as the album title/statement points out otherwise. But which De La Soul is it that we listen to today? If we pre-write De La Soul based on previous notions of what the group did, then perhaps De La Soul as it existed in the past might not exist in the same way. The *Dead* flowers suggest that we halt and consider which group we are about to listen to.

An album cover could be considered an accessory to the work as a whole, as a paragon, "a form which has as its traditional determination not that it stands out but that it disappears, buries itself, effaces itself, melts away at the moment it deploys its greatest energy".[13] A record cover may attract a potential listener's attention, only to have a diminished impact once played.[14] While the same is true generally with *Dead*, De La Soul deliberately subverts the traditional listening experience through both the cover and the insert, and more importantly the album itself. In the narrative of which the cover is merely a part, three gangsters do indeed declare "De La Soul is dead". But then of course De La Soul is the author of precisely those words, on the cover and in the voice of the gangsters. This double negative of negation somehow brings us to the conclusion that De La Soul is indeed alive – but changed.

Unlike Magritte, whose paintings suggest via Foucault "the impossibility of defining a perspective that would let us say that the assertion is true, false, or contradictory",[15] the self-naming of De La Soul feels like more of an obligation: if the group is not technically dead, their image may be – and that is different. It's not common practice among rappers to declare their deaths (though some, like Tupac, may indeed predict it), but rather their *power*. As LL Cool J raps so memorably in "Mama Said Knock You Out": "Don't call it a comeback". But De La Soul projects a power through diffusion, through its feints, and bits and pieces, and,

12 Erlewine, "De La Soul", *VH1*.

13 Derrida, p. 61.

14 There's no doubt I'm taking this comment out of context from the whole of Derrida's work here, which is a large-scale critique of Kant and other philosophers and Cezanne's comment in a letter about finding the "truth in painting". See Derrida, p. 2. Our inquiries are similar but not the same – mine is of a much smaller scale but is dealing with a similar indeterminacy.

15 Michel Foucault, *This is Not a Pipe*, trans. and ed. James Harkness (Berkeley: California University Press, 1983), p. 20.

most importantly, its commandeering of audience expectation. *De La Soul Is Dead* is thus not a declaration of death but a co-opting of audience reaction and community standard. The group does so in many ways, in many voices, not only their own, but dozens of others who fight with De La Soul, kill their incestuous fathers, ask them to listen to demo tapes, kick ass, eat porridge, metaphorically cut loose their drug-addled brothers, pick on fast food counter workers, eat Chinese food, preach, dj, and keep the faith. Those voices are more than personas – they are audience members, and I deliberately obfuscate through the pronoun "they" who "they" was – De La Soul or the audience members – as they do. Like good postmodern authors, their author hands are all over the narrative and difficult to trace back to their autobiography.

In this particular case, *De La Soul Is Dead* can be judged by its cover, definitely and partially. The calligram that constructs it is a clue that what is on the inside will be clever and worthy of listening. However, the cover only hints at what one will find. And because De La Soul seemingly (though not definitely) disavows it later, we have to be skeptical of the motive behind the album cover art and who was responsible for its concept, though we do not have to be as skeptical about the clever title.

The music and lyrics of the album accentuates the audience's involvement with the narrative of the work. A young boy finds a tape of the album in a garbage can and subsequently gets beat up by three bullies who proceed to take the tape from him. As the record unfolds, we hear songs punctuated by comments from the bullies, one who hates the album, another who is negatively inclined toward it, and a third who likes it – and is beaten when he expresses his affection. Apparently, although this new album is somewhat "harder" (it's for example more outwardly sexual and sexist) than their previous work, De La Soul knows that it's not quite hard enough to suit those who want more traditional rap (though to characterize any type of rap as more traditional than another is to diminish rap music's diversity of thought and music, which is extensive). So while they are claiming a new spot within the rap world, they also convince the audience that they remain their own brand of rappers, neither soft, nor too hard, but just right, or rather just themselves – funny, interesting, and unable to be pigeonholed.

Still, in the narrative of the record, and in the title itself, De La Soul declares its own persona, that of rap hippies, to be dead. There's little indication of this in the first two songs, "Oodles of Os", and "Talkin' Bout Hey Love", both fun but inconsequential in terms of the album's message. The album's central theme comes out in "Pease Porridge in the Pot". The song begins with a dance beat straight out of the tap dancing 1940s, as we overhear a conversation about De La Soul, their strengths and weaknesses, and with the ultimate result that these young men are going to the club ("The Donut Hole") to challenge De La Soul. Then follows another conversation between young women, who describe a fight De La Soul was in, and end up wondering, "I thought it was supposed to be about peace signs…". Then we hear from De La Soul, who make this statement: "Just because we want peace, does not mean we can't throw no joints", joints being punches. Then we hear from someone, in an Indian accent who bemoans De La Soul's violence, an imitation of Kermit the Frog about his love of porridge, and we go back to the chorus: "Pease Porridge in the Pot, Nine Days Old". So in this song alone, we hear from ten voices, with varying degrees of support for and displeasure with De La Soul's violence. It's clear that De La Soul feels its violent response is justified, but it's also as clear that they recognize others might not do so. In the words of Adam Krims, the song "both critiques 'hardcore' images in hip-hop culture and challenges those fans who would deny 'hardcore' status to artists advocating peace".[16]

This song marks the most direct comment on De La Soul's need to seem tough; the rest of the album, excluding the periodic skits by the hoodlums, is less straightforwardly self-referential, save for two funny songs, "Bitties in the BK Lounge" and "Ring Ring Ring (Ha Ha Hey)", in which they describe their bouts with fame; the first describes how the indifference of a restaurant worker changes when she realizes it's De La Soul; the second describes their inundation in demo tapes after they became well known. The rest of the album straight out picks up where the *Three Feet* lets off – funny with interesting samples and good beats. They are less afraid to talk about sex directly ("Let, Let Me In", a song recounting a consummated seduction), and less afraid to confront issues directly ("Millie Pulled a Pistol on Santa", a song about incest turned revenge). But the hoodlums are not pleased with this continuation of *Three Feet*. Clearly the gang leader likes gangster rap, and De La Soul does not want to be gangster rappers. So De La Soul is not dead, in fact, except to these rappers. Appropriately, they use the album's title to conclude the album. To their listeners, in providing a multi-vocal response to their audience's expectations, De La Soul successfully negotiates a new identity, one as serious rappers, but not ones listeners can pigeonhole. They, in fact, are probably more self-assured in their follow-up, *Buhloone Mindstate*, where Mase exclaims, "I'm the greatest MC in the world".

De La Soul also deals with a past largely of their own making but also one

16 Adam Krims, *Rap Music and Poetics of Identity* (Cambridge: Cambridge University Press, 2000), p. 68.

in which they repudiate their past and take aim at those who shaped their career although their musical repudiation will have to wait until *Buhloone Mindstate*. De La Soul presents a work, prepackaged for all their critics, anticipating their intended audience. In a sense, this is both a call and response of the postmodern kind, or to use a mathematical sign (call+response). It's a call to the audience, to pay attention to the back and forth contained within the dialogue, and a response to the same audience, which wants the rappers to remain as they are.

In a real sense, De La Soul's three albums represent a true narrative of identity, a trilogy of different forms of engagement with their audience. The ironic twist in this particular narrative comes in the third album, *Buhloone Mindstate*, and in the song, "Patti Dooke", which obviously refers to Patty Duke, though I confess I'm at a loss for the precise interpretation of what the song means, save for the fact that Patty Duke played two very white identical cousins on *The Patty Duke Show* in the 1960s – a show that De La Soul growing up in the 1970s in Amityville, Long Island would have seen repeatedly.[17]

The cover of *Buhloone* features the faces of De La Soul in a way they were absent in *Dead*; the cover is a depiction of their reflection in a body of water, blurred with a dominant hue of green. While we've discussed the symbolic reason for daisies gracing the cover of *Dead*, there might be another. "Patti Dooke" is a song about crossing over, in which Posdnous contemplates the idea of "the boys from Tommy plant bridge crossin' to a larger community". His commentary on resisting white influence ("White boy Roy cannot feel it/But the first to try and steal it/Dilute it, pollute it, kill it/I see him infiltratin' to the masses") is inter-spliced with scenes from the movie *The Five Heartbeats*.[18] Marvin J. Gladney writes that in the movie "a record company first proposes that a white group record a black group's song, substituting white faces for black talent, and then deletes a picture of the group from the record jacket because the firm doesn't believe that the Heartbeats' image will sell". Gladney points out that, "in this way, De La Soul dramatically portrays the historical precedents for the image posturing that is fundamental to the contemporary music/hip-hop industry".

Whether this is specifically about *De La Soul Is Dead* and its faceless cover is debatable, but the central questions regarding De La Soul's liminal identity on *De La Soul Is Dead* remain. Their first album, they explain, captured a white audience largely because they grew up in suburbia. According to an interview with Posdnous, "I'm very sure us living where we did had an effect on the way we looked at things... What surrounded us was suburbia". But in the interviews done right around the time that *Dead* was released, he was careful to let read-

17 They live in the same metro broadcast area, New York City, as I did growing up in Connecticut – the show was on repeatedly when I was a child.

18 Marvin J. Gladney, "The Black Arts Movement and Hip-Hop", *African-American Review* 29:2 (Summer 1995), pp. 291–301.

ers know that he "lived both lives". He lived in Amityville, but "stayed with my cousins in the Bronx...".[19] The Bronx is a code word for the ghetto, according to Tricia Rose, a crucial element in hip-hop identity: "Even though rappers are aware of the diversity of their audiences and the context for reception, their use of the ghetto and its symbolic significance is primarily directed at other black hip hop fans".[20]

De La Soul truly is marginal in this particular stance, according to Robert Park's old definition that describes groups (in particular, the Jews) existing in two worlds, neither giving up one or the other. Their distance from more traditional rap allowed them to cross over in the netherworlds of critical attention; yet, they remained three African-American rappers, and all that that may mean to some in white America. Again, the album cover reflects this uncertainty – was it a compromise cover, a negation of identity, a clever play on words, or some of all?

At this point they remain between (and betwixt), caught between defending themselves as tough young men and creative, funny artists whose range steps beyond almost anyone in sight. They take rap to places that pop and rock music can only dream to go. In recent years, Wilco's *Yankee Foxtrot Hotel* has been lauded as experimental with its weird radio hissing noise; several years before, Beck's *Mellow Gold* and *Odelay* received the same type of hype, mostly deserved, for Beck's collage work mixing sounds and ideas. But De La Soul not only collages, they rummage and collect – taking sounds as diverse as traditional '40s dance music to the voice-beat of the in-and-out to a traditional funk beat to a house beat to a rock beat to a tap-dancing beat, which *Yankee Foxtrot Hotel* and *Odelay* do, but nowhere to the same degree that *De La Soul Is Dead* does. In his review for *Rolling Stone* (one of the few places that rated *Dead* higher than *Three Feet High*), Scott Poulson-Bryant says *De La Soul Is Dead* is "crammed full of startlingly inventive samples and an intelligent, well-spoken defensiveness bred in the onrush of sudden fame and fortune". Poulson-Bryant believes that De La Soul "are true hip-hop scholars, redefining in jam after jam (with the help of producer Prince Paul) how we listen to, dance to, live with and abide by hip-hop".[21] In any case, De La Soul samples everything with the idea of showing there is nothing on the shelf they – and the listeners – won't and can't use in the pursuit of truth-telling, self-revelation. It has much more in common, and I apologize here for the discordant insertion, with Ralph Ellison's obsessive use of folklore in *Invisible Man* than it does anything else.

In writing *Invisible Man*, one thing Ellison did so powerfully, like Langston Hughes before him, was to show how the experience of African Americans

19 Sean Taylor, "Soul Destroyed – De La Soul Are Dead. Long live De La Soul/The Reborn Rappers in the Post-Daisy Age", *The Guardian*, 2 May 1991. *Lexis-Nexis* (accessed 20 March 2005).

20 Tricia Rose, *Black Noise: Rap Music and Black Culture in Contemporary America* (Hanover, NH: Wesleyan University Press, 1994), p. 12.

21 Scott Poulson-Bryant, review of *De La Soul Is Dead*, *Rolling Stone*, 30 May 1991. http://rollingstone.com/reviews/cd/review.asp?aid=16266&cf= (accessed 20 March 2003).

and the American experience fit together, not in a puzzle or even in a traditional narrative, but as mysterious parts of an unknown whole.

While *De La Soul Is Dead* is not *Invisible Man*, either in literary achievement or in the depth of its scope, but the trope of invisibility becomes relevant when looking at the cover. The invisibility of the narrator in *Invisible Man* is a temporary state, from which the narrator hopes to emerge. The cover, taken with the contents of the album, suggests a similar invisibility for the group, who in *De La Soul is Dead* stake out a liminal position between the day-glo hippie life portrayed on the cover of *Three Feet High and Rising* and the more ambiguous cover of *Buhloone Mindstate*. The group is not only absent from the cover, but it proclaims their death. The invisibility, while not as explicitly political and centered on race as the invisibility of the narrator in *Invisible Man*, does suggest the type of retreat and advancement he undertakes.

De La Soul Is Dead also recalls *Invisible Man* in the way it uses diverse sources. It reminds us of the diversity of sound available to the modern listener, of the pop traditions beyond traditional pop, and, thematically, of the invisibility/visibility of the modern black man. Brent Staples postulates in his canonical essay "Just Walk on By: Black Men and Public Space" that it is often necessary to identify oneself as a particular type of African American – he uses whistling classical music as an example.[22] De La Soul does the music equivalent in drawing itself as tough rappers with a philosophical side, similar to the move that African-American author Walter Mosley does with Easy Rawlins in the mystery color novels (of which *Devil in a Blue Dress* is one) and Socrates Fortlow in *Always Outnumbered, Always Outgunned*. These characters not only defend themselves but also illuminate the racial divide in ways both subtle and broad. They serve as reminders that the political, practical, and artistic are never separate but intertwined.

De La Soul is itself worried about its own irrelevance in a different way, caught between black and white communities. The mainstream loves them because they are "peaceful", not angry. *Dead* is a reaction to reclaim their blackness. Some reviewers, like Karen Schoemer from the *New York Times*, do not get their predicament. She writes, "... ever since the release of 'De La Soul Is Dead last year, the group has seemed intent on proving that they're just tough guys in disguise... Tough-guy posturing is a necessary part of rap, but what once made De La Soul special was that it offered a lighthearted alternative".[23] Without even combating her misguided double standard – if tough guy posturing is indeed a necessary part of rap, then why can't De La Soul do it? – it shows the dilemma De La Soul faced when trying to find an audience.

22 Brent Staples, "Just Walk on By: Black Men and Public Space", *Ms.*, September 1986.

23 Karen Schoemer, "De La Soul's New Image: Toughness", *New York Times*, 18 February 1992.

Their response was *De La Soul Is Dead*, a work which served to interrogate the continuing questions of what powers authors and audiences have, what an author can do with his or her work to shape perception of both work and artist, and, finally, what the means of production has to say about such a relationship.

Enough people got and get De La Soul to know they were different than traditional rappers. The group and their producer Prince Paul contributed heavily – or should have – to the ongoing conversation about postmodernism and rap. If rap is postmodern because it is self-referential, what do we make of De La Soul, whose self-referentially is itself self-referential? The multiple layers of artifice they lay in, on, and through their work become even more remarkable when there is a group at the center of it. We don't lose the group's authorial voice, even as they weave samples and multiple narratives throughout. Instead of the voice becoming diffuse, it becomes unified through this paradox of engagement and disengagement. This paradox begins with the cover, a simple image of a desiccated flowerpot, and stenciled lettering indicating De La Soul's death and ultimately proving how alive the group really is.

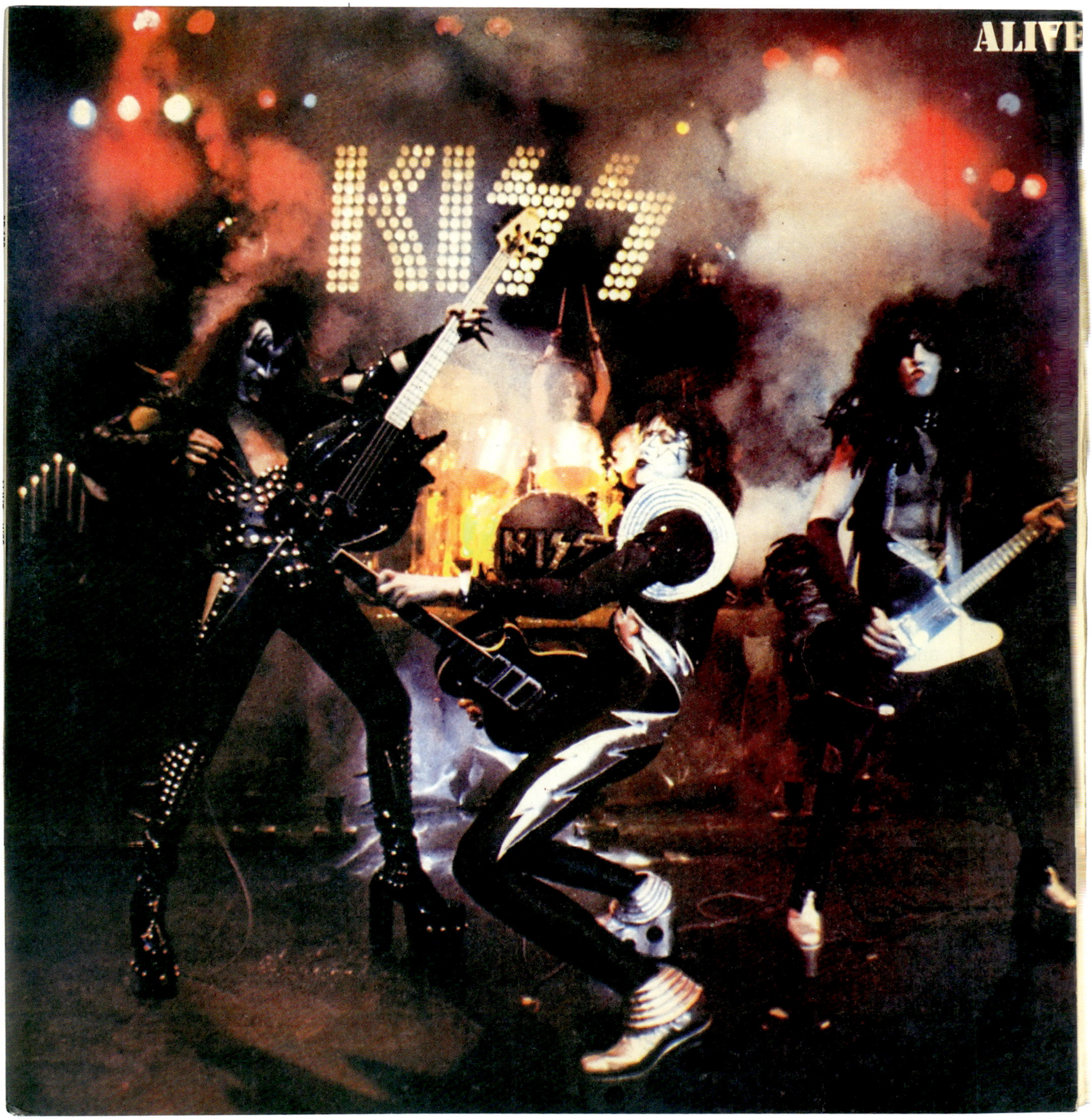
ALIVE
KISS

KISS: *Alive!*

An Iconographical Approach

Ian Chapman

KISS, *Alive!*, album cover, 1975. Casablanca Records. Cover concept and photography fin Costello.

Currently, there exists no proven scholarly method for the evaluation of album cover art. While Roger Dean and David Howells have contributed much to the elevation of album covers to a distinct art form through the publication of their *Album Cover Album* series, their stated goal is to "celebrate the art of the album cover and to bring it to the attention of a wider audience".[1] Thus, while providing a valuable resource and useful chronology for the development of the album cover, such publications attempt little analysis, nor do they suggest how analysis might be conducted. The authors do, however, make several salient observations. For instance, in dismissing the notion that album covers function merely as packaging, Dean and Howells argue that within album cover design there are always signs, codes and symbols that provide musicians with both identity and image, to the extent that an 'aware' audience may identify at a glance a specific 'type' of music and a more general musical and visual ambiance.[2]

Supporting this notion, Nick de Ville, author of *Album Style and Image in Sleeve Design*, suggests that album covers offer "pictorial representations of the self-consciously adopted aesthetic values and worldly interests of specific, identifiable lifestyles, subcultures, urban tribes and other self-determined communities".[3] I concur with these views and, via the adaptation and application of a defining interpretive method from art history, in this essay I will identify the signs, codes and symbols present in a specific album cover. From this information I will then extrapolate how these covers might have conveyed cultural purchase to myself as a consumer. While length constraints prevent a complete, overarching application in this essay, the intention is to demonstrate that the model is an appropriate one.

My introduction to KISS occurred in 1975, in Hamilton, New Zealand. This event left a lasting impression on me, as it provided a blatant demonstration of the power of album cover art. I can clearly recall perusing the record collection of a

1 Roger Dean and David Howells, *Album Cover Album 4* (Surrey: Dragon's World Ltd, 1987), p. 10.

2 Ibid.

3 Nick de Ville, *Album Style and Image in Sleeve Design* (London: Octopus Publishing Group, 2003), p. 8.

new boy who had just started at my school, having recently emigrated from England with his family. I was fifteen years old and, although a popular music fan, I was totally unaware of KISS until I came across *Alive!* while flicking through his albums.

My introduction was thus purely a visual one, with no prior biographical knowledge of any kind, nor any initial aural reinforcement. Yet, I was certain that I would like this band, a summation arrived at purely through a visual appraisal of the cover. And so it was to be. One of my primary aims in conducting this analysis, then, is that I might understand better how this was so. How and what did the cover art communicate to me? At the time I considered music to be a defining personal statement and, while I certainly did not think of it in such clear terms at the time, aligning myself with a subculture was all-important to me. What, then, did I immediately seize upon as being of cultural purchase?

Prior to beginning a visual analysis I will further define the parameters of my investigation. Art historian and methodologist Ernst Gombrich suggests that "interpretation proceeds by steps, and the first step on which everything else depends is the decision to which genre a given work is to be assigned".[4] Gombrich is, of course, referring to genres of paintings, and to underline the importance of correct genre attribution, he then describes the misreading of hieroglyphics during the Renaissance because of fundamental misconceptions about Egyptian script.[5] In addressing album covers, however, we are not dealing with centuries-old painted images, seeking to discern long-lost associations and meanings from symbols and signs that may have become foreign to the modern eye.[6] Rather, we are dealing with a clearly delineated medium that dates back only to 1940, when Columbia Records issued the 78 rpm recording *Smash Song Hits by Rodgers & Hart* in the first pictorial sleeve.[7] Specifically, we are dealing with a printed-paper or cardboard cover used for housing gramophone records from 1940 until the late 1980s, at which time the primary format for the distribution of music switched to the digital compact disc. In using the term 'album cover art', I make no distinction between album covers consisting of photographs and those that utilize paintings or other media.

I do not address questions of artistic or commercial intention. How much of what is discernable from the KISS album cover was intentionally planned by the band, their management and/or record company, is – for the purposes of this discussion – a moot point. Indeed, as art historian Michael Baxandall warns, "once we start inferring causes and intention in a picture we are doing something that is obviously very precarious indeed".[8] When looking at album cover art in particular, the question of where advertising and marketing consid-

4 Ernst H. Gombrich, *Symbolic Images: Studies in the Art of the Renaissance* (London: Phaidon, 1972), p. 21.
5 Ibid.
6 Notwithstanding the fact that occasionally an album cover may consist of a reinterpretation, a parody, or even an exact reprint of a historic artwork.
7 de Ville, p. 25.
8 Michael Baxandall, *Patterns of Intention* (London: Yale University Press, 1985), p. vi.

erations might begin and end presents itself very early on. However, any attempt to address this unavoidably requires entering into the much wider debate of art versus commerce. And before even beginning, it would be critical to ascertain the level of control artists have regarding album cover decisions. To avoid this, and thus pull the project back to manageable proportions, I confine all analytical discourse to such evidence as may be gleaned from a formal appraisal of the work itself. In so doing, I place myself in direct contrast to those analytical approaches to art history that require the reconstruction of the artistic vision as a central component.[9]

Art historians Baxandall, Richard Leppert, Lyckle De Vries, Thomas Heck and others agree there can be no definitive method for evaluating visual imagery. De Vries, however, suggests that of those available, Erwin Panofsky's is one of the best.[10] Intended for the interpretation of images in renaissance and baroque works of art, I believe the major strength of the method is its flexibility, and it is for this reason that I loosely employ it here. Panofsky's is a long-established, three-stage method of analysis, whereby data gleaned from one level forms the basis for each subsequent level of investigation. Adapted for my application to *Alive!*, my approach is to firstly describe the cover using words alone in order to compile primary data for use at the next level, a process Baxandall describes as "a written representation of a picture".[11] This step requires that one disregards what may be represented by the collected data. The second stage is an interpretive one – to identify signs, codes and symbols found within the primary data and to determine how these might communicate specific themes or concepts. In the final stage I conduct an investigation into what lies beyond the specific themes or concepts identified previously, and draw conclusions regarding the message(s) that the cover might communicate to an informed or semi-informed audience. De Vries summarizes Panofsky's method thus: "[It would] start with the visual image of the material object and work towards understanding its cultural context – not the other way round".[12] This description of the method remains valid for album cover analysis, and this current application is by no means the first time it has been put to use outside that for which it was originally intended. Laurie Schneider Adams, for instance, applies Panofsky's method to an exploration of how the image of cartoon character Mickey Mouse takes on many different meanings as a cultural icon.[13]

As is the case for others who employ the model, my goal in adopting this formal approach to analysis is that I might proceed beyond the simple, primary level of subject-matter identification.

9 See Otto Pacht, *The Practice of Art History: Reflections on Method* (Munich: Harvey Millar Publishers, 1999), p. 69, and Baxandall, *Patterns of Intention.*

10 Lyckle De Vries, "Iconography and Iconology in Art History: Panofsky's Prescriptive Definitions and Some Art-Historical Responses to Them", in Thomas Heck (ed.), *Picturing Performance: The Iconography of the Performing Arts in Concept and Practice* (New York: University of Rochester Press, 1999), p. 64.

11 Baxandall, p. 3.

12 De Vries, p. 49.

13 Laurie Schneider Adams, *The Methodologies of Art: An Introduction* (Colorado: Westview Press, 1996), pp. 37–38.

The first stage is a purely descriptive one and has been kept to a minimum in this essay. This is largely because the image itself is reproduced here for the reader; however, it should be noted that those employing Panofsky's method often devote considerably more space to it to ensure that no detail is omitted.

The cover is a photograph of a rock band in what appears to be a 'live' concert situation, a summation backed by the word *Alive!* at the top right corner. The predominant colors are black and red, with patches of light or dark blue evident, and bright yellow light bathing the drum-kit and drummer. The bright lighting silhouettes the drummer's upwardly extended arms and drumsticks that effectively point toward the word 'KISS' above. 'KISS' appears again on the bass drum, written in silver glitter outlined by black. In the foreground, in the space occupied by the other three band members, the stage is bare except for guitar leads and what appear to be pyrotechnic devices (commonly called flash-pots) positioned between the figures and the drum riser. The only other object evident on the stage is a lit candelabrum on the left.

The four musicians are presented in highly stylized dramatic poses. They have their faces distinctively painted and they wear highly individual black and silver costuming and platform boots.

This, then, is a brief summary of what the viewer has seen upon first perusal of the cover. I shall now proceed to the second stage, equivalent to Panofsky's second level and summarized by De Vries thus: "to read themes and concepts in these objects and events".[14] Before I do so, however, I must briefly address the nature of viewing. Even though I had no knowledge of KISS prior to seeing this album cover, in 1975 at age fifteen I was utterly incapable of viewing the work with no presuppositions – a state of seeing that Gombrich terms 'the innocent eye'.[15] I had a working knowledge of both existing and previous rock music iconography, especially, in my case, regarding glam rock. Therefore I had reference points that consciously or unconsciously helped inform my view from the moment of setting eyes upon the cover – effectively combining both the first and second levels of the method simultaneously. Gombrich, in debunking the notion of the innocent eye, suggests:

> It postulates that we can, and possibly should, attend to all messages which the eye receives from the visible world with neutral impartiality because to be selective in our attention introduces a bias and therefore a distortion of the objective truth... this demand is quite unrealistic.[16]

14 De Vries, p. 49.
15 Gombrich, *The Sense of Order: A Study in the Psychology of Decorative Art* (New York: Cornell University Press, 1979), p. 105.
16 Ibid.

One instantly absorbs, from the visual image, a selection of recognizable signs, and comparative associations are made. In the case of album covers, I suggest these initial responses constitute a search for style allegiance. As Leppert suggests, "the means by which visual art 'says' something to us is in part unique... Sight is a 'device' for recognition, prediction and confirmation".[17] And as Taylor points out, because this process is so instantaneous, separating the steps by which we absorb a visual image is something of an arbitrary exercise.[18] Baxandall describes the process thus:

> Obviously the optical act of scanning is not all there is to looking; we use our minds and our minds use concepts... Within the first second or so of looking we have a sort of impression of the whole field of a picture. What follows is sharpening of detail, noting of relations, perception of orders...[19]

Recognizing the impossibility of viewing with an innocent eye does not, however, render impossible the successful application of the first level of this method. All that is required is that any such acknowledged associations as may exist be purposely left until level two where they may be treated specifically as such. While acknowledging the flux, it is possible to accurately describe signs, codes and symbols in writing, without attribution, by consciously confining oneself to a simple data collection exercise. Indeed it is precisely this disciplined, structured, methodical process – designed to prevent the ad hoc and premature blending of content and meaning – that art historians such as Heck regard as the major strength of Panofsky's method.

Our task at the second stage is to make sense of the compiled information. How might the components that we have identified function as signs, codes and symbols of a more specific theme or concept? Of foremost importance to our current application of the method is the question of style alignment; to what popular music style does this band belong?

It can be safely assumed that the band's name is KISS as, in addition to the word appearing prominently twice on the cover, two of the band members provide further visual support by having their red or black painted lips pursed as if in the act of kissing. The bass player's extended tongue can be regarded similarly, albeit in a more direct sexual reference. Also of a sexual nature the thrusting of the guitars at crotch level clearly fulfills the "extension of the male body" criteria for cock-rock as defined by Sheila Whiteley and others.[20]

The fact that all four musicians have painted faces immediately suggests

17 Richard Leppert, *Art and the Committed Eye* (Colorado: Westview Press, 1996), p. 5.
18 Joshua C. Taylor, *Learning to Look: A Handbook for the Visual Arts* (Chicago: The University of Chicago Press, 1981), p. 52.
19 Baxandall, p. 3.
20 Sheila Whiteley, *Sexing the Groove: Popular Music and Gender* (London: Routledge, 1997), p. 43.

an alignment with glam rock. While many glam rock artists did not wear face paint to this degree, some of those who did, and who were active in the three years immediately preceding the KISS release, include David Bowie (as Ziggy Stardust) and Alice Cooper, and – to a lesser extent perhaps – Steve Harley & Cockney Rebel, Chicory Tip, Roy Wood & Wizzard, Sweet, and even Lou Reed around the time of his 1972 *Transformer* album. Equally, the style of the face painting may also be regarded as reminiscent of comic-book heroes such as Spiderman and Batman, thus introducing a fantasy/science fiction theme into the mix, a component which de Ville considers a "preoccupation of heavy metal art".[21]

The platform boots strengthen the glam rock association further, as does the obvious theatrical posing that is also a hallmark of the visually flamboyant, image conscious, glam rock performance style. Equally, the sequins and shiny silver material on the costume of the guitarist in the foreground, and the feathers around the shoulders of the guitarist on the right are convincing glam signifiers. Yet, overall, the black clothing of the band members throws an element of contradiction into the analysis. Glam rock artists almost never wore black.[22]

In combination, the makeup and costuming introduces a significant androgynous element to the image of the band. Overall, this strongly suggests a glam rock affiliation, because as Todd Haynes has it, "[glam] presented to the world a new and radically fluid model for sexual identity; no longer defined by its permanence, but by the multi-colored result of constant change and reinvention".[23]

The dominance of black and red on the cover is, according to Weinstein, a heavy metal signifier,[24] and these colors are prevalent in gothic horror imagery also. There is a close relationship at work here, as gothic horror is a central theme of heavy metal. As Walser suggests, "The development of heavy metal in the late 1960s and its continuing popularity through the 1970s and 1980s coincides exactly with the period of the greatest popularity horror films and books have ever known".[25] The candelabrum is another gothic representation on the cover.

The bass player's clothing resembles medieval body armor, seemingly consistent with his aggressive, war-like stance, his war-paint and overall aggressive countenance. War is a common theme in heavy metal[26] and the elements of smoke and fire evident on the KISS cover – in collusion with the aggressive stance of the band members – enhance this stage-as-battlefield interpretation. This is consistent with Weinstein's summation that "The heavy metal code specifies that what is depicted must be somewhat ominous, threatening,

21 de Ville, p. 151.
22 With the notable exception of Suzi Quatro – the sole female artist associated with the style, and, at times, Alice Cooper.
23 Todd Haynes, "Foreword", in Barney Hoskyns, *Glam: Bowie, Bolan And The Glitter Rock Revolution* (London: Faber and Faber Ltd, 1998), p. xi.
24 Deena Weinstein, *Heavy Metal: The Music And Its Culture* (New York: Da Capo Press, 2000), p. 28.
25 Robert Walser, *Running with the Devil: Power, Gender and Madness in Heavy Metal Music* (Connecticut: Wesleyan University Press, 1993), p. 161.
26 Ibid., p. 163.

and unsettling, suggesting chaos and bordering on the grotesque".[27] Allied to this war allusion, the configuration of the SS letters of KISS resembles the Nazi Storm-trooper's insignia, with Roy Shuker regarding Nazi insignia as one of the primary heavy metal signatures,[28] and Weinstein commenting on the prevalence of what she terms the "thunderbolt motif"[29] in heavy metal, evident in the work of many bands including Black Sabbath. In addition, this stylized S brings to mind Bowie's *Ziggy Stardust* backdrop, and also the painted motif he wears on his face on the cover of the *Aladdin Sane* album (1973). The configuration of these letters thus serves the dual role of providing both a glam rock reference and a heavy metal one.

The overall style of costuming, with black leather and silver studs being much in evidence, may also be read as representational of biker regalia. Equally, the Saturn rings and star-flecked costume of the guitarist in the foreground can be seen as science fiction imagery – each of these themes being identified by Weinstein as archetypal for heavy metal.[30] Yet a further reading of the bass player's costuming, focusing upon the cutaway at the thigh, suggests a sadism & masochism element to the costuming; another heavy metal signature.[31]

In summary: four of the most common heavy metal signifiers have been identified at this second level of analysis: gothic horror, war, sex and science fiction. The latter two themes apply equally to glam rock, while aspects of the costuming, the androgynous presentation, and the overriding blatant theatricality of the staging also support this assertion. De Ville suggests that an album cover can make clear the "genre allegiance of the performer".[32] From the analysis thus far, does the *Alive!* cover clearly project a genre allegiance? On balance, our analysis suggests that the primary genre allegiance of KISS is heavy metal. Yet some of the stylistic signals are confusing, even contradictory. In particular, fingerprints of glam rock are very evident. While today there exists a specific sub-genre termed 'glam-metal',[33] in 1975 no such term existed and I suggest that by blending imagery of the two styles so blatantly, genre allegiances were challenged rather than clarified.

With regard to my initial personal response to the KISS cover, it is pertinent to consider for a moment the degree to which I was an 'informed audience'. Although in 1975 the popular music industry was nothing like the fragmented, stylistically independent market that it is now, at age fifteen I was fully conversant with the terms 'heavy metal' and 'glam rock'. I owned Black Sabbath albums and knew them to be heavy metal. I also owned T Rex, Slade, Sweet and David Bowie albums and knew them to be glam rock. With the possible exception of Alice Cooper, there was nothing I was aware of that I would have con-

27 Weinstein, p. 29.
28 Roy Shuker, *Key Concepts in Popular Music* (London: Routledge, 1998), p. 161.
29 Weinstein, p. 28.
30 Ibid.
31 Ibid., p. 30.
32 de Ville, p. 10.
33 Walser, p. 124.

sidered a combination of the two styles, and I believe this blurring of stylistic signifiers contributed much to my fascination with this cover. As a music fan in 1975 – enormously concerned with what I would now regard as alignment with a subculture – I was attracted by the spectacle inherent to glam rock and also by what I regarded as the power of heavy metal. Eighteen years later, Walser would correctly describe KISS as the "founders of spectacular metal".[34]

At the final stage we may now go on to explore intrinsic meaning, that which Panofsky describes as the "history of cultural symptoms or 'symbols' in general (insight into the manner in which ... essential tendencies of the human mind were expressed by specific themes and concepts)".[35] This is the most challenging level for the researcher as, in our case, analysis proceeds beyond determining style(s), to the stage where historical precedents for specific components are explored. Far-reaching and bound by fluid parameters, the threads requiring investigation in the case of *Alive!* include gothic imagery, the history of horror as a specific genre, science fiction, color analysis, photography, textiles, costuming, gestural analysis, and beyond. For reasons of space, my investigation into the most obvious of these factors is limited, but it is my intention, nevertheless, that the following should provide an overview of the possibilities for more thorough research.

It is immediately evident that the band members are unified in their manner of dress, while at the same time possessing clearly discernable individual characteristics. The band wears a uniform made from non-naturalistic materials – a choice of textiles that Mablen Jones regards as immediately suggesting an other-worldliness[36] – and the full-face makeup of the band members enhances this overall homogeneity. Such unification in costuming, as Colin McDowell reminds us, always projects an air of power and total authority,[37] and the gestural projection of the four figures fully supports this conviction in their cohesively blatant, arrogant, aggressive demeanor.

While the predominant use of black and red in the stage lighting, costuming and makeup was earlier identified as being consistent with a wider gothic horror ambience borrowed by heavy metal, at this level of analysis we may extend this line of enquiry to a deeper exploration of the significance of these colors. Almost any text dealing with the historical significance of color aligns black with power, elegance, death, evil and mystery; and red with energy, war, danger, passion and desire.[38] As Rebecca Arnold suggests with regard to costuming, "[the] connotations of the deadly, the repeated use of black and blood red, run deeper than just the clothing itself. The imagery of fashion has become fascinated with the notion of threat ... forcing a confrontation with inner fears".[39]

34 Ibid., p. 125.
35 Erwin Panofsky, cited in De Vries, p. 50.
36 Mablen Jones, *Getting it on: The Clothing of Rock'n'Roll* (New York: Abbeville Press, 1987), p. 124.
37 Colin McDowell, *Dressed to Kill: Sex, Power & Clothes* (London: Hutchinson, 1992), p. 129.
38 See, for instance, Edith Anderson Feisner, *Colour: How to Use Colour in Art and Design* (London: Laurence King Publishing Ltd, 2001), pp. 118–120. Also John Gage, *Colour and Meaning: Art, Science and Symbolism* (London: Thames & Huson Ltd, 1999).
39 Rebecca Arnold, *Fashion, Desire and Anxiety: Image and Morality in the Twentieth Century* (New Jersey: Rutgers University Press, 2001), p. 59.

Operating at a deep level then, and regardless of whether this is subconscious or conscious, through color choices the *Alive!* album cover taps into universal, primordial human emotions.

Allied to this, one must also consider the history and wider implications of the use of masks in theatrical performance. As David Griffiths affirms, masks have been part of theatrical tradition since Greek drama, Roman theatre, and the Commedia.[40] In addition, Japanese *Noh* theatre has a history spanning six centuries, and it is arguably this tradition of mask that is the most pertinent to this discussion. According to Laurence Senelick, in Japanese theatre the base color of white eliminates individuality, elevates the wearer above the ordinary, and allows the presentation of archetypes rather than individuals.[41] Upon these archetypes an audience may project their own readings and experiences for a personal interpretation of meaning. The painted faces of KISS closely resemble the mask-types of gods, monsters and demons identified by Diana Devlin as inherent to *Noh*,[42] and also those of the closely associated *Kyogen* comical plays that feature animals and specific human types (e.g.: lover, thinker, criminal, etc).[43] Thus, the face of a KISS member denies human individuality and offers in its place a theatrical caricature – in the case of bassist Gene Simmons, a caricature of the demonic – in a portrayal totally supported in the costuming and therefore fully adhering to Mablen Jones' belief that "successful rock costume is a type of expressionistic caricature that eliminates all detail that does not contribute to a specific character".[44] Onto this unified presentation the popular music consumer may then project their own personal take on the monster/demon figure in much the same way as intended in Japanese theatre. Indeed, in the case of the *Alive!* album cover, any potential doubts regarding the character-alignment of individual band members – such as may exist in the mind of a consumer following a visual appraisal – are further assuaged by the personally signed notes purportedly penned by each of them in the inside sleeve. The character traits evident within these brief texts adhere rigidly to the caricatures of 'the cat' (Peter Criss), 'the demon' (Simmons), 'the lover' (Paul Stanley), and 'the spaceman' (Ace Frehley).

Closely allied to this denial of human individuality and projection of archetype is androgyny, in itself a form of gender-masking. Senelick suggests that "gender tokens are magical, and to abuse them will transform and denature the abuser. It confuses signifier with signified".[45] In glam rock, androgyny provided a critical shock element, a touch of danger that challenged traditional western concepts of morality. Historical warnings against androgynous practices can be found in the Bible, specifically in Deuteronomy 22:5: "No woman

40 David Griffiths, *Acting Through Mask* (Amsterdam: Harwood Academic Publishers, 1998), p. 37.

41 Laurence Senelick, *The Changing Room: Sex, Drag and Theatre* (New York: Routledge, 2000), p. 87.

42 Diana Devlin, *Mask and Scene: An Introduction to a World View of Theatre* (Hampshire: MacMillan Publishers Ltd, 1989), p. 60.

43 Ibid., p. 61.

44 Jones, p. 11.

45 Senelick, p. 18.

shall wear an article of man's clothing, nor shall a man put on a woman's dress for those who do these things are abominable to the Lord your God". To display gender signifiers of two sexes is an act that clouds perceived notions of gender authenticity. As is the case with masks, the effect is, as Whiteley asserts, the intentional forfeiture of gendered individuality.[46] Kari Weil regards the employment of androgyny as "a psychological and poetic ideal, a transcendence of sex, self and language".[47] Just as the aim of white face paint in Japanese theatre is designed to elevate the wearer above the ordinary, so too the employment of androgynous imagery presents an ideal above the concept of fallible individuality. As Senelick believes, this promotes the transcendence of the actor's personality and gender, thus creating an artificial construction of an ideal.[48]

Overall, the combination of color, masking, costuming and gesture results in the successful creation of archetypal myth figures. Jones describes this as "the spectacle of excess at its outermost limits of agony and ecstasy ... the evocation of primordial images from the wellsprings of archetype".[49]

My investigation into the "intrinsic meaning" of the album cover must end at this premature point, although certainly there is more to explore. The cover is, by any standard, a visual feast. The multi-faceted combination of components – of which color, masking, costuming, androgyny and gesture are arguably the most important but by no means the only factors – results in an extraordinarily cohesive picture that operates on several levels.

As stated earlier, one of my primary goals in conducting this research was to better understand how the album cover garnered such a positive response from me upon first viewing. As a result of this three-tiered process of analysis, I conclude that it did so through the blurring – or outright denial – of the individuality of the four band members, and the replacement of this by the presentation of historical archetypes upon which I was able to project my own fantasy meanings. While I certainly don't suggest that I was cognizant of this process at the time, the cover nevertheless afforded me a level of interpretive freedom that no 'real' image could have matched. Crucially, in addition to functioning in this manner for me personally, the cover conveyed a far more widespread appeal due to the universality of the underlying primordial human emotions portrayed within the *mise-en-scène* overall. This, surely, must go a long way toward accounting for the enormous success of the album and the manner in which it launched KISS into the 'supergroup' category of artists. Through the denial of specificity within multiple components – and operating at several levels – the ambiguity of the image afforded the opportunity for personal readings *en masse*. This, I suggest

46 Whiteley, p. 200.
47 Kari Weil, cited in Whiteley, p. 200.
48 Senelick, p. 89.
49 Jones, p. 7.

constitutes something of a marketer's dream and supports Dominy Hamilton's assertion that "fantasy is attractive because it allows the possibility of infinite change and manipulation whereas reality does not, and is therefore not an asset for someone who wants to sell things".[50]

I believe that album covers constitute a clearly delineated medium and, as such, the employment of formal analysis is crucial in order to unpack not only personal interpretations such as that carried out here, but also to work toward a wider understanding of how specific examples – or even specific styles – might impact upon music consumers at large. As Taylor suggests, "analysis serves to broaden our experience by refining our perception of the individual work, leading us toward the definition of quality that can be completed only within the depths of our personal understanding".[51] While no single, purpose-designed method of album cover analysis currently exists, the formal application of a 'borrowed' proven, evaluative method such as I have used here may nevertheless serve to facilitate useful, in-depth analysis. I do not suggest the method I have employed is definitive for the task of analyzing the visual imagery of album covers – indeed a purpose-designed interpretive method may well serve the medium more fully. However, in the absence of such a 'new' method, I consider this to be a credible starting point.

50 Dominy Hamilton, "Introduction", in Dean and Howells, p. 23.

51 Taylor, *Learning to Look*, p. 62.

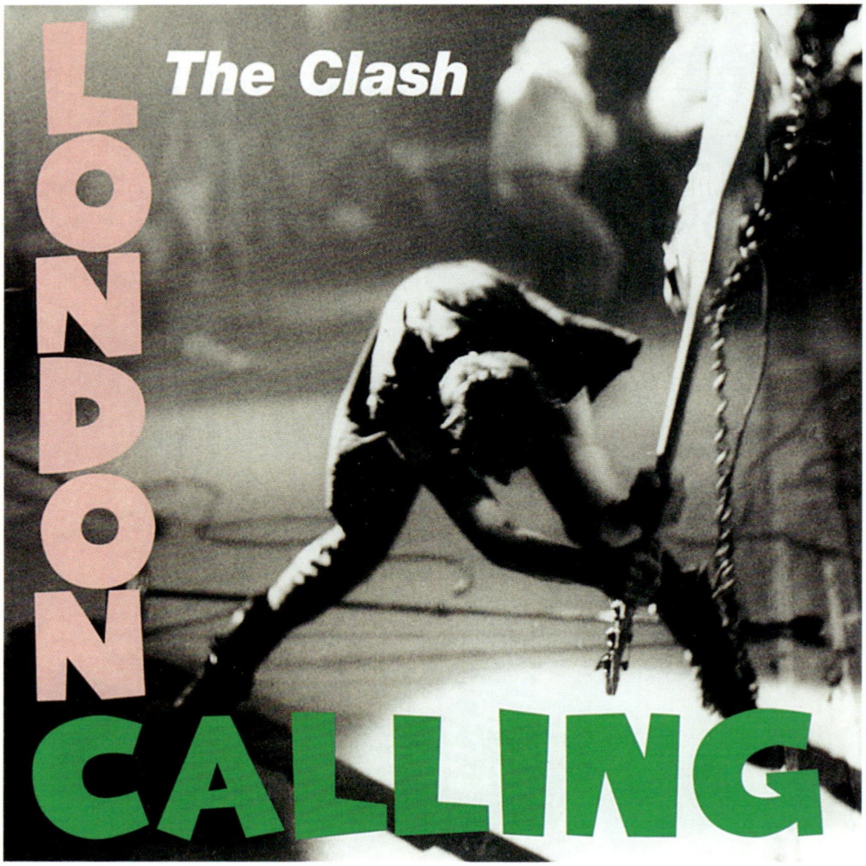

The Clash, *London Calling*, album cover. Design: Ray Lowry. Photo: Pennie Smith, 1979. © Pennie Smith/Sony Music.

Stars as Human Beings – and Timeless Icons

Pennie Smith's and Anton Corbijn's Artist Portraits

Sigrid Lien

Ever since record covers stopped being neutral, brown paper wrappings some time in the late 1950s, the face, the artist portrait has been their central visual element. In this essay, I will examine the role of the portrait as sign of authenticity in the image constructions of the music industry, particularly on the record cover. The material I have selected will be the star portrait of the punk and post-punk periods as it came to be expressed in the works of the now-legendary photographers Pennie Smith and Anton Corbijn.

Each in their own way, these two contributed to radicalizing the artist portrait as genre from the end of the 1970s. Smith's cover shot for The Clash's *London Calling* (1979), for example, has now achieved iconic status. It is a key work, which is still being quoted in new contexts. This unclear, partially unfocused shot in grainy black and white shows a bent-over Paul Simonon in vigorous motion on-stage under the spotlights of *The Palladium*, New York – about to smash his bass guitar.

Anton Corbijn has made himself known with visually striking cover photographs for, among others, U2, Depeche Mode, Nick Cave and The Rolling Stones. However, one of his finest works is the portrait of Don Van Vliet/Captain Beefheart – presented on the cover of his last record, *Ice Cream for Crow* of 1982. In contrast to Smith's action-oriented on-stage photography, Corbijn's portrait of Van Vliet has a more quiet "location feel" to it. The musician and painter Vliet poses in an arid desert landscape, he is in the foreground and in focus. This captures the object of the portrait in vivid detail: the pores of the skin, the wrinkles around the eyes and mouth and the intense gaze.

But at the same time as Smith's and Corbijn's very dissimilar artist portraits in black and white represented a renewal of the portrait aesthetic of the music industry, their works can also be seen as a continuation of an older tra-

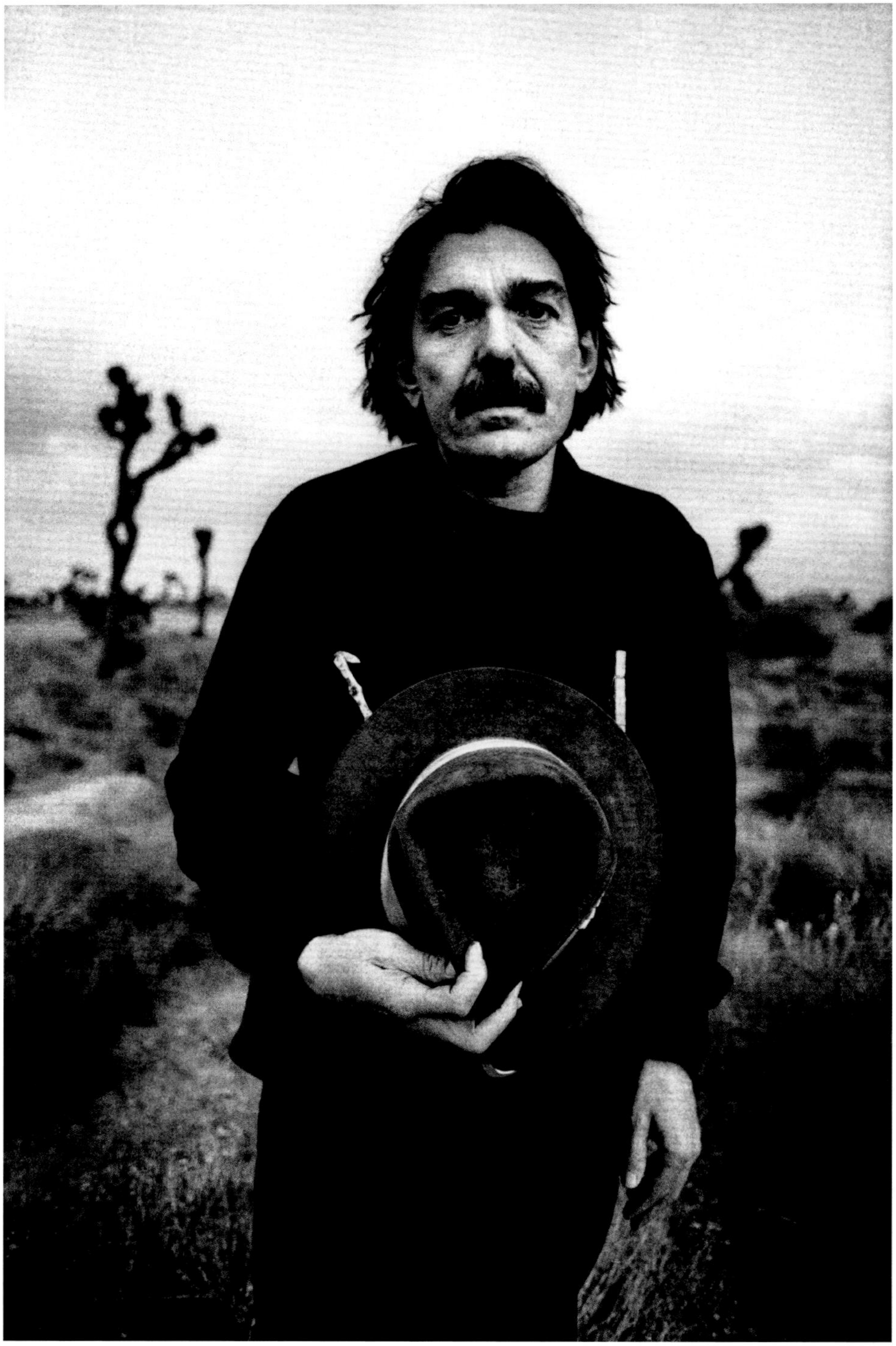

Captian Beefheart, *Ice Cream for Crow*. Photo: Anton Corbijn, 1982.

dition of portraiture. I want to argue that there is a certain continuity between the modern character portrait in visual art and the photographic portrait which manifests itself in the iconography of popular music. So it becomes relevant to ask why this historical genre has kept its strength. In the discussion of this question, I will use the ideas of the British art historian Michael Baxandall from *Patterns of Intention* (1985).

In his work, Baxandall argues that all forms of cultural products – images or other objects – must be understood as an outcome of problem solving processes. His most important point is that whoever makes an image or other forms of historical artefacts are human beings dealing with a problem. The finished cultural product can be seen as the final, concrete solution to this problem. In order to understand the cultural product, one must attempt to reconstruct both the problem and the specific context of the problem solving process. But factors of a more fluid nature, related to the general cultural orientation of the actors – intellectual stimulation, provocation, articulation of ideas and thoughts, criticism, etc. – also fit into Baxandall's model of understanding.

So I will search for an explanation of the continuity of character portraits in the music industry within the close production context of the idol photograph, in the problem solving situation itself. But at the same time, I will consider the wider cultural-historical contexts in which these actors operate. Another relevant issue here is the intermedial mode that characterizes the artist portrait as genre. The artist portrait doesn't just manifest itself on record covers, but across a wide range of visual media. Even though Pennie Smith and Anton Corbijn originally made their mark as photographers in the British music press, their photographs achieved a multi-medial impact. Their work which was originally presented as feature and cover story photographs in the music press came to manifest itself as record covers, as book illustrations, t-shirt prints, etc. Anton Corbijn has also expanded from still photography to making moving images in the form of music videos and feature films.

In order to make a historic reconstruction of the near context for Smith's and Corbijn's problem solving processes, I have interviewed the involved parties, not exclusively the photographers. I have examined the activities of the image makers in an interaction perspective through interviews with actors on several levels. In addition to the photographers, I have interviewed their employers in the music press, record companies, and management and design agencies.[1] Using this as the foundation, I will approach the essay's fundamental question: what brings a specific photograph – for instance Smith's portrait of the bass-smashing Simonon or Corbijn's desert photograph of Van Vliet – to the record

1 This essay is based on material from my Ph.D. thesis, "'Slap-dash' og sterke bilder. En studie i punk- og postpunkperiodens portrettestetikk" (University of Bergen, 1999). When otherwise not stated, the quotations from the different actors, photographers, editors, etc., mentioned in this text, come from interviews I have done with them during the process of writing this thesis.

cover? But let us first look closer at Smith and Corbijn's approach to the artist portrait. The photographers themselves have published photographic works in books like *The Clash: Before & After* of 1980 and *Famouz: Photographs 1976–88* of 1989. These books provide broader access to their respective works.

The Clash: Before & After **(1980) and** ***Famouz: Photographs*** **1976–88 (1989)**

The cover photograph for *London Calling* is a part of the series of images which Smith presented in her book on The Clash. This indicates a process perspective, as does the title. Pennie Smith followed the band throughout six years, and the book takes the shape of a diary from this period, a period that coincided with the apex of the band's career. The diary theme and the "on the road"-feel that characterizes the book is visualized from the outset. The very first photo shows the members of the band leaving a plane just after landing, en route to their next destination. Through the camera lens, Smith persistently follows her subjects through their hectic touring. The scenario is always this: airport terminals, tour buses, hotels, press conferences, meetings with concert promoters and fans, back and on-stage environments, etc.

The pictures are also tagged with brief, humorous comments, either by the members of The Clash or by the photographer herself. Sometimes these comments are in a dialogic relationship to each other. The various actors comment on each other's comments. This amplifies the diary feel of the book. We are not just sharing Smith's point of view of the reality represented in the photographs, but also that of the band. Pennie Smith herself has compared touring with The Clash to watching "a commando raid performed by *The Bash Street Kids*". And her photographs show us some of this. With the interplay of the comments of the band and the photographer, the pictures are given a certain appealing naivety which can be reminiscent of the cartoon form. The musicians of The Clash appear as comical anti-heroes rather than heroic rock idols, uninhibited by star status or the role of being an idol. Joe Strummer, for instance, is constantly grinning at us with his bad teeth, and central members of the band seem not to mind exposing their pale, English bodies or their anything but athletic builds, by the poolside.

Corbijn's portrait object, Don Van Vliet, on the other hand, is photographed in a setting far from concert venues and tour life. The spectator immediately wonders what this musician is doing out among the cacti and parched vegetation, presented almost as a Mexican field worker. But fans of his work will probably say that nature *is* the only "proper" setting for the nature-mystic ecofreak Beefheart, who settled down in the rural U.S.

The photographer's presence is palpable in different ways in the portraits that we have now described. Van Vliet/Beefheart appears to enter humbly into collaboration with his portrayer. He meets Corbijn with something which can be read as sombre respect, ready to be the "co-creator" of the portrait and to "reveal himself" in the "decisive" moment of companionship in the taking of the picture. Smith's portrait, on the other hand, seems to be almost a snapshot of a more or less random episode – where the object of the portrait appears to be absorbed in his own performance, and where the presence of the photographer is not reflected in the portrait.

Like Pennie Smith's subjects, the artists depicted in Corbijn's book are mainly figures with a central position in the pop and rock culture of the latter half of the '70s and a large portion of the '80s. Many of them can more accurately be characterized as punk or post-punk artists: Johnny Rotten (Sex Pistols), Nina Hagen, Lux Interior (The Cramps), Siouxsie Sioux (Siouxsie and the Banshees), Viv Albertine (The Slits), Sting, Elvis Costello, Cabaret Voltaire, Marc Almond, etc. But Corbijn has also taken portraits of a number of bigger "names" reaching further back into the history of popular music, like Leonard Cohen, Stevie Wonder, Roy Orbison, Miles Davis, Ry Cooder – and Captain Beefheart. While The Clash stands as the collective theme for Smith's photographs, the thematic thread in Corbijn's work is that all these famous artists have been photographed by him.

The whole presentation of Smith's and Corbijn's photographs further underscores the stylistic differences between them. Both work in grainy black and white photography. But where Smith mostly lets the lighter tones of the greyscale dominate, and her frequently symmetrically arranged compositions seem elegant in their simplicity, Corbijn's works are characterized by dramatic contrasts. He makes great use of darkness and pits formal elements against each other in the picture space in a way that always gives them a striking visual style. And where she consistently keeps a certain distance to her subjects (The Clash are without exception depicted either in full figure or in a "head to hip"-crop), Corbijn tends in many of his photographs to get close to his subjects, through tight, intimate, ultra close-ups.

Despite the differences between them, the work of both these photographers appears to be attempts to create psychological portraits. Both Smith's and Corbijn's photographs give the impression that what they want to display is something different and more *authentic* than the traditional, glamorized image of the rock star. In this way, these portraits inscribe themselves into a tradition rooted in the portraiture of modernism. But what is a modernist portrait photograph? What characterizes this photographic portrait-aesthetic?

The Modern Character Portrait and the Myth of the Exposed Self

In arguing that it is possible to speak of a modernist portrait photograph, I will first bring up the issue of modernist portrait painting. To clarify my point here, I will refer to the British art historian Andrew Graham-Dixon, who has described the modernist portrait painting as something which – in opposition to the earlier, representative portrait – rests on the mythical supposition that the truth about a human being will always be hidden.[2] In the modern practice of portraiture, then, the self of the subject of the portrait is no longer something to be mythologized, but something to be mercilessly exposed. Graham-Dixon holds Van Gogh and Munch to be the pioneers of this tradition.

But as John Berger among others have pointed out, the portrait painters of the modernist tradition drove the portrait to the brink of dissolution through their experimental approaches to the genre.[3] Picasso's famous portrait of the art dealer Kahnweiler is one early example of this. Through producing portraits which made it impossible to identify the portrayed, the major modernist painters created portraits that in some sense ceased to be portraits.

Parallels can also be drawn between the modernist portrait painting of the early twentieth century and the portraits of its contemporary photographic modernism: for example the portrait photography of Alfred Stieglitz and Alexander Rodchenko. Both of these photographers declared their intention to preserve the so-called "photographic" aspects of their works. In reality, they both came to produce photographs that paradoxically combined many aspects of other media, respectively: the contemporary, abstract painting and the formalism of literature.

Stieglitz, in his portraits, abandoned the idea of capturing the character of the subject in a single image. Instead, he almost consistently worked with *photo series*. His portrait series of his life partner, Georgia O'Keeffe, is the most well known of these. Rodchenko did not want his camera to create unity or synthesis. Instead, he was looking for an "aggregating, analytic style".[4] Like Stieglitz, he went for a more snapshot-like portrait, which at least could communicate what he thought of as fragments of the truth.

But this modernist tendency can also be located in early nineteenth century portrait photography. For instance, there are many good reasons to char-

2 Andrew Graham-Dixon, "The official versions", *The Independent*, London, Thursday, 18 May 1991.
3 John Berger, "The Changing View of Man in the Portrait", in *Selected Essays and Articles: The Look of Things* (London: Vintage Books, 1972).
4 Alexander Rodchenko, "Gegen das Syntetische Porträt für den Schnappschuss", in Wolfgang Kempf, *Theorie der Fotografie II* (Munich: Schirmer/Mosel Verlag, 1979), p. 82. My translation.

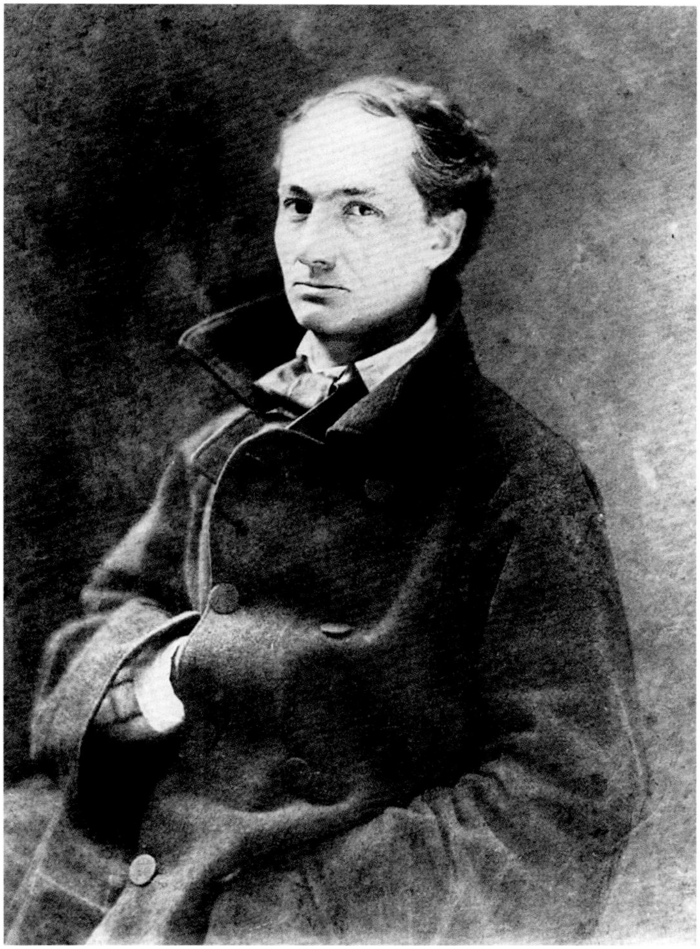

Félix Nadar, "Charles Baudelaire" (1856–1858), Musée d' Orsay, Paris.

acterize the French photographer Félix Tournachon Nadar (1820–1910) as one of the very first portrait modernists in the history of photography.[5] Even though Nadar worked with single photographic portraits and not series, he – like Stieglitz and Rodchenko – wanted to establish a modernist portrait aesthetic, in the psychological sense. His goal, in other words, was to uncover the "actual" character of the subject under what could be thought of as a protective facade.

The pioneering age of the photograph is historically coincidental with the time where physiognomy gradually lost its credibility. This school of thought held that one could, in "scientific" terms, decode the moral and psychological character based on outer physiological traits. It was to a large extent based on Johann Caspar Lavaters work of 1783, *Physiognomische Fragmente zur Beförderung*

5 I base this on the following texts: Roger Cardinal, "Nadar and the Photographic Portrait in Nineteenth-Century France", in Graham Clarke (ed.), *The Portrait in Photography* (London: Reaktion Books, 1992); Gisele Freund, *Fotografi och samhälle* (Stockholm: PAN/Norstedt, 1977); Rosalind Krauss, "Tracing Nadar", in Thomas F. Barrow et al. (eds.), *Reading into Photography, Selected Essays 1959–1980* (Alberquerque: University of New Mexico Press, 1982); Elizabeth Anne McCauley, *Industrial madness: Commercial*

der Mennschenkenntnis und Menschenliebe. In Lavater's system, which also came to enjoy great prestige throughout the nineteenth century, narrow lips were for example considered to be an indicator of avarice and greed.

But such ideas about the character of human beings as something which could be more or less passively registered on the surface were gradually replaced by the idea of the individual's character as something hidden; something which must be made the object of an entirely different, much more thorough type of interpretation. This shift would obviously come to have consequences for the practice of the photographic portrait. In Nadar's portraits, one can also find a tension between the real and the staged; between working towards creating a specifically photographic mode of expression and solutions related to the formal solutions of the painting. Nadar's photographs seem both to be characterized by objectifying accentuation of the moment and staged emotion. They are, in other words, a sort of combination of theatre and science. In the act of taking the picture, the photographer waits, while at the same time using lighting, costumes, etc. to signal that he is operating from an idea of what he wishes to bring out in the portrait. In addition to being a mimetic, instant representation of the subject, the photographer consolidates what he perceives to be the self of the portrayed.

It is precisely this combination of approaches that seems to characterize the modern photographic character portrait. For example, Anton Corbijn can be seen as an heir to Nadar when he professes to want to depict "the real" – by "exposing new sides of the character of his subjects". Smith likewise says, "I ought to be able to capture anybody off their guard". In her will to expose the subject, she also reveals her firm belief that it is possible to capture the character of a person in a fleeting moment. And Corbijn is also on the same horizon of ideas when he expresses his reasons for portraying musicians instead of actors. This is because actors will unwillingly use one role after another in front of the camera, thus making the "final" character portrait an impossible project.[6]

Smith, in the same way, strives to enter the working situation by simply trying to see what she can "find" there and then. She works hard to avoid being bound by a predefined concept or the artist's own desired image: "I'm not taking anybody's directions. I can't be bothered with bands who know what they look like". In a similar manner, Corbijn has not encouraged personal preferences on behalf of the portrayed. In this way, they both seem to be uncompromising in their demand for authenticity – a strategy that requires a great deal of sovereignty on the part of the photographer in the interaction with the subject. Bono, the vocalist of the Irish rock group U2, tellingly states, in an interview with the

photography in Paris 1848–1871 (New Haven and London: Yale University Press, 1994); Phillipe Néagu and Jean-Jacques Poulet-Allamagny (eds.), *Nadar*, Tome 1, *Photographies* (Paris 1979).

6 Anton Corbijn quoted in Kathy Acker, "Strange Gaze", *World Art*, no. 13 (1997), p. 35.

British music publication *Q*, that it can be a serious hassle being portrayed by Corbijn:

> Most people say, We're in Paris, let's put you under the Eiffel Tower – but Anton will take you halfway across the world to shoot you in a laneway. I can remember real rows with him. This is the most important lamppost in the world, is it Anton? And we've been up all night just to get this lamppost, have we? Of course, just out of spite, that would be the best shot.[7]

The most striking thing about Corbijn's problem solving is that he chooses strategies which do not just accentuate the portrayed, but also the creative self of the photographer. He dramatizes his subjects with an aestheticizing gravity and pathos, which can make even the most speculative of pop's ephemera to appear as timeless icons. If Smith shows us the star as an "average person", Corbijn does the opposite. He practically makes the artists of the music industry "vibrate" with aesthetic integrity in his portraits. But what still seems to unite them is that they both ground their aesthetic choices in a reference to a concept of authenticity.

The Star Portraits of Punk

This accentuation of authenticity must also be understood in the context of the photographer's association with the punk aesthetic, and the opposition to what was considered a well-directed, decadent and remote cult of personality around the stars of the music industry. And what sorts of idol-visualizations did the so-called punk photographers place themselves in opposition to? Roughly speaking, one can trace two dominating tendencies in artist photography in the 1970s.

On the one hand, we find a conceptual tendency, where the photographer operates on a comprehensive register of effects and visual solutions in line with the rise of image and market orientation, which characterized the pop climate of the 1970s. Stars such as Gary Glitter were created for a certain market with a certain image. According to the British photographer Gered Mankowitz, who made his mark with a string of conceptual record covers at the time, it was expected that the photographers should realize a predefined image strategy. In advance of the actual taking of the portrait, the photographer had to present his suggestions and the expected cost of the shot to the record company for approval: "And then we would begin to present ideas to them, like Gary Glitter sitting on a

7 Mark Ellen, "If I Could Be a Camera. Anton Corbijn", *Q Magazine*, January 1995.

rainbow or something. And then I would have to tell them how much that would cost and we would either do it or would not".

The photographer didn't just function as a director, but also as a scenographer. And naturally, most of the work had to be done in a studio. Mankowitz actually photographed Gary Glitter standing on white clouds under a kitschy, arced rainbow while wearing a tight-fitting, silvery, science fiction costume (1974). He also photographed Slade dressed in shimmering, fluorescent white suits against a deep black background; the singer Dana Gillespie (who had received attention for a song entitled *Weren't Born a Man*) posing as a sailor, casually seated in her berth, looking at sexy pictures of herself (1973); Peter Wingfield (a mid-'70s one-hit-wonder) playing a burning piano under a freeway near London's Shepherd's Bush (1976); Kate Bush on all fours in a lion outfit (1978) and Elton John as a cricketer (1976). The photographer carefully constructed sets, moods and lighting themes, inviting the viewer into the world of fiction.

The other dominant branch of idol photography in the 1970s was the moment-oriented live shot. The artist was portrayed in action on the stage in the big arenas – in colour and without any spectacular effects. This live photography was therefore primarily directed towards registering the intensity of the performance moment: concentration, sweat and charisma in the spotlights of the pop arena. One of the central practitioners of this kind of photography was David Redfern. Through his long career, he has produced live portraits of such different artists and bands as ABBA, Alice Cooper, Eric Clapton, Stevie Wonder, and Tina Turner.

These tendencies – the conceptual cover photo and the colour-based live photograph – each in their own way had overtones of rock ideology. First of all, the kitsch visualizations of the conceptual tradition can be read as an indication of the transformation of 1970s rock from counter-culture to spectacular entertainment – and the resulting status of the rock artist of becoming any sort of audience-adapted and well-directed entertainer. Second, it is not a stretch to interpret the live portrait, or rather the continual attraction of the "arena" portrait, as an effect of the need for documentation, which developed apace with the growing consciousness of the cultural history of rock. This tendency towards historical mythologization meant that the major stars of rock came to be seen through a veil of temporal distance and mythological heroification.

This is what the artist photographers of punk were trying to subvert. "I tend to see people as ordinary people", Pennie Smith says, adopting a sceptical attitude to the precondition of the cult of personality: the belief in the star as exceptional and superhuman. Her photographic ambitions have therefore been

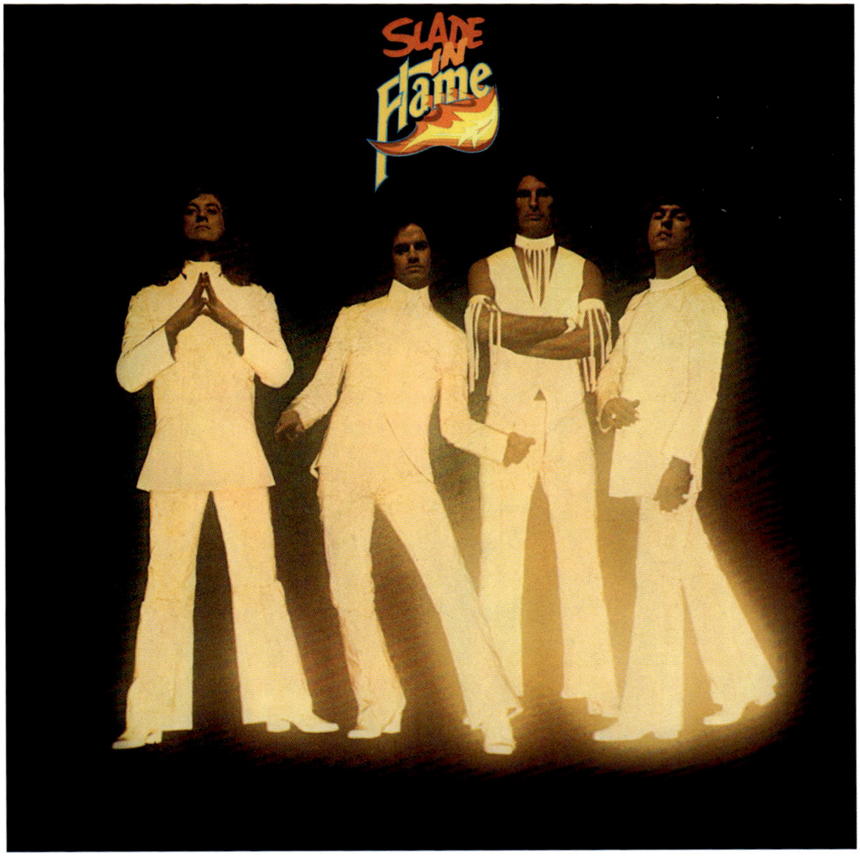

Slade, *Slade in Flame*, 1974. Photo: Gered Mankowitz. © Gered Mankowitz/Polydor Records.

directed towards democratizing or demystifying the rock and roll idol: "I mean rock stars aren't rock stars, they are people doing a job. Perhaps there isn't any rock-star, apart from in the eye of the fan". She doesn't hide her displeasure at working with what she sees as "inauthentic" artists, corrupted by the industry and a slick marketing concept: "There are many dilettante bands that I would not touch. Sort of pretty boys that somehow have been arranged by the record company".

The Clash must therefore have seemed like the ideal portrait subject to Pennie Smith. The band was definitely not a part of the avant-garde of punk music. It placed itself in a mainstream layer which, as Simon Frith puts it, appeared to be happy repeating its well-rehearsed repertoire of *rage and riot*. So The Clash were far from being postmodern experimenters on a par with The Sex Pistols and McLaren. It seems more appropriate to interpret their demeanour and how they strove to keep their "gutter credibility" intact as a sort of non-ironic attempt at subculture theory in practice. This desire to appear as spokesmen for the urban proletariat is also reflected in many of the band's lyrics:

> I don't wanna hear about what the rich are doing
> I don't wanna go to where, where the rich are going
> They think they're so clever they think they're so right
> But the truth is only known by the gutter snipes.
> *The Clash, "Garageland" 1977*

Smith sees her portraits of The Clash as a sort of photographic continuation of the band's music: "Basically we had this thing. I enjoyed the noise they made most of the time, and I was taking the sort of pictures they would take, if they had taken photographs. So it worked on an artistic level really". She also thinks of her documentary black and white style as a visual equivalent to the intentions of the band to unambiguously communicate the realities of life:

> It [colour photography] tends to be what you actually see. Colours don't seem to bring out the graffiti on the wall or the exit signs – only cheerful faces – somebody looking bright. But the whole rock side is a lot seamier, it's a hard job of working people – people who get the flu and get spots. ... I was doing documentary stuff with them [The Clash]. It was run instead of articles. It was descriptive of the style of the band. Rather than being a photographed pop group, it made the band look like human beings.[8]

Smith's attitude to the genre of star photography can therefore be said to be related to what contemporary punk photographers (for instance that of Derek Ridgers) did, by turning their back to the artist on stage in deep fascination towards the audience. Her Clash photographs can be seen as a translation of the punk photographers' "ideology of sub-cultural honesty" into the sphere of the idol portrait. And through her portraits of The Clash, Smith became the foreground figure in the development of punk-associated music photography.

But Pennie Smith's photography can also be seen as something beyond this. Despite their touch of a rough "random" aesthetic, her black and white photographs of The Clash place themselves far from the otherwise widespread flash-based rawness of punk photography. This is because Smith also followed the band *out* of the dark basements of their concert venues. She photographed a punk band as a group of people in motion, in more than one sense. The portrait

8 Mari Girling and Stuart Franklin, "Interview: Pennie Smith", *British Journal of Photography*, vol. 128, 23.1 (1981), pp. 95–97.

subjects are displayed in constantly changing surroundings and moods. In her series of photographs, the tour which The Clash is on also becomes a "mental journey" from one place to another.

In this exploration of people and environments, her photographs show a familial relationship to American rock photography. The early Leibovitz emphasized taking a "neutral" position, "obliterating one's own self", and moving with the portrayed. Smith also emphasizes the necessity of maintaining an emotional distance to her subjects: "I try not to get too emotionally involved, because you've got to keep that distance up to record. I try to keep myself out of it".

She doesn't plan her portrait sessions, and instead of directing, she leaves herself open to the play of coincidence. She is always "on the way" and always registering changes in lighting, landscape and scenery. In this way, Pennie Smith also takes up the inheritance of Robert Frank's on-the-road classic of the 1950s, *The Americans*. The anecdotal technique in this work, clearly derived from the same impulses as the so-called Beat poets, is something which reappears in Pennie Smith's Clash series. Like *The Americans*, Smith's tour photographs are a visual story about America, seen with the eyes of a European. But they are also much more than this. Where Frank sees a bleak, forlorn America in a way which makes it natural to interpret the photographs as a reflection of his own isolation or alienation in this unknown landscape, Smith is playful in her pastiche-like treatment of this theme.

Smith's photographs communicate a sort of "Americana-romantic" *déjà vu* experience rather than melancholy and unease. The photographer appears to be attracted to the slightly repugnant. She is approaching American conformity and conventionality with humour. However, her work is more explicitly influenced by that of Winston Link, the American "railroad photographer" of the 1950s. His use of natural light has been a source of inspiration for Smith, who uses light to conjure up beauty and mystery in the apparently trivial. The photo of Joe Strummer in the mist by an English channel is an example of this; so are the many bus and airplane scenes where sunlight and shadows surround the subjects of the portrait. In this way, Smith's photography becomes something more than humoristic, anecdotal documents.

If we now turn our attention to Anton Corbijn's work, we will be able to see more clearly that his portrait aesthetic, or his technical direction, really crosses or is tangential to Smith's at several points. Like his female colleague, Corbijn finds the reasons for his long preference for black and white photography in his adherence to a realistic programme. His portraying method, which has later been characterized as a process where the photographer "depicts icons turning into human beings", obviously has something in common with Smith and other punk photographer's respectless attitude to stereotypical idealizations.[9]

But where Smith observes and documents, Corbijn's activities are directed towards directing "strong images". The photographer himself sees this as a result of his Dutch cultural background. His frequent use of dramatic lighting and partially of theatrical, tableau-like set-ups may also be read as reminiscent of Dutch seventeenth-century painting. And if Smith tries to place herself as an equal in the interaction with the subject, her male colleague places himself in the role of the artist, and the star: "I think I am a photographer, but I'd like to be an artist. That's how I see myself. I am interested in people who are not working on the music scene, who are what you call real artists". As Kathy Acker has noted, realism – or the realist impulses in Corbijn's star portraits – are woven into an expressive, romantic discourse. Anton Corbijn photographs what he sees as a romantic, alienated visionary.[10]

As presented in books, Smith's and Corbijn's works appear as free and independent artistic projects. But most of the photographs in these publications came to be made as a result of the photographers' connection to the British music press. They both began their careers in the weekly music publication *NME* (*New Musical Express*) in the latter half of the 1970s.

"Insights into their character" – from *NME* Features to Record Covers

As a result of the advances in the late 1960s towards establishing an ideology of rock as art, the popular music press came to change character over the course of the 1970s. The feature material came to be more comprehensive, and the interviews became more "serious".[11] Like their role models in American *Rolling Stone*, which throughout the latter half of the '70s had distinguished itself with large-format covers and portrait works by the star photographer Anne Leibovitz, *NME*, with Nick Logan as editor-in-chief, worked to profile itself through good photography. This tendency was strengthened in the second half of the '70s, when Smith and Corbijn became attached to *NME*. More than being decorative page filler, the photographic material should now speak its own language.

Related to this new profile, a status-differentiation of the various kinds of photographic assignments evolved. Live photography was at the lowest rung, while feature and cover photographs were at the top of the ladder. The editors placed different demands on the different kinds of assignment. For example, Neil Spencer (Logan's assistant editor) expected the feature photograph to op-

9 Acker, p. 37.
10 Acker, pp. 33–34.
11 For a historical perspective on the development of the British music press, see Simon Frith, *Sound Effects. Youth, Leisure and the Politics of Rock'n'Roll* (New York: Pantheon, 1981), pp. 165–177.

posed to so-called "live shots") to be a character portrait: "I always thought they [the photographs] should show you what makes a person 'tick' as we say. They should show you what makes somebody 'tick': what somebody is about, give you some insights into their character".

Through the music magazine, Smith and Corbijn got basic training in delivering portrait photographs that were supposed to say something about the characters of the individual artist or band. And they both advanced quickly in the assignment hierarchy, from the first fumbling concert shots to the most prestigious cover assignments. The photographers both had a stylistic individuality, which also made it possible for them to succeed in the power plays that followed the increase in the prestige of the photo. Corbijn, for example, could allow himself to deny the editor's aesthetic directives. According to one of the employees of *NME*, this happened when the editorial staff wanted him to leave black and white for colour: "We had problems. Anton particularly was unable to take colour, or he was reluctant to take colour. And at that time NME was just moving into colour. He would say, 'No, no, black and white is much better'". In the same way, Pennie Smith has said no to assignments which she feels would conflict with her personal style of photography: "I say no if it is something that I would not like doing. I don't get asked to do bands like say Aerosmith, because they're not in line with my style. Either not been asked by The Stones, because my style and theirs is quite incompatible".

The individual styles of Smith and Corbijn also finally led them to a position where they could allow themselves to choose their clients independently of the music paper. Through *NME*, the photographers had the opportunity to make contact with a number of artists, which would then later contact them directly as clients. The portrait subjects, represented via record companies or design agencies, came to compete with the music paper for the role as the primary employer of the photographers. Smith photographed as we have seen for The Clash, and Corbijn became the band photographer for U2 and Depeche Mode. These assignments were obviously more economically lucrative than their work for *NME*. The editorial staff and picture policy of the music paper thus contributed to a culture where the individual photographer's biggest competitive advantage was their aesthetic individuality – and where the image production was directed towards displaying the artist's "true self" in the form of "serious" character portraits. In this way the paper came to function as a display window for the photographers – a window which would open up for new, external assignments: among them record covers.

The Artist Portrait and the Myth of the Unique and Authentic Subject

Based on this, in closing, I want to return to the overall issue addressed in this essay – and the question of what brings a specific photograph to the record cover, where it gains a sort of signal value. If we look at Smith's and Corbijn's works as they are produced within the framework of the photo book, we meet the individual photo as a fragment: a singular element of a large and richly varied series of photographs. The same goes for the artist portrait as it is presented as a part of a feature spread, or as an element in the rhythmically structured image flow of the music video. On the record cover, the artist portrait receives another communicative role. Isolated and torn loose from other flows of images, it approaches the functions of the monument: a visual expression that collects the essentials; something that the eye should dwell on, something that will remain.

In its entirety, Smith's series of Clash photographs connote the appeal of rock in its last phase of rebellion, and a version of the star mythology which is easy on the digestion: an unruly and charming punk band on their way up. The cover photo of Paul Simonon – floodlit, bathing in atmospheric light at the New York Palladium stage – compresses all of this. It radiates young energy and untamed vitality – ideals that represent the very core of the punk rock aesthetic. Through visual references (motif, composition and layout) to the early live photography of the 1950s – specifically to Elvis Presley's debut album – a rhetorical link is established with the canonized history of rock and the youthful rebellion of earlier generations. And even if it is unfocused, Smith's photograph also has striking aesthetic qualities that make it stand out from the *keep the needle in the middle and hope for the best* state of mind that characterized punk photography. The photograph becomes punk poetry in an old rock tradition – the image of uncompromized rock mentality.

A similar experience of correspondence between musical and visual expression may have been what has brought Corbijn's desert portrait of Captain Beefheart to the cover of *Ice Cream for Crow* (1982). The jangly, unpolished and apparently improvized "sound" is in some ways reminiscent of the sound of punk. This raw edge is also something which characterizes the photograph itself. The intimate crop, with the stubbly beard and the staring eyes seems brutalizing – but also monumentally aesthetisizing. The portrait "grates" on the spectator, like the artist's sore, untamed voice does. And the mercilessly grand desert landscape which frames the depiction further underscores this play between aesthetics and brutality.

It should be noted that such a reading of these cover photographs bases itself on the old myth of the portrait as a telling expression of the subject's inner qualities. The continuity of this tradition is not caused solely by the fact that the marketing machinery of the music industry still seems to be organized around the romantic myth of the unique and authentic subject. It must also be seen in context with the demand for recognizability or realistic presentation on one hand, and the demand to signal artistry and integrity on the other. The cover photo is therefore made to reveal and display the music industry's stars as human beings – but also to monumentalize and immortalize them as timeless icons.

Translated from the Norwegian by Martin Grüner Larsen

Profaning the Sacred

Goth Iconography, Iconoclasm, and Subcultural Resistance

Jeffrey Andrew Weinstock

Self-styled "goths" should be considered as a "subculture" in Dick Hebdige's popular sense of the word – that is, as a minority population defined by "expressive forms and rituals"[1] that signal a "refusal" of the status quo and "represent symbolic challenges to a symbolic order".[2] Goth culture, as with punk, rave, and other subcultures, is organized around patterns of dress, make-up, and bodily manipulation; distinctive musical forms; recurring themes and images; and a generally disdainful attitude toward "mainstream" values and social trends. As J. Gordon Melton details in his exhaustive *The Vampire Book*, what he terms the "Gothic movement" developed in the United Kingdom in the late 1970s as a segment of youth culture and "merged the mood, themes, and conventions of Gothic literature and film with punk and post-60s psychedelica" in order "to celebrate the dark shadowy side of life".[3] The movement was organized around a particular style of music derived from 1970s punk and heavy metal and initially popularized by groups such as Bauhaus, Siouxsie & the Banshees, The Cure, and The Sisters of Mercy.[4]

An important component of this music and the culture that grew up around it was (and remains) its rebellious stance. According to Melton, "Gothic music, as all counter-cultural forms, articulated an explicit nonconformist stance vis-à-vis the dominant establishment". In particular, "[i]t opposed narrow sexual mores and traditional established religions".[5] The movement reached its peak in the early 1980s in England and the early 1990s in America. Although the number of goth subculture participants has declined worldwide since the mid-1990s, goth culture persists to varying degrees in most metropolitan centers and in some smaller towns and cities as both well-entrenched goth bands such as The Cure, The Mission U.K., and Skinny Puppy, as well as new goth acts such as Bella Morte, Voltaire, and Diva Destruction, continue to release albums.

True to its rebellious roots, one of the ways in which the goth subculture has resisted and persists in troubling mainstream values and mores is by de-

1 Dick Hebdige, *Subculture: The Meaning of Style* (London: Methuen, 1979), p. 2.

2 Ibid., p. 92.

3 J. Gordon Melton, *The Vampire Book: The Encyclopedia of the Undead* (Detroit, Washington D.C. and London: Visible Ink, 1994), p. 265.

4 Ibid., p. 264.

5 Ibid., p. 265.

ploying iconoclastic images that profane the sacred by linking religious icons to crass commercialism and/or perverse sexuality. Adopting a strategy drawn directly from Gothic novels of the late eighteenth and early nineteenth centuries, contemporary goth artists seek to shock and titillate – and in some cases critique – by presenting on album covers images of nuns and angels in sexually provocative poses, and debased images of saints, priests, and even Christ himself. While certainly not limited to goth artists and not by any means a strategy employed by all goth acts, this profanation of the sacred still occurs with sufficient regularity on goth album covers to be considered an important component of goth's "refusal" of the status quo. In this essay, I will examine goth music's strategic deployment of profaned sacred imagery with particular attention to the album covers of French act Die Form, German band In Strict Confidence, and seminal American goth act Christian Death. Before concluding, I will also attend to album art featured on recent releases by American goth artists The Empire Hideous and Voltaire. In each case, I will emphasize the ways in which the album's iconoclastic iconography not only violates expectations of taste and decorum, but precisely through these violations seeks to subvert conventional or conservative attitudes toward religion and often sexuality and/or capitalism as well.

An obvious starting point for such a conversation is with French gothic/industrial act Die Form. Die Form (with, at the time of this writing, an astounding 36 releases to its name) has made a career out of dwelling on non-standard sexual practices and the dark side of human desire. Chiefly the project of French artist Philippe Fichot, who is usually accompanied by singer Eliane P., Die Form's provocative black and white album imagery worries conventional standards of good taste by presenting artistically accomplished and often strikingly beautiful images of morbid sexuality and debased religion. The clash between elegant image aesthetics and subversive content raises questions about the nature of beauty itself that the band's music then pursues through its lyrical preoccupation with alternative sexual practices and forms of spirituality.

A recurring image in the Die Form *oeuvre* is a familiar trope of the literary Gothic: that of the sexually provocative or perverse nun. The relatively understated front cover for the band's 1993 *Ad Infinitum* release, for example, features Elaine P. presented in a nun's veil (called a wimple) with a meditative or pious look on her face. However, a corset replaces the traditional nun's habit and her chest is bare from her neck to her nipples, the latter of which are not quite covered by the corset. Furthermore, her head is encircled by a wreath of thorns that form a sort of visor across her face and block her already shadowed eyes.

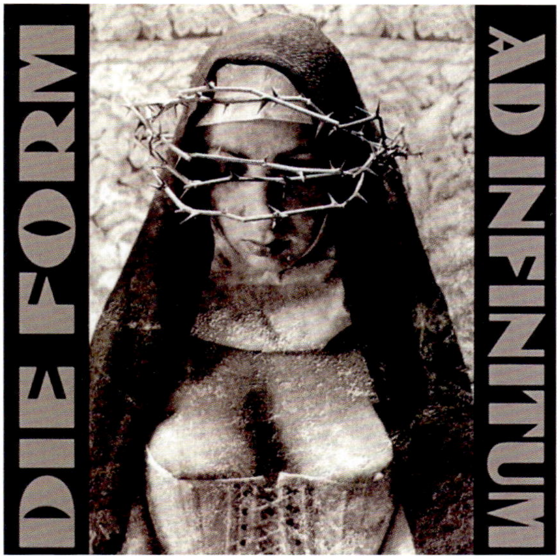

Die Form, *Ad Infinitum*. Courtesy of Die Form.

The anomalous elements of the image are, of course, the thorny visor and the corset in place of the anticipated nun's habit, and these elements divide the image into two vertical halves unified by the sweep of the viewer's gaze. The thorns, while alluding to Christ's passion, are not on the figure's head and do not puncture her flesh – she is not presented as a tormented or tortured Christ figure. Instead, the thorns form a barrier between the figure and the viewer. They render her eyes visually inaccessible and suggest that her serene face is untouchable. By extension, what is rendered forbidding and inaccessible is conventional religion itself – the solemn, motionless nun in traditional desexualizing wimple and her passionless faith presented in the upper half of the image are not available to the viewer.

What remains accessible is not her saintly head, but her eroticized body. The lower half of the image presents a jarring contrast with the upper half and contradicts the expectation of demure chastity associated with nuns. The inaccessible serenity of the nun's face is counterpoised by the provocative sensuality of her body. The corset emphasizes her breasts and the visibility of her nipples highlights the transgressive re-sexualization of this nun.

The cover art to *Ad Infinitum* clearly signals Die Form's antagonistic attitude toward conventional Christian beliefs, as well as the band's preoccupation with fetishistic sexual practices (for which it is most famous). The elegant image with its provocative content titillates through its flirtation with the taboo. Interestingly, the image does not seem to emphasize the sexual hypocrisy of the

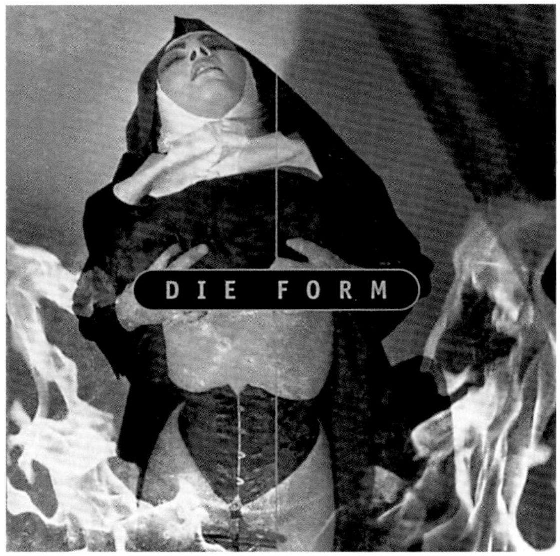

Die Form, *Vicious Circles*.
Courtesy of Die Form.

Church (although that element is certainly present here), as much as Western culture's inability to see women as anything other than sex objects. In a sense, it is the viewer of the image that undresses the nun; it is not her desire that is represented – her face remains devout and serene – but that of the viewer for the forbidden. Therefore, even as the image titillates, the incongruous elements of the image seem to implicate the viewer in sexual objectification of women.

Die Form elaborates on these same elements in the much more salacious cover image to the band's 1996 "best of" compilation, *Vicious Circles*. The cover art for *Vicious Circles* again features Die Form band member Eliane P. dressed as a corseted nun. However, this time, she is surrounded by flames and writhes in simultaneous ecstasy and agony as she raises her habit and holds her breasts. Unlike the stationary and serene figure of the nun that appears on the cover to *Ad Infinitum*, this nun clearly is in the throes of sexual ecstasy. That she wears her corset (and apparently nothing else) beneath her habit and massages her breasts suggests the hypocrisy of religious belief systems and Bible-thumping moralists who preach abstinence and mortification of the flesh even as they themselves indulge in hidden vice. The flames that surround her are simultaneously the heat of sexual ecstasy and the fires of perdition.

As with the cover to *Ad Infinitum*, the cover to *Vicious Circles* is clearly intended both to shock and titillate. The strategic placement of the band's name in the center of the cover and over the nun's breasts draws attention directly to the nun's fondling of herself, and forges an association between the band and

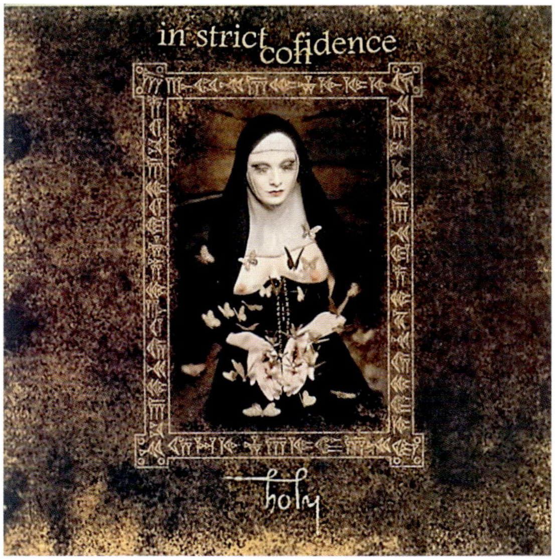

In Strict Confidence, *Holy*. Courtesy of Metropolis Records.

the represented illicit sexual act – in a sense, it is precisely Die Form that is both undressing and obscuring the nun, and thereby provoking the viewer. The profanation of the sacred through the iconoclastic representation of "deviant" sexuality in this instance positions the band itself as transgressive through its disdain for both conventional religious beliefs and sexual practices.

Representation of what one might refer to as the "naughty nun" to foreground a band's subversive or resistant stance toward conventional sexual and religious mores is also the primary device in the striking artwork accompanying German gothic/industrial act In Strict Confidence's 2004 release, *Holy*. Borrowing heavily from Die Form's famously fetishistic album art, the cover to *Holy*, as well as the series of aesthetically accomplished images taken by photographer Jens Howorka and included within the booklet accompanying the CD, features a beautiful young woman dressed in a nun's wimple and black corset with exposed breasts. Each album image subtly or explicitly scandalizes conventional religious belief by intertwining profane and sacred elements in such a way that the nature of "holiness" itself is called into question.

The juxtaposition of sacred and profane elements that organizes the iconography of *Holy* is readily apparent in the cover art to the album. As in the cover to Die Form's *Ad Infinitum*, the cover to *Holy* features a young, beautiful woman in nun's wimple and black corset with eyes averted downward and a calm, serene expression. Her breasts are exposed and her hands, bearing the wounds of the stigmata, are held out in front of her, palms facing upward. Butterflies, which may have been released from her hands, flutter around her hands and torso. The restricted color palette of the artwork for the album as a whole, with its emphasis on shades of brown, simulates the sepia tones of antique photographs and daguerreotypes and "ages" the images. The antique aspect of the images is heightened by the pale skin, exaggerated make-up, and emphasized eyes (see especially In Strict Confidence's *Holy*) of the model used which call to mind a silent movie-era filmstar. Also adding to the sense that the image is an antique photograph is the absence of background – the woman is seemingly posed in a sort of dark corner or against a backdrop of fabric – in the curious frame that encloses her and is decorated with cuneiform script.

The combination of incongruous elements in this composition results in an image that is highly suggestive but resists any single concrete interpretation. As with the cover to Die Form's *Ad Infinitum*, the nun's corset and naked breasts are clearly intended to provoke the viewer's interest by suggesting something deviant or fetishistic inherent in Christianity. However, the absence of passion in the nun's serene expression intimates that the desire to violate taboos, in this case to violate the chastity of the nun, is the viewer's. In place of a visor of thorns, this nun is distanced from the viewer by virtue of the frame and, interestingly, a blockade of butterflies. The frame, with its archaic cuneiform script, participates with the sepia tone of the composition in "dating" the image – Christianity is presented as something ancient and inaccessible or unreachable. The butterflies present a fascinating juxtaposition with the nun's stigmata. The repulsive nature of her bleeding wounds is offset by a sort of natural affirmation offered by the butterflies. And underneath it all is the title to the album, *Holy*, itself written in a sort of "Biblical" or ancient looking script suggestive of a medieval illuminated manuscript.

Based solely on the cover image, the exact message being communicated about conventional Christianity by In Strict Confidence's *Holy* is difficult to determine. Catholicism is presented simultaneously as ancient, inaccessible, fetishistic, and gruesome, and natural, beautiful, and soothing. However, when the cover image is considered together with the other images included in the packaging of the album, a decidedly more negative impression of Christianity is conveyed.

The nun from the cover is also presented in a portrait in which she cups her naked left breast as blood flows from her nipple. Her gaze confronts the viewer with pornographic directness, demanding that one observe the stream of blood, and perhaps challenging the viewer to suckle from her bleeding breast. Her right hand stretches across her waist, and thereby both draws attention to

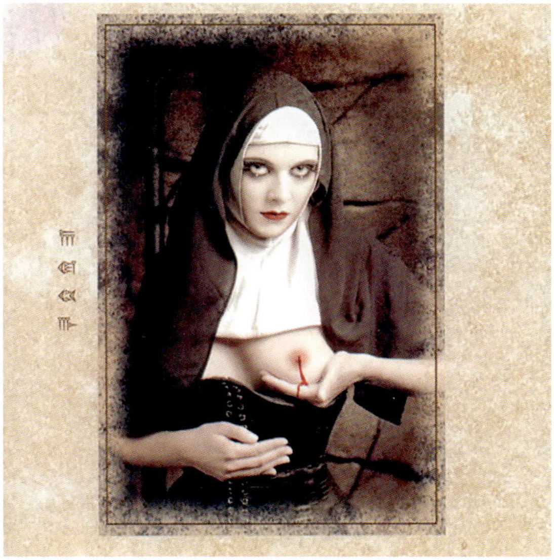

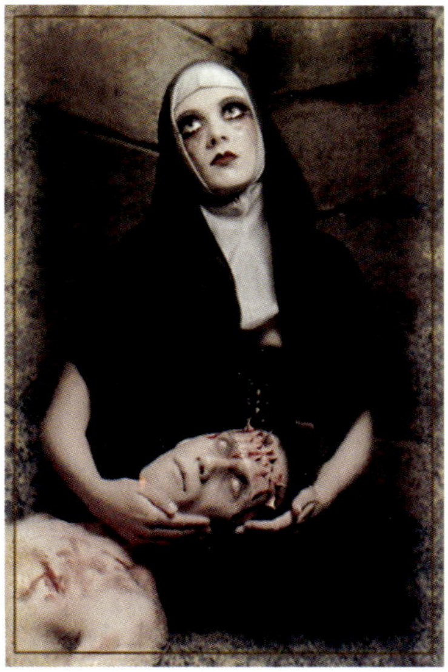

In Strict Confidence, *Holy* booklet images. Courtesy of Metropolis Records.

her black leather corset and directs the viewer's attention to her exposed and bleeding breast. Unlike the cover image, there are no butterflies or other natural imagery to offset her wound. The clear suggestion of this image is that, instead of nourishing milk, what Christians imbibe is blood – and, by extension, pain, violence, and death.

Perhaps the most scandalous image included in the American CD packaging for *Holy* is the image of our nun seated and cradling the head of a dead figure that can only be referred to as "FrankenChrist". Most disturbing here are the bloody thorns that protrude from the brow above the milky lifeless eyes of the deceased giant. Rather than being tortured by a crown of thorns imposed from without, the monster/Christ figure in the image has had the thorns emerge *from within* – they have burst through the skin from inside his head. The deformation of the dead Christ figure, in conjunction with the internal thorns, can be read as suggesting that Christianity, with its emphasis on Christ's Passion and martyrdom, creates masochistic monsters. Also notable in this image is the expressionless face of the nun who gazes wide-eyed, not at the dead figure in her lap, but off into the distance. The false tears affixed to her face suggest the facades of devotion that many professing Christians erect, while her corset and the glimpse of flesh beneath her wimple reveal the sinful nature that lurks beneath the pious exterior.

Die Form and In Strict Confidence thus both share a disparaging attitude toward conventional forms of Christianity that they communicate through

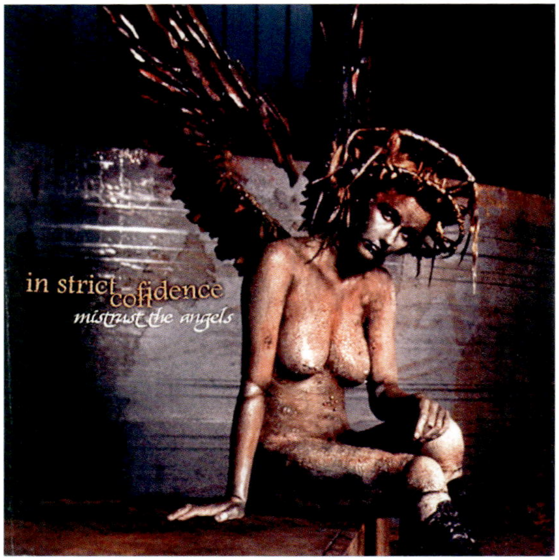

In Strict Confidence, *Mistrust the Angels*. Courtesy of Metropolis Records.

iconoclastic cover art depicting bare-breasted nuns in fetish attire. These images function strategically to establish the bands as transgressive or "non-mainstream" and to titillate the viewer. In Die Form's case, the sexually provocative images of nuns foreground both a disdainful attitude toward Christian sexual hypocrisy and the inevitable objectification of women in patriarchal culture. While In Strict Confidence's images perform the same critique, the grotesque aspects of the cover art and packaging for *Holy* also paint a picture of Christianity as a religion obsessed with pain, suffering, violence, and death.

Since my intention in this essay is to establish the ubiquity within the goth genre of the strategic profanation of sacred images as a form of symbolic challenge to the status quo, space does not allow me to devote too much attention to any one band. However, I do feel that another set of images from the German band In Strict Confidence, this time the images associated with the band's 2002 release *Mistrust the Angels*, merit some analysis in this context, both for their fascinating representations of debased angels and for their aesthetic beauty.

The stunning cover to *Mistrust the Angels* features a seated voluptuous female angel, naked except for her black leather boots. The setting is very dark, hard, and cold – the color palette for all the artwork associated with *Mistrust the Angels* emphasizes blues, grays, and rusty oranges – and the angel appears to be seated upon a rusted steel platform of some sort, perhaps a loading dock. Behind her is a dirty metal retaining wall and, above that, a nighttime sky can just be glimpsed through a barred window.

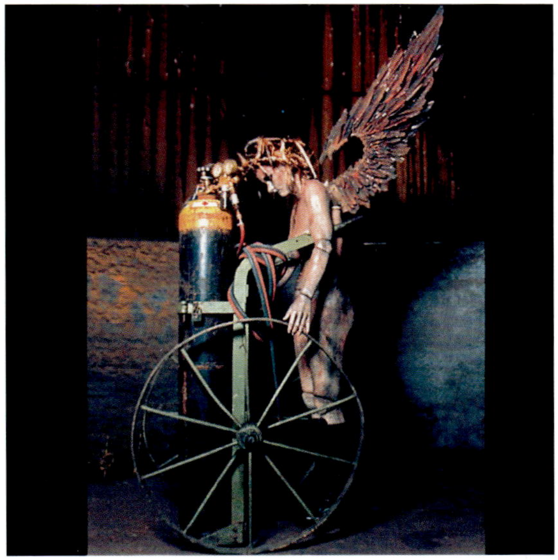

In Strict Confidence, *Mistrust the Angels* booklet image. Courtesy of Metropolis Records.

What stands out about the image, however, is the angel herself. Aside from being naked and voluptuous, she appears ashen, filthy, and perhaps even rusted – as if she either is made of metal, or works in an industrial setting like a foundry (the rest of the packaging tends to support this latter interpretation). On her head is a two-tiered twisted scrap-metal halo, and behind her extend two dangerous looking rusty steel wings. She gazes apathetically – or perhaps exhaustedly – out at the viewer, and one can almost imagine that she is taking a cigarette break between shifts at a steel mill.

The booklet that accompanies the CD features an intriguing selection of images featuring this angel, along with shots of members of the band. In each instance, settings are extremely dark and cold and figures are dirty. Among the most intriguing of these images is the one which features the angel standing wearily within the arms of an old-fashioned, dented handtruck. Strapped to the handtruck is a large pressurized tank of what may be oxygen or some other gas. Here, as on the cover, the angel appears to be naked except for her boots, and her body is filthy. Noticeable in this image are dark bands at her wrist and around and below the elbow that almost suggest she may be a mannequin rather than a living being.

Whereas the artwork for *Holy* – especially the images contained within the CD booklet – clearly are intended to offer a critique of Christianity, the imagery of *Mistrust the Angels* is less a direct interrogation of Christianity than an expression of cultural exhaustion or postmodern malaise. The worldly, filthy

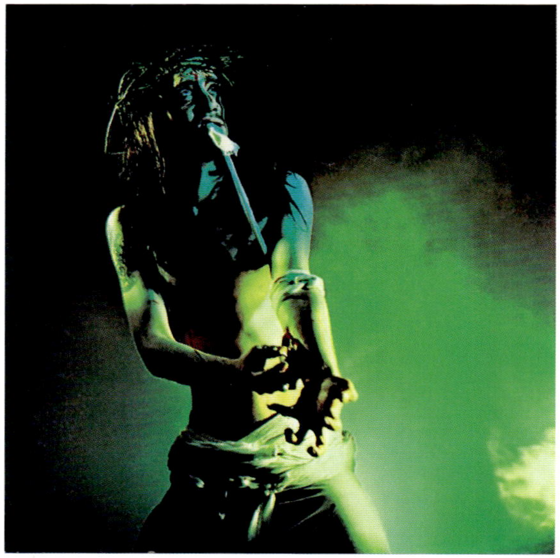

Christian Death, *Sex and Drugs and Jesus Christ*. Reproduced courtesy of Jungle Records, www.jungle-records.com.

angel with her rusted iron wings and her imposing boots cynically suggests that industrial capitalism "puts religion to work" in the service of profit. Spiritual purity or innocence is nowhere to be found in the proletarian world of modern wage labor. Most telling is the image of the angel with the oxygen tank – exhausted and filthy, she can barely keep her head up and one wonders if the oxygen is not in fact for her.

As opposed to the images of perverse nuns addressed above, the primary purpose of the naked, voluptuous angel represented in the artwork accompanying *Mistrust the Angels* is not to titillate or to foreground Christian sexual hypocrisy. Rather, the angel – and, by extension, religion itself – has been stripped bare and sullied by a world dominated by greed. Her exhausted, knowing look signifies the murder of purity and innocence at the hands of industrial capitalism. Religion is portrayed as being on life-support, so to speak, unable to respond adequately to the exigencies of the modern world in which profit is the new god.

The exhaustion or corruption of religion is the central focus of the goth band most notorious for the profanation of religious iconography: seminal American goth band Christian Death. Founded in 1979 by singer Rozz Williams (who committed suicide in 1998), the band's name reflects Williams' rejection of his religious upbringing.[6] The band, according to Baddeley, claimed not to be attacking the teachings of Jesus per se, "but of those in the Church who have perverted his creed to their own ends". The band's name and logo, a cross with

6 Gavin Baddeley, *Goth Chic: A Connoisseur's Guide to Dark Culture* (London: Plexus, 2002), p. 245.

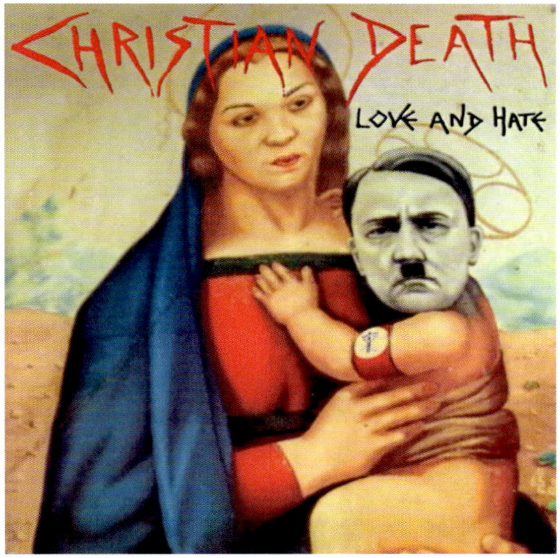

Christian Death, *Love and Hate*. Reproduced courtesy of Jungle Records, www.jungle-records.com.

a superimposed X made of bones, "were based on the observation that Christianity, purportedly the religion of love, takes as its symbol the device used to execute the messiah".[7]

The band's aggressively defiant attitude toward conventional Christianity is evident to some extent in almost all of its album covers, but is perhaps most immediately obvious on the covers to *Sex and Drugs and Jesus Christ* (1988) and *Love and Hate* (1993). Calculated to offend and banned from many stores, *Sex and Drugs and Jesus Christ* naturally became one of Christian Death's biggest sellers. The cover to the album features a dimly-lit grimacing Jesus shooting up heroin. Unlike the elegant aesthetics of Die Form and In Strict Confidence, and more in keeping with Christian Death's punk-influenced "deathrock" format, the image is neither subtle nor alluring. The unnatural green light that illuminates the Jesus figure from below highlights the claw-like hand of the figure that reaches out toward the viewer as the drug is injected. The figure is gaunt and hairy and appears substantially more like a junkie than a religious savior.

Love and Hate is equally inflammatory. The cover features a stylized rendering of Mary and the Baby Jesus. However, Jesus' head has been replaced with that of Hitler, and he wears a red Nazi armband with the swastika replaced by a cross. In contrast to the rest of the image, the pasted-on Hitler's head is in black and white, giving the impression of a low-budget cut-out aesthetic.

Both of these Christian Death record covers launch a clear assault on Christianity. *Sex and Drugs and Jesus Christ* suggests that Christianity is mor-

7 Ibid.

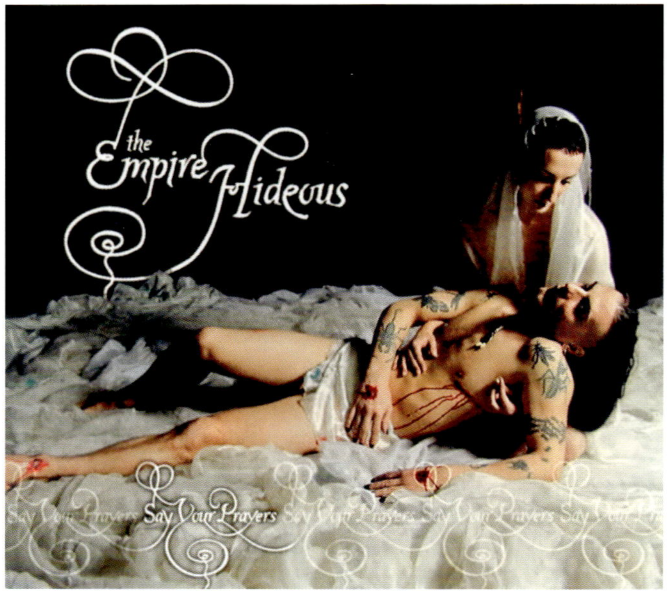

The Empire Hideous, *Say Your Prayers*. Courtesy of Middle Pillar. Photo: Kyle Cassidy.

ally bankrupt. The cover is clearly intended to offend Christians and to position Christian Death as counter-cultural mavericks. The cover to *Love and Hate* associates Christianity with Nazism. The message that it sends is that, rather than love, what Christianity has given birth to is hatred, violence, and genocide. More so than Die Form or In Strict Confidence, foundational goth band Christian Death uses its album aesthetics, and specifically its iconoclastic profanation of the sacred, as a strategic form of cultural refusal. Sharing a resistant attitude toward conventional religion with goth bands in general, Christian Death militantly voices this symbolic challenge to Christian hegemony both in its album imagery and in its very name.

Before concluding this survey of iconoclastic goth record album aesthetics, I would like to consider briefly two album covers by more recent participants in the goth scene. The first image, the cover to New York goth act The Empire Hideous' 2004 release, *Say Your Prayers*, participates directly in goth's subcultural refusal of conventional religion through its explicit iconoclasm. The second cover, from New York City goth crooner Voltaire's 2002 release, *Almost Human*, departs from the goth's usual aggressive rejection of conventional religion through its use of humor.

The cover to The Empire Hideous' *Say Your Prayers* release features Empire Hideous founding member and lead singer Myke Hideous (notable also for a brief stint as lead singer for the punk band The Misfits) portrayed as a dying Christ being supported on Mary's lap after having been let down from the crucifix. He is attired only in a loincloth and the wounds on his feet, hands, and side are readily apparent. He and Mary rest on a bed of billowy white fabric and the blackness of the background reflects a sense of isolation. The conventionally dressed Mary (no corset or revealed bosom here!) gazes down upon him solemnly.

For the most part, this is a reasonably conventional representation of Jesus dying. What renders it scandalous is the substitution of Myke Hideous with his prominently tattooed arms for Jesus and the juxtaposition of the band's name and the album title with the scene of Myke Hideous/Christ dying. Substituting Myke Hideous for Christ equates the two and, from a conventional religious perspective, simultaneously debases Christ by comparing him to a mortal and hubristically elevates Myke Hideous by equating him with a supernatural God-figure. The arm tattoos are potent signifiers in the image, establishing what might be referred to as a "punk Jesus". Inasmuch as tattoos are still associated with transgressive, lower socio-economic subcultures, Jesus is not just rendered mortal in the picture, but associated with social "deviance". This demotion of Christ and the elevation of a "punk" in his place, of course, is distasteful (if not heretical) from a conventional religious perspective that ascribes absolute purity to Christ and differentiates between his supernatural nature and that of mortal man.

However, the full impact of the image is only available if the name of the band and the album are taken into consideration. The prominently displayed name of the band, "The Empire Hideous", forges an association between name and image and functions almost as a title or caption for the image. When connected, the "hideous empire" seems to be that precisely of conventional Christianity and the substitution of Myke Hideous for Christ implies a reconceptualization of Christianity in which the facade is stripped away and what is revealed is not a god, but a man – a punk, an outcast, an "undesirable", literally "Mr. Hideous"! The title of the album, then, *Say Your Prayers*, acts as an ironic commentary on religion. Once the "sham" that is Christianity is revealed, once the sanctity of Jesus is revealed to be a joke, to what or whom does one pray?

In keeping with goth's distaste for conventional religious belief and practice, The Empire Hideous' profanation of the sacred undermines conventional religious faith by parodying and thereby calling into question the divinity of Christ. In place of a universe ordered and ruled by a divine presence, the Empire Hideous, through the juxtaposition of image and band name, substitutes an existential void. In such a universe, devout religious faith is revealed to be either naiveté or a willful refusal to accept the fact of God's absence.

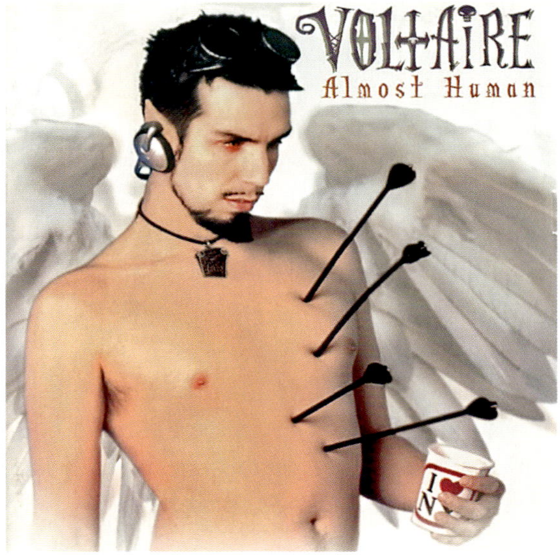

Voltaire, *Almost Human*. Courtesy of Sam Rosenthal and Project Records.

The last cover upon which I would like to focus, that to Voltaire's *Almost Human*, deviates from the established pattern of religious iconoclasm that I have detailed above through its use of humor, yet still maintains the characteristically goth critique of organized religion. Voltaire is a New York based artist whose contributions to the goth genre feature an unusual mix of orchestrated ballads and up-tempo songs (Voltaire records and performs with a string section) notable for the sardonic and at times self-deprecating humor and playful romanticism of his lyrics. A "nothing's sacred" attitude informs all of Voltaire's releases as songs move easily from mocking religious zealots to poking fun at members of the goth subculture itself.

Voltaire's lighthearted iconoclasm is evident on the cover to his 2003 release, *Almost Human*, which features a portrait of Voltaire himself as a hybrid angel/devil/contemporary St. Sebastian. On this cover, Voltaire reproduces the devilish facial features that previously characterized him on his debut release, *The Devil's Bris*: pointed ears and a distinctive pointed black goatee. However, rather than a pointed tail or batlike wings, which one might anticipate to complement the devilish facial features, angelic feathery white wings extend from his back. St. Sebastian-like, his hairless naked torso is punctured by four deeply embedded arrows.

If this interesting amalgamation of religious iconography constituted the entirety of the image, one might perhaps be entitled to read the representation as symbolizing the human mediation between heaven and hell: Voltaire himself, one might suggest, embodies both the angelic and demonic – and suffers from the pains that inevitably result from the negotiation of these competing components or inclinations.

However, what complicates this reading and alters the tone of the image from serious to comic are the "I Love NY" coffee cup in Voltaire's hand, the Walkman headphones covering his ear, and the old-fashioned motorist's goggles on his head. (The pendant necklace around his neck may also participate to a lesser extent in the humor as well, but is not visually distinct enough to make a major impact.) The humor of this cover derives precisely from the unexpected juxtaposition of contemporary consumer items with the "timeless" mythical religious icons. The devil and angels belong "outside time", so to speak, and they neither desire nor require material goods. Saints, while tied to specific historical moments, also become part of mythic/religious time after their deaths and, perhaps even more so than either angels or the devil, are defined by their self-abnegation. Thus, inasmuch as piety is conventionally associated with self-denial and rejection of material pleasures, the representation of St. Sebastian with a coffee mug in his hand – and a kitschy "I Love New York" mug at that – breaks with the traditional expectations for representations of saints and angels by reattaching the image to our specific cultural moment and indicating the figure's participation in consumer capitalism.

The Walkman headphones and motorist's goggles amplify this "desacralization" of religious iconography within the image. As with the coffee cup, the headphones undermine conventional associations between sacredness and both timeless universality and asceticism. Further, they suggest that the figure, rather than attending to the prayers and pleas of the devout, is absorbed in listening to music of its own choosing – perhaps even that of Voltaire! The goggles, while on the surface especially anomalous, can be read as a knowing wink toward the goth subculture consumers who will purchase the album – an established component of goth fashion, particularly for what Voltaire has called "cybergoths", are such goggles.

Ultimately, what one discovers when attending closely to the juxtaposition of sacred and profane in the cover image to *Almost Heaven* is a condensed figure for the "skewering" of religion in general being performed by Voltaire. The object of Voltaire's scorn is the commercialization of religion – saints, Satan, God, and angels, or, more particularly, those who take traditional religion too seriously and presume to know God's plan for the world, are all playfully mocked in album lyrics that foreground the ways in which religious discourse have been used to justify bigotry and hatred ("God Thinks") or present comic yet sensitive renderings of "immoral" sexual practices ("Dead Girls").

Voltaire skillfully walks a fine line between playful impishness and open disdain for conventional religion with the visual imagery and lyrical content of *Almost Human*. Rather than aggressively attacking conventional religious beliefs through shocking iconoclasm, Voltaire makes use of humor as a strategy, gently to mock religious hypocrisy. St. Sebastian with a coffee mug in his hand acts as a humorous yet potent symbol for the commodification of belief in a world dominated by greed and intolerance.

The analysis of the repetition of religious iconoclasm – the profanation of the sacred – on album covers in the goth genre makes clear one strategy that the goth subculture employs to communicate its disdain for conventional religious beliefs and mores and to maintain its transgressive edge. Through images of debased nuns, angels, saints, and Christ himself, goth bands attempt to shock the mainstream and thereby call attention to themselves. In many cases, this may be purely a marketing strategy. However, the images still serve to communicate a negative appraisal of conventional religious belief and, in conjunction with lyrical content addressing religious hypocrisy and intolerance, can serve as a means to critique religious ideology. Profanation of the sacred is one prominent means whereby the goth subculture enacts its challenge to the dominant culture.

Painting Sound, Playing Color

The Multiple Voices of Ornette Coleman's *Free Jazz* and Jackson Pollock's *White Light*

Hilary Moore

> "Total control ... denial of the accident ...
> States of order ...
> Organic intensity ...
> Energy and motion made visible ..."
> *Jackson Pollock, undated*[1]

When Ornette Coleman's *Free Jazz* came out in 1961, the sounds exploding from gramophones were unprecedented, shocking, and seemingly anarchic. Yet for attentive buyers, the music should not have come as a complete surprise. The sounds were heralded by the album's cover art: a depiction of Jackson Pollock's *White Light*.

White Light, like many Pollock paintings, reverberates with multiple narratives, transcending the static nature of paint on canvas, with lines of color in dynamic conversation. In the following, I will explore the ways in which an understanding of Pollock's work can enrich our interpretation of the aesthetic, structural, and ideological voices in Coleman's *Free Jazz*. Through an analysis of Coleman's music, I highlight parallels between the two men's conception of their art, particularly their mutual struggle to reconcile polarities of freedom and structure, and group expression and individual voice. Further similarities in the two men's lives, both in their position within American society and within the development of their art, add power to the linking of their names.

I also consider the use of a pre-existing work of art to illustrate, advertise, and narrate upon music. How does the cover of *Free Jazz* impact upon the history of jazz album covers as a whole? And to what level can we meaningfully

1 These words are an extract from a surviving Pollock doodle, quoted in Pepe Karmel (ed.), *Jackson Pollock: Interviews, Articles, and Reviews* (New York: Museum of Modern Art, 1999).

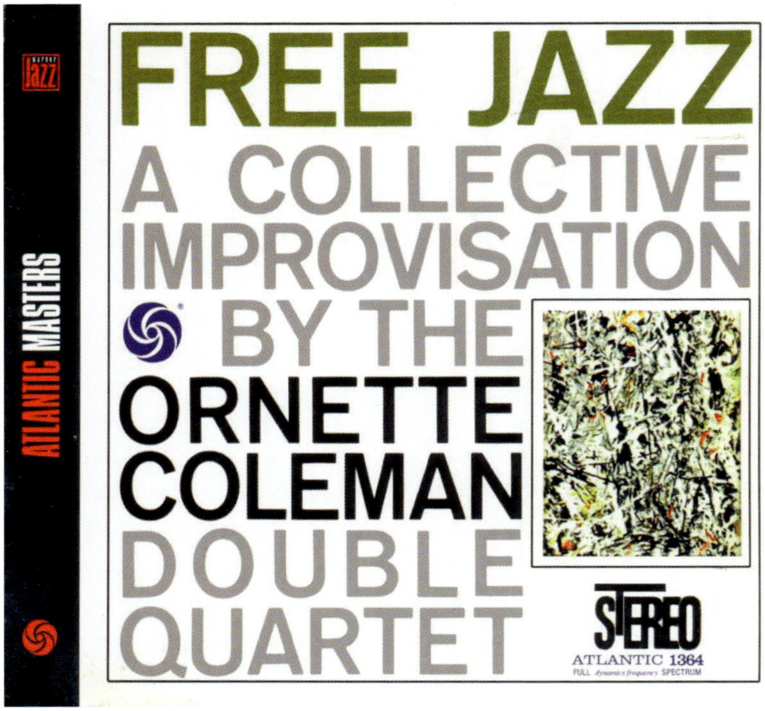

The Ornette Coleman Double Quartet, *Free Jazz*, album cover. Courtesy of Warner Music.

Jackson Pollock, *White Light*, 1954. New York, Museum of Modern Art (MoMA). Oil, enamel, and aluminum paint on canvas (122.4 × 96.9 cm). The Sidney and Harriet Janis Collection. 337.1967. © 2009. Digital image, The Museum of Modern Art, New York/Scala, Florence.

transfer ideas of conception and creation from a visual art form like painting to a sonic one like jazz?

According to Amiri Baraka, Coleman expressed a "rapport" with Pollock's work around the time of his *Free Jazz* release. In a second interview, the saxophonist described Pollock as "in the same state I was in – doing what I was doing".[2] Little else is known about his deeper thoughts on the painter's approach. In fact, Coleman was not the one to decide upon the *Free Jazz* album cover, and it is possible that *White Light* could simply have been a casual attempt to signify a modernist aesthetic; a fitting accompaniment to the groundbreaking music. Yet, as Nick Cook suggests, to consider the images that accompany music as mere "optional accessories" is to employ an overly narrow analytical framework. Instead, album covers can be considered "as agents in the cultural process, sites where meaning is negotiated through the act of consumption".[3] Supporting this view, I suggest that deeper parallels between the artists can enhance our understanding of *Free Jazz*. Pollock's work can be exploited as an interpretative tool, a relatively unexplored influence upon Coleman's musical approach. Pollock's work also represents an iconic cluster of both ideological and aesthetic stances

2 See Amiri Baraka, *Blues People: Negro Music in White America* [1963] (New York: William Morrow, 1999), p. 234; and Chad Mandeles, "Jackson Pollock and Jazz: structural parallels", *Arts Magazine*, L VI/2, October 1981, pp. 139–141: ill.

3 Nick Cook, "The Domestic Gesamtkunstwerk, or Record Sleeves and Reception", in Wyndham Thomas (ed.), *Composition-Performance-Reception: Studies in the Creative Process in Music* (Aldershot: Ashgate, 1998), pp. 105–106.

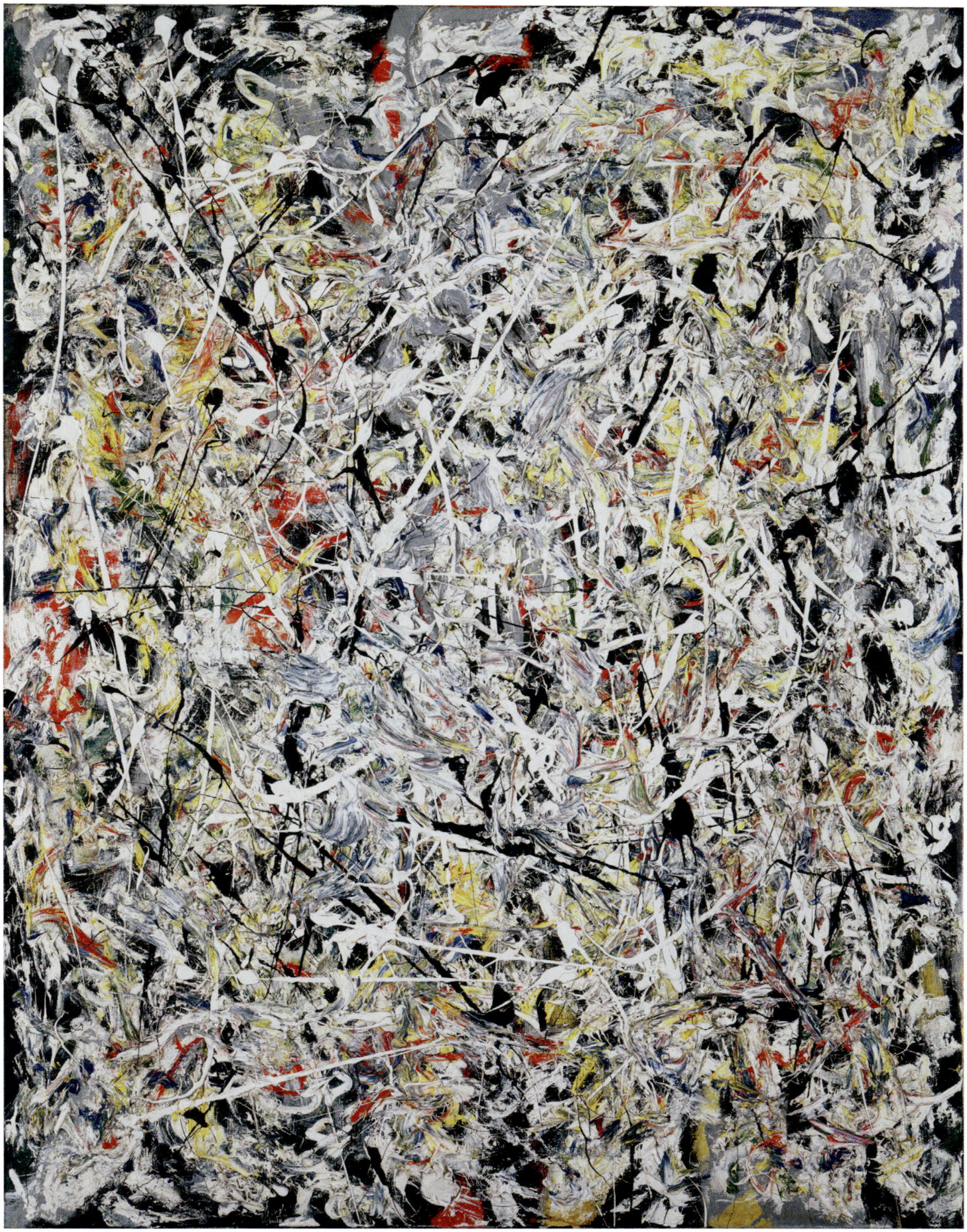

with which Coleman may have wished to align himself, influencing the way his music would be heard and interpreted by his audiences.

Pollock, who died in 1958, was influenced by jazz of a slightly earlier genre. His wife, Lee Kasner, claims he believed jazz to be the only other innovative art form in America. She explains that Pollock "would get into grooves of listening to his jazz records – not just for days – day and night, day and night for three days running ... the house would *shake*".[4] In a synthesis of the two creative processes, Pollock would frequently paint while listening to music, emphasizing the crucial role of his own physical movements; the aural rhythms and timbres of the music inspiring the pace and pulse of his paint strokes, drips, swings, and slashes, in Matthew Rohn's words his "motion-orientated dynamics".[5] Perhaps as a result, his paintings sing of the creative process, embedding the act of creation within the end product's power and meaning. As art critic Harold Rosenberg explained, "what was to go on the canvas was not a picture but an event".[6] Pollock himself described his painting as "energy and motion made visible".[7]

Regarded by many at the time as threatening, anarchic, or plain ridiculous, the emphasis upon movement and the breaking down of the larger structural constraints prevalent in earlier forms of painting was frequently considered synonymous with a quest for (and expression of) 'freedom': a powerful, if ill-defined cluster of ideas, which I shall discuss in detail when considering the avant-garde jazz scene in the 1950s and 1960s. Pollock's art has been consistently framed in terms of 'freedom' since it rose to national and international prominence in the late 1940s. In the wake of World War II, art critic Clement Greenberg described Pollock's painting as an icon of "liberation – a setting free of the natural spiritual flow within us".[8] Similarly, biographer B.H. Friedman claimed that Pollock's name was "synonymous with the expression of freedom".[9] Pollock's work, in flouting even the limited structural coherence of European cubists such as Picasso and Klee, provided not merely an aesthetic change but a democratization of artistic voices. Critics, unable to recognize the complex levels of control and artistic discretion employed in his paintings, frequently represented its uncompromising energy and innovative flair as free from intellectual control. A visual evocation of the spirit of America, it seemed vulgar, invigorating, dynamic, unrestrained, and unafraid. In this tangled crux of misrepresentation, innovation, and freedom of expression, Pollock's work intersects powerfully with jazz of the 1950s and 1960s.

4 Francine du Plessix and Cleve Gray, "Who was Jackson Pollock?", *Art in America* 55:3 (1967), p. 51.

5 Matthew L. Rhon, *Visual Dynamics in Jackson Pollock's Abstractions* (Ann Arbor: UMI Research Press, 1987), p. 59.

6 Harold Rosenberg, "The American Action Painters", *Art News*, September 1952, p. 22.

7 Karmel, p. 24.

8 Quoted in Jeremy Lewison, *Interpreting Pollock* (London: Tate Gallery Publishing, 1999), p. 7.

9 B.H. Friedman, *Jackson Pollock: Energy Made Visible* (London: Wedienfeld & Nicholson, 1972), p. xi.

Free Jazz: Ideology and Aesthetics

The artistic aims and philosophical approaches displayed in *Free Jazz* grew from the larger musical and political context of late 1950s and 1960s America. Ideas of freedom were inextricably linked with avant-garde jazz, not least because of Coleman's album. They have influenced writing on American jazz of the sixties onwards.[10] Yet the idea of freedom itself has been used (or misused) in numerous ways, its definitions proving highly elusive. An ideological backbone for America's resistance to fascist or communist ideologies, the concept was just as likely to be used as state-sponsored propaganda, than as a tool of self-assertion for oppressed minorities. In the context of American cultural initiatives, it could also be read as a promise of liberation from European cultural dominance. Not least, 'freedom' came to represent an escape not only from oppression, but from consciousness, materialism, intellect and the 'slavery' of self-control. All of these discourses proved pertinent to the free jazz movement, an intensely political and emotional struggle, which is often portrayed in terms of active resistance to white American or Western hegemony.[11] Frank Kofsky describes the avant-garde movement in jazz as "a musical representation of the ghetto's vote of 'no confidence' in Western civilization and the American Dream", and as "the expression of outraged protest".[12] He quotes Archie Shepp, who declares that jazz is "anti-war; it is opposed to Vietnam; it is for Cuba; it is for the liberation of all people".[13] Defining the music through its pro- and anti-stances, Shepp places 'liberation' in opposition to violence and oppression perpetuated by white Western power-holders. However, many musicians, including Ornette Coleman, did not speak about their music in this way.

Both Shepp and Kofsy attribute musicians' failure to articulate political resistance through the 1960s to fear.[14] Undoubtedly, livelihoods could come under serious jeopardy as a result of political proselytizing. However, I would like to consider the possibilities of free jazz less as resistance and more as an escape from hegemony through the creative enactment of individual and communal voices. This distinction is inspired by W.E.B. Du Bois' concept of "negative and positive sides of freedom", set out in 1915. Du Bois stressed that Negroes "must not simply be free from [enslavement and oppression] ... but must have power: the power of men, the right to do, to know, to feel and to express".[15] Not simply freedom *from*, then, but freedom *to*: the freedom to create a space of expression that simply *is*.[16] It is this freedom ideal – the freedom of doing, of unrestrained expression that is non-referential, independent, and not explicitly oppositional – that is central to the free jazz movement.

10 See Baraka, *Blues People*; Frank Kofsky, *Black Nationalism and the Revolution in Music* (New York: Pathfinder, 1970); Ronald Radano, *New Musical Figurations: Anthony Braxton's Cultural Critique* (Chicago: University of Chicago Press, 1993); Scott Saul, *Freedom is Freedom Aint: Jazz and the Making of the Sixties* (USA: President and Fellows of Harvard College, 2003); David Such, *Avant-garde Jazz Musicians Performing 'Out There'* (Iowa City: University of Iowa Press, 1993); Peter Townsend, *Jazz in American Culture* (Edinburgh: Edinburgh University Press, 2000); Brian Ward (ed.), *Media, Culture, and the Modern African-American Freedom Struggle* (Florida: University of Florida Press, 2001); and Val Wilmer, *As Serious as Your Life: John Coltrane and Beyond* [1977] (London: Serpent's Tail, 1992). The exceptions here are Ekkehard Jost, *Free Jazz* [1974] (USA: Da Capo Press, 1994) and John Litweiler, *The Freedom Principle: Jazz After 1958* [1984] (New York: Da Capo Press, 1990), which pay relatively little attention to the political context and concentrating, though with very different analytical approaches, on the music itself. Jost goes so far as suggesting that "the variety of musical formative principles existing in the stylistic conglomerate of free jazz has so far been obscured rather than brought to light by the sociological approach predominant in contemporary jazz literature". See Jost, p. 9.

11 See in particular Baraka, *Blues People* and *Black Music* [1967] (New York: Da Capo Press, 1998); A.B. Spellman, *Black Music: Four Lives in the Be-Bop Business* (New York: Limelight, 1967); Wilmer, *As Serious as Your Life*; and statements by Archie Shepp and Max Roach.

12 Kofsky, pp. 131, 57.

13 Ibid., p. 64.

14 See Wilmer, *As Serius as Your Life*, p. 155, and Kofsky, pp. 56–63.

15 Quoted in Richard H. King, *Civil Rights and the Idea of Freedom* [1992] (New York: Oxford University Press, 1996), p. 20.

16 Sherrie Ortner and Guthrie Ramsey (2003) warn against the danger of perceiving all black activity as defined by its relationship to whiteness. Doing so can result in the internal

I would like to shape this freedom around two key concepts: the desire to escape beyond the limitation of time, space, and the body; and the attempted enactment of an ideal society through the interaction and expression of individual and communal voices. In considering these two aspects of the freedom ideal, parallels with Pollock and the modernist art movement in American should become clear.

Escape

The desire to transcend and push beyond the limits and prejudices of material life and break from the constraining languages and structures of more traditional jazz is a common narrative within free jazz and its scholarship. Sometimes this desire is expressed in an explicitly spiritual context, particularly in the work of John Coltrane and Albert Ayler.[17] Yet just as often, the space 'beyond' is defined in terms not explicitly spiritual. The desire for complete separation from the mainstream is described by Radano in his study of Anthony Braxton and the AACM,[18] and is reflected by the aspirations of black power, and more extremely, the Nation of Islam. Sun Ra's insistence that he comes from beyond this planet, and his refusal to acknowledge his own parents, his birth, or his name evokes the same ideals,[19] a desire to "generate a space outside the very framework of domination".[20]

Coleman is frequently described as having developed and pursued his art outside the realms of societal and musical constraint: we shall see later how this is reflected in his album covers. Wilmer declares that he "made music that was as natural as breathing".[21] Don Cherry explains that Coleman's music "really lives because you can see there is no time period. Style is only related to a certain period, Ornette's music goes beyond".[22] David Ake describes Coleman as a "cultural outsider", particularly alienated from traditional forms of embodied masculinity. Ake explains that Coleman went as far as to consider castration in an attempt to distance himself from mainstream narratives of masculine domination.[23]

Ironically, the idea of artistic transcendence can be linked with myths of the lone male genius through the cultural and intellectual history of the 'West'. It is a trope that can be detected in many representations of Jackson Pollock. Jeremy Lewison explains that the public viewed Pollock's "paintings [as] created with mindless speed and extracted from the unconscious", helping to create "an image of the artist as shaman".[24] He highlights the frequent reference to Pollock's birthplace of Cody, Wyoming (a town named after Buffalo Bill), sug-

complexities of black life being erased and distorted. It also denies blackness the right to be defined upon its own terms; an agenda surely central to the free jazz movement. See Radano, *New Musical Figurations* and Saul in particular.

17 See Saul, pp. 254–260; Wilmer, *As Serious as Your Life*, pp. 31–40, 92–99.

18 See Radano, *New Musical Figurations*.

19 See John Szwed, *Space is the Place: The Lives and Times of Sun Ra* (New York: Da Capo Press, 1997).

20 Ajay Heble, *Landing on the Wrong Note: Jazz, Dissonance, and Critical Practice* (London: Routledge, 2000), p. 125.

21 Wilmer, *As Serious as Your Life*, p. 61.

22 Ibid., 64.

23 David Ake, *Jazz Culture* (Berkeley: University of California Press, 2002).

24 Lewison, p. 7.

gesting that Pollock willingly perpetuated his own image as outsider, living on the wilder peripheries of American society, with inborn understanding of Native American and other naturalistic beliefs and outlooks.[25]

Ideas of artistic transcendence reflect upon both creator and the created. Implicit in the outsider status of artists, and their inspired transcendence from day-to-day realities, is the idea that what is being created is in fact art. For Pollock, the heritage of his field could hardly be questioned, although his own contributions were often accused of destroying its legacies. For Coleman, jazz had rarely been credited as an art form at all, more often being perceived as an instinctual, anti-intellectual entertainment. The picturing of modern art on the *Free Jazz* album cover can be viewed as contributing to the positioning of jazz as art form; a contentious issue among jazz musicians and scholars, which will be discussed in more detail below.

Voice and the Enactment of an Ideal Society

In Amiri Baraka's opinion, most avant-garde reed players "are intrigued by the sound of the human voice".[26] Coltrane's revolutionary use of timbre, adopted and extended by Coleman, Shepp, and Ayler among others, did not merely represent an expansion of the instrument's tonal repertoire, but a reinterpretation of its very objectives. Listening to Ayler's intensely human vibrato as he weightily lingers over the spirituals' melodies, or to Coltrane's high-octane screams, which seem to break from all forms of referentiality, one can hear the musicians forging new spaces of expression: a "radicalisation of sound" to embrace "the cries of animals, the screechings of machines, the susurrations of the natural elements, the conversational twitterings of evoked harmonics and the gorgeous jazz ballad tone".[27]

Pressing's list of sonic possibilities (which could easily be longer) captures the multiplication of voices, sounds, and subject positions important in free jazz. This democratization of voices was not without precedent and can be detected to varying degrees in some earlier jazz music: in the timbral range of Ellington's orchestral work, and the unrestrained contrapuntalism of New Orleans, for example. However, the way in which these voices interacted, and the extension of expressive possibilities particularly within the rhythm section, was new and integrally linked to the political climate of mid century America. While taking their art back to a realm that reflected a more personal, essential emotionalism, the avant-gardists were also extending many of hard bop's musical and political directions. They drew inspiration from Mingus' focus on black

25 Ibid., pp. 70–73.

26 Baraka, *Black Music*, p. 75.

27 See Jeff Pressing, "Free Jazz and the Avant-garde", in Mervyn Cooke and David Horn (eds.), *Cambridge Companion to Jazz* (Cambridge: Cambridge University Press, 2002), p. 204.

roots music, unfettered religious emotionalism, liberated vocal and instrumental cries, and collective improvisational approach. They also absorbed the politicized stances of Mingus and his contemporaries; Max Roach, Abbey Lincoln, and Sonny Rollins, among others.[28]

The two decades after World War II sparked intensified debates about freedom, democracy, racial equality, and the nature of the 'ideal society'. These were chiefly fuelled by disillusionment with American forms of democracy and capitalism, or as Kofsky suggests, the "American Dream". America's victorious engagement in World War II had been justified by the destruction of German fascism, yet segregation and lynching were common experiences for America's own black population, many of whom had served their country in the war.

The McCarthy era had reached a climax of fascistic paranoia in the late 1940s and early 1950s. Peaceful civil rights demonstrators were being beaten and killed by the National Guard and police on American streets, while the Vietnam War saw America embroiled in a moral quagmire of indiscriminate killing. Both Vietnam and McCarthyism were justified in the name of freedom and the moral superiority of capitalism over alternative social arrangements, which, at least superficially, appeared to champion equality over commerce. In America, it seemed that the tenets of individual respect the government claimed to champion were only reserved for some. The capitalist structures of jazz production and performance, along with the crushing institutional prejudice of record companies, club owners, and the critical establishment, led to a situation of virtual apartheid: logistical institutions that profited from jazz were overwhelmingly white while the majority of jazz producers were black and paid minimal wages for the creation of a national music.

America's fierce individualism and materialism offered neither justice nor equality of opportunity for African Americans. They were also incompatible with African-originating ideologies of group participation and community dialogue. An important ethos in Free Jazz and the civil rights movement was the philosophical and practical negotiation of forging individual freedoms with alternative narratives of group power.[29] As I shall show in the analysis of *Free Jazz*, this translated into an ambivalent, if not conflicting, relationship between the expressive rights of the individual and the group; a tension also embedded in the diverse and multiple 'authorial voices' of Pollock's paintings. It is the negotiation of diverse artistic strands (individual and communal), between unfettered freedom and the structures of coherent, communicable thought, which I shall consider in further detail for Coleman's *Free Jazz* album and its *White Light* cover.

28 See Kofsky; Saul; Spellman; Townsend, "Free Jazz".

29 See John Corbett, "Ephemera Underscored: Writing Around Free Improvisation", in Krin Gabbard (ed.), *Jazz Among the Discourses* (Durham: Duke University Press, 1995); Charles Hersch, "Let Freedom Ring: Free Jazz and African-American Politics", *Cultural Critique* (Winter 1996), pp. 97–123; Pressing; Radano, *New Musical Figurations*; Saul; and Such.

On Listening to *Free Jazz*

A fleeting sense of busy incoherence subsides to reveal energetic dialogues of thought, gesture, and momentary inspiration. Horns jostle with one another. Sometimes selfish, sometimes giving, they comment, laugh, scream, and chatter. One arcs above them, teeters, and plunges down. Another grabs a three-note whim, extends to four, and accelerates. One murmers underneath, dragging its heels, sceptical, as the last spirals seemingly directionless to settle on a quarter tone. The driving pulse of the bass underlies all, as the drums shimmer and crash through multiple, splintered melodies.

Free Jazz provides thirty-seven minutes of unbroken music, the majority of which is free of pre-composition. To unprepared ears, the piece initially sounds formless and anarchical (and was certainly accused of being so at the time of release), yet the music actually represents a subtle balance of meta-structure and expressive freedom. Coleman provides an overarching form by dividing the piece into sections, each with a designated instrumentalist as principal soloist. During the performance, he indicates when these sections should begin and end. The solo sections are separated by short interludes with predetermined shape and concept, but freedom of pitch choice. Every instrument in the ensemble, including drums and basses, is given a designated section in which to solo. Surprisingly perhaps, and in clear contrast to accusations levied by contemporary critics such as Ira Gitler or Philip Larkin, *Free Jazz* is indeed structured, and quite traditionally so: as Peter Niklas Wilson explains, "the 'free' in 'free jazz' can only be understood in a limited, or relative sense".[30]

The sequence of theme-solo-theme is mostly adhered to and the traditional time-keeping role is demanded from the rhythm section (especially from Haden and Blackwell). The well-established hierarchy between rhythm section and horns is reinforced through the ordering, and length of the solos (Coleman's is the longest, and the explications of the drums and bass are much shorter and placed towards the end). Most of the freedom comes from the absence of harmonic progression and consequent liberation of pitch choice. The rules that constrain the choice of note and define the note's function within an overall tonality (or tonal 'scape') have been broken.

30 Peter Niklas Wilson, *Ornette Coleman: His Life and Music* (Berkeley: Berkeley Hills Books, 1999), p. 371.

Individual and Communal Voices in *Free Jazz*

> The most important thing was for us to play together, all at the same time, without getting in each other's way, and also to have enough room for each player to 'ad lib' alone... When the soloist played something that suggested a musical idea or direction to me, I played that behind him in my style. He continued his own way in his solo, of course[31]
> *Ornette Coleman, Original Album Notes, 1961*

> Although everyone is a soloist in Free Jazz – relatively independent and equal with the seven others – the word solo in this case has to be reinterpreted. There is no one soloist, and there are no merely supporting accompanists. Everyone is equal, and in a sense everyone is at all times simultaneously leading (soloing) and supporting (complementing).[32]
> *Gunther Schuller, Additional Notes, later edition, 1997*

Both Coleman and Schuller place a heavy emphasis on the musical self-determination of each part. It is clearly the intention that each player expresses his individual musical ideas and relates those contrapuntally to the surrounding activity: the emphasis is on individual, rather than communal expression. The disjuncture between the different instrumental timbres and styles is intentional. This is made clear by Coleman's insistence that each musician should continue in his own style, even when reacting to another's contributions, that enough room should be left for players to ad lib on their own, and that each should avoid getting in another's way. Yet freedom, equality, and self-determination are not mistaken for isolation or independence.

Musicians listen and respond to one another intently. The horns consistently develop motifs along similar lines to Coleman's own methods of melodic elaboration.[33] Charlie Haden, when talking of the experience of recording *Free Jazz* and working with Coleman, consistently emphasizes the need for intense listening.[34] Ekkehard Jost describes and provides analyses of the "abundance of motivic interaction" between instruments.[35]

A fine balance is being negotiated between each musician's self-determination and the inevitable constraints of playing as an ensemble. Despite the freedom of individual voice being paramount, Coleman includes necessary

31 Ornette Coleman, quoted by Martin Williams in the original sleeve notes to *Free Jazz* (Atlantic, 1961).

32 Gunther Schuller, CD liner notes, *Free Jazz*.

33 See Jost; Litweiler; and Wilson.

34 Palmer, "Charlie Haden's Creed", *Down Beat*, 20 July 1972.

35 Jost, p. 59.

counterbalances of cooperation and equivalency. Each section has a designated soloist, yet the prominence of the soloist fluctuates a great deal as he competes with the other instruments for attention; often becoming embroiled in the timbral mix, before rising again to assert 'dominance'.

Like other American saxophone players of the 1960s,[36] Coleman dropped the piano from his ensembles when he abandoned harmonic pre-determination. The piano's traditionally harmonic role would perhaps undermine the attempt to create contrapuntal independence, forcing a more vertical, and therefore hierarchical, musical whole. One can imagine the undesired 'anchoring' effect of a piano's harmonic and timbral solidity within this mesh of 'equal' voices. While four horns can intermingle and imitate one another over the softer, multivalent percussion and bass sounds, the piano's timbre would remain unmistakably its own: by drawing attention to itself as a unique entity, it would undermine the less aggressive individuality of the other instruments.

The balance between instruments is also prescribed in the interludes. Within a few measures of the start, for example, the horns play patterns of notes in sequence with one another, rather than in harmony, thus creating an abstract, 'composite' melody. This technique, termed by Coleman as 'melodic unison', provides a valuable illustration of his overall approach. Rather than several musicians fulfilling different roles to create a whole, each takes a fragmented share of the soloist's role. Each instrument supplies a relatively self-contained and equally significant element within an overall sound that is defined as much by the activity of its parts as it is by its overarching effect.

Free Jazz, therefore, creates a texture of numerous voices talking partly to one another, and partly independently. The overall motive, it seems, is to unleash the potential for a larger spectrum of expression. Ironically though, with the exception of the bass and drum solos, the overarching soundscape is surprisingly mono-textural, "emotionally static", in Jeff Pressing's words.[37] The extremity of musical individualism and communication is in the end suppressed by an almost accidental communal voice: the relatively unchanging sound of eight concurrent attempts at self-expression.[38]

I suggest that this is a tension within Coleman's collective improvisation ideal. While every player must feel free to follow his own musical instincts, no player may take the 'liberty' of stealing the show.[39] Peter Niklas Wilson claims that it was only in the 1970s, after his experiments with Joujouka, that Coleman "was able to realize an orchestral music in which the group sound, not the musi-

36 Kevin Leander Williams (Freidwald et al. 2002, p. 171) declares that "Everyone knows that saxists of the 1960s swore off the piano because of chordal constraints". See Williams, p. 171. See also Pressing, p. 205, for a discussion of the piano's apparent limitations in free jazz.

37 Pressing, p. 209.

38 A similar phenomenon is mentioned by Radano in reference to the music of AACM. He explains that for extended sections, "all players perform in parallel, creating a non-interactive multi-linear web". He suggests that this approach creates a "quality of anonymity" in some recordings. See Radano, *New Musical Figurations*, p. 108.

39 This stance is reflected in Coleman's liner notes to *Change of the Century* (Atlantic, 1959), in which he declares that "I let everyone express himself just as he wants to" while explaining that his collaborators resist grandstanding, and that the music is "at all times a group effort". Saul explores the relationship between individual and community in his study of Hard Bop. He represents the combination of individual and communal agendas as a successful and radical expression of freedom, defined in opposition to the individualist and consumerist definitions posited by Europe and mainstream America at the time. While he makes room for the idea of struggle within his paradigm, he defines the sound and act of struggle as freedom itself, and seems unambiguous in presenting jazz musicians' expressions of freedom as fully realized, strengthened rather than weakened by their underlying contradictions. David Meltzer concurs, declaring that "In essence, a jazz performance is a real-time utopia, a collaborative effort supporting individual expression", *Reading Jazz* (San Francisco: Mercury House, 1993), p. 4. Nathaniel Mackey also suggests that "black music – especially that of the sixties, with its heavy emphasis on individual freedom within a collectively improvised context – proposed a model social order, an ideal, even utopic balance between impulse and group demands", *Discrepant Engagement: Dissonance, Cross-culturality, and Environmental Writing* (Cambridge: Cambridge University Press), p. 34. Radano (p. 97) takes a different view; while he acknowledges the potential for black culture to

cal individuality of the participants, was the crucial thing".[40] Robert Palmer also reports a conversation he had with Coleman around the same time, in which the saxophone player declares his previous frustration at being forced to choose between musical freedom and audience connection: two divergent agendas I suggest can be aligned with the enactment of musical process and the creation of musical product. It seems possible that Coleman himself regarded *Free Jazz* as only a partial fulfillment of his visions of freedom.[41]

Pollock's Multiple Voices

In staring at the painting ...

Thin white lasers scatter like spillikins upon a canvas thick with colors, paint, shapes. Daubs of purity, splashed white, collapse into feathered curves of grey. Black figurines (an accident, an apparition?) dance behind, trailing veins that circle, shape and scar the image-coated canvas. Yellow and red, like submerged foliage, burn one another, sometimes thick, sometimes absent, they oscillate with grey behind branches of white. They hide, fiery, beneath indifferent turmoil, an ever-shifting illusion of layers encompassed by flatness: a sense of overwhelming activity immersed, anaesthetized even, by the changing same of paint. Tangling above, below, tangling over, under itself, its lines and colors quarrel and sing in constant transition.

I have shown how *Free Jazz* can be viewed as collapsing the hierarchy between overarching musical product and the microcosm of motivic interaction and multiple voices functioning within, but partly independently of, the resulting 'picture'. Rather than numerous colors blending to create one image, the quarrelling and conversing of separate strands of shade, texture, and tone formed the centerpiece of the art work itself. Pollock's paintings can be analyzed in a similar way. Persistent in refuting misconceptions of his art as chaotic, anarchic, uncalculated, or uncontrolled, Pollock would describe his work more in terms of a loosening of previous 'rules' (bound inextricably to the realities of 1950s American life) and a dynamic enactment of the artistic process.[42]

Mathew Rohn analyses Pollock's painting in terms of their balance between "microstructures" (small shapes, individual strands, splashes and gestures) and "Primary structural configurations" (larger-scale shapes or colors that dominate, frame, and define the overall dynamics of the painting). He notes that "the microstructures generate the principal expressive activity in most Pollock abstractions" and explains that modernist painters, in search of

challenge "the ideology of a fiercely competitive, capitalist state" he expresses the ironic and limiting nature inherent in black struggles for freedom when exploiting the tools of the system from which they are trying to escape. See also Daniel Fischlin and Ajay Heble (eds.), *The Other Side of Nowhere: Jazz, Improvisation, and Communities in Dialogue* (Middletown: Wesleyan University Press, 2004); Jost; and Marshall Soules, "Improvising Character: Jazz, the Actor, and Protocols of Improvisation", in Fischline and Heble.

40 Wilson, p. 58.

41 Even Litweiler, one of Coleman's most passionate supporters, concedes that while the album's objective may have been to create a "spontaneous ensemble structure achieved through responsive, simultaneous motivic development", its aim was at best "nearly realized" and that *Free Jazz* shows more a "potential for unity" through collective improvisation, than a realization of that potential. See Litweiler, pp. 47–48.

"a more egalitarian form of expression" have sought to "divest their works of the [prior] dominance [of] primary structural configuration". They regard the "collective action among components themselves as the most essential and revealing source for values".[43]

The negotiation between hierarchical structures and the egalitarian expression of individual voices can easily be perceived in a survey of Pollock's abstractionist paintings. *Blue Poles* of 1952 shows a canvas split (though not completely) by prominent dark slashes of paint. Their angles oscillate to create a dynamic, flowing pulse, behind which numerous colors swim and scatter against one another. *Out of the Web* (1949) has an equally clear metanarrative, with thick, curving oscillations of brown superimposed upon gestures that are thinner and more complex. In both paintings, the underlying colors are shaped by an overarching structure.

The hierarchy is less clear in *Reflection of the Big Dipper* (1947). A large purple daub, just off-center is covered with swinging arcs of black. The ribbons of black meld into increasingly splintered detail, making it more challenging to define where large and small statements begin and end. *Number 27* (1950) has acrobatic swirls of light brown and heavy areas of black, gray, and white. Their relationship to one another contributes to the spatial narrative of the painting, yet it is difficult to define what is key and structural: there is no one focus, but a multiple network of movement.

Number 1A (1948), *Number 1* (1949), and *White Light* are further along this continuum. All three contain various elements that catch the eye, yet each gesture seems small, almost isolated. The action encapsulated within numerous, localized gestures form the lynchpin of the paintings' impact. The microstructure and movement of inner voices form the event itself.

When Rohn describes the "qualities of motion and energy that course through [this] work ... paint strokes erupt[ing] in a frenzy of activity, vy[ing] with one another for prominence",[44] he evokes a heteroglossia of multiple voices defined through their dialogical engagement in one expressive space.[45] Coleman's freedom ideal is based on the same premise: the active expression of multiple voices within a single sonic moment. Coleman's description of Free Jazz concentrates overwhelmingly on the experience of performing it, the thoughts and aspirations of the musicians while playing. He spends little time discussing the quality or effect of the sounds that will be produced. Just as in the "action painting" Pollock pioneered, Coleman's end product, rather than being a predetermined aim, is an enactment of the creative process, what Wilmer refers to as "living music".[46]

42 See for example his description of his art as involving "total control ... denial of the accident ... energy and motion made visible", in Karmel, p. 24.

43 Rohn, pp. 45, 102.

44 Rohn, pp. 59, 104.

45 Mikhail Bakhtin, *The Dialogical Imagination: Four Essays* [1935] (Austin: University of Texas Press, 2002).

46 Wilmer, *As Serious as Your Life*, p. 63. See also George Lewis' distinction between Afrological and Eurological approaches in jazz, in which Lewis personifies most free jazz as Afrological in its concentration upon the process of music-making and renunciation of harmony. George Lewis, "Improvised music after 1950: Afrological and Eurological perspectives", in Fischline and Heble.

While it is difficult to estimate the care with which this specific painting was chosen for the album cover, it does seem that *White Light*'s near disregard for metanarrative, along with its focus upon individual gestures of overlapping color (superimposed upon one another but rarely blended), is startlingly similar to the approach of the musicians in *Free Jazz*.

Coda

By placing *White Light* on his album cover, in conjunction with the bold lettering of his name and the declarative, genre-defining title, Coleman extended the strong imaging of his music already established by earlier album covers. Both Contemporary and Atlantic labels, with which Coleman recorded in 1958 and 1959, portrayed Coleman and his music differently from traditional jazz imaging of the day. Titles such as *Tomorrow is the Question!, The Shape of Jazz to Come,* and *Change of the Century* declare the uniqueness of Coleman's sound. Implying the saxophonist's role as conduit or guide to a jazz future few could yet envision, they place themselves at the center of jazz history-making. Perhaps the most obvious precursor for this would be *Birth of the Cool* (1949), but titles such as *Blue Train* (1957), *Round About Midnight* (1956) and *My Favorite Things* (1960) were far more typical, helping to frame jazz within individual spaces of the imagination, denying the more architectural developments traditionally associated with an 'art form'.

The albums' photographic portrayals of Coleman generally reinforce the image of epochal innovator, while also manipulating the relationship of the musician to his music beyond traditional jazz representations. Common practice at the time, perhaps most epitomized by the Blue Note record covers, would picture suave musicians in 'hip' poses, instrument in hand, with mood lighting and deep shadows, reinforcing "jazz mythologies" of the cool, night club hipster.[47]

Coleman's albums depict a more disjointed relationship between musician and music, while avoiding the nightclub image all together. In *Something Else!!!* (1958), a black and white photo of Coleman in the bottom left hand corner is dwarfed by the red and blue headline album title. Dressed in a woolen pullover and clearly absorbed in the act of playing, his own image seems subsumed by the power of his creation. *Tomorrow is the Question* (1959) offers a close-up of Coleman without instrument and seemingly in deep contemplation. Eyes hooded, he gazes past the camera as if viewing the future evoked in the title. Taken in strong sunlight, against a sandy-colored background, shaded with patterns like tree bark, there are overtones of the naturalist or African visionary.

47 See Townsend, *Jazz in American Culture*.

The implication seems to be that his music is a product of his visions, not of his saxophone playing. The image of Coleman as contemplative visionary, bereft of saxophone, is repeated several times in the late 1950s and early 1960s, for example in *Change of the Century* (1959) and *Town Hall* (1962). *This is Our Music* (1960) also pictures the quartet members without instruments. In a clearly posed photograph, they seem detached from the act of music making. In contrast to Cherry, Blackwell, and Haden, Coleman stares uncompromisingly forward, with a purity and certainty of representation that hints at his unshakeable artistic vision.

Even when Coleman is holding his saxophone, techniques are employed to decontextualize him from traditional jazz symbolism. In *The Shape of Jazz to Come* (1959), he stands clearly posed, against an uncompromising red background, dressed again in a woolen pullover. In *Beauty is a Rare Thing* (1961), he is pictured sitting on the earth, half concealed by a tree branch, reinforcing his almost mystic connection with nature and music beyond the realms of style.

Within this context, *Free Jazz* can be viewed as continuing a process of rewriting jazz through its sounds *and* images. Coleman is dropped from the front cover altogether, finalizing separation of musician from music. In replacing his image with one of contemporary art, Atlantic removes jazz from its club environment, and evokes instead the cultural currency of 'Western art' forms and modernist aesthetic values. Through the use of a Jackson Pollock, Coleman is aligned with a national icon of artistic innovation and expressive freedom. The level to which Coleman was instrumental in his own marketing is unclear, but his music and the imaging of his music were both groundbreaking. Like Pollock, he redefined not only the rules, but the definitions of his art.

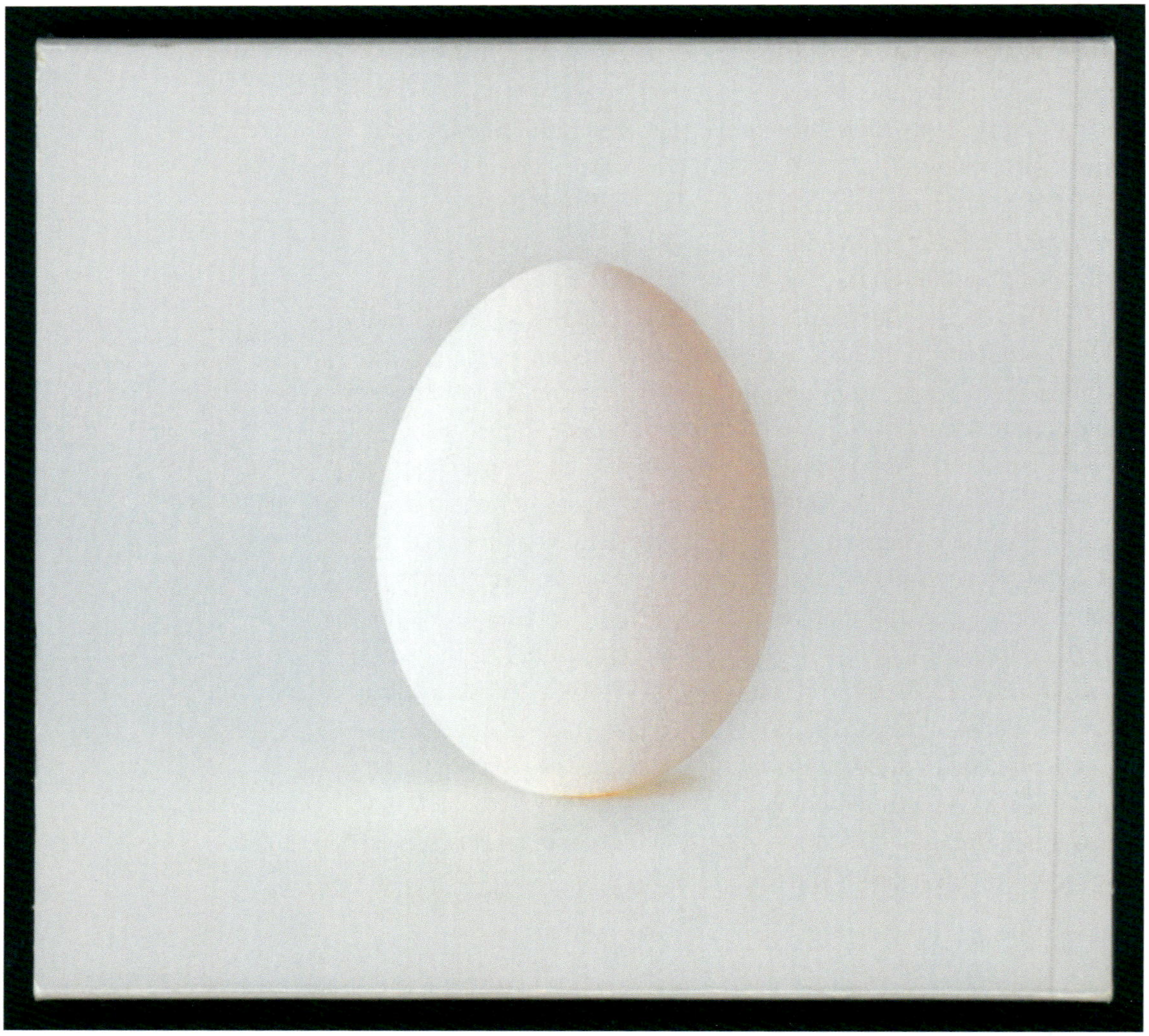

Wilco, *A Ghost is Born*. Courtesy of Dan Nadel and Peter Buchanan-Smith / PictureBox Inc. www.pictureboxinc.com

Interview with Dan Nadel

Asbjørn Grønstad & Øyvind Vågnes

In this interview, Grammy-award winning sleeve designer Dan Nadel talks about his work with Wilco's A Ghost is Born, *the various influences that have shaped his distinct stylistic output, the significance of changing formats for the aesthetics of the album cover – and the egg as an icon of everyday life.*

G&V: How did your work with Wilco come about?

DN: I publish an anthology of design, art, comics, and illustration called *The Ganzfeld*. In early 2002 I got really interested in rock and roll books, specifically the Wings book, *Hands Across the Water*,[1] which is basically a collection of snapshots from around the tour. You hardly see the band in the book, and there are no shots of the band playing at all. It's a great book about traveling across America, being bored on tour, and the kind of beautiful monotony of a rock tour. So, I thought that it might be interesting to apply the multi-disciplinary visual book model of *The Ganzfeld* to a rock band, making a rock project as wonderfully off-kilter as the Wings book. Wilco was and is one of my favorite bands, and since they didn't have a concrete visual identity, but did share some common interests with me, I thought it might be fun to try to make a book with them. I sent their manager some books of mine, they liked them, and we took off from there. The concept was to make a fully collaborative book about music in general, and Wilco in particular by looking at the world they've created for themselves. So, we explored their creative process, but also the processes of their guitar tech – how he thinks about guitars. And we interviewed their sound guys on their approach to sound in general and live concert sound in particular. Things like that. The idea being that a non-Wilco fan could pick up the book and learn a lot about making music in general. We also wanted to avoid rock clichés, so there's only one shot in the entire book of the band performing on stage. The book was eventually published in October 2004. In the middle of working on the book, the band began to record a new record, and since we'd been working with them so well on the book, they asked us to design the record.

1 Storm Thorgerson and Peter Christopherson (eds.), *Hands Across the Water* (London: Paper Tiger, 1978).

G&V: Could you describe how your cooperation with the band worked, and how you arrived at what became the cover of *A Ghost is Born*?

DN: We sat in on the recording sessions, listened to songs, and talked to the band about what they wanted. The general consensus was that they wanted some kind of concept behind the visual, and they didn't want it to look like a normal flimsy CD. That was pretty much it. We came up with a variety of images and treatments, and the egg resonated the most with them (and with their title). We then combined the egg with the narrative idea: so the egg cracks, then opens, as you unsheathe and open the CD. This brings the viewer into the world in a gentle, but direct way.

G&V: What particular challenges did you meet in working with album cover art? How were these different from those you've met in your previous work?

DN: The biggest challenge was coming up with an image as indelible and affecting as the music it was representing. That was daunting. It was different in having to tell a story through a short sequence of small images. Also, you have to think about how the object will be handled, opened, and so on. It means designing with an eye towards real use of the object, rather than only reading, as with books.

G&V: You mention the Wings book as a source of inspiration for your work on the Wilco book.[2] In creating cover art, are there any other artists or styles both within the genre of record sleeves specifically and that of visual art more generally that have particularly affected the way you work?

DN: Hipgnosis was a big influence. They managed to make compelling images that stand on their own regardless of the music. It's image making rather than problem-solving graphic design, per se, and seems best suited to holding up against musical bombast.

G&V: The struggle to paraphrase different forms of visual art is usually regarded as a notoriously difficult one. It strikes us that the attempt on part of visual art to capture the abstractness of music must be even harder. Would you agree that recorded music seems to be fundamentally unquotable, and, if so, how do you come to terms with this unquotability in your own work? Granted, representing or reproducing music visually is neither possible nor even desirable, but there

2 Peter Buchanan-Smith and Dan Nadel, *The Wilco Book* (New York: PictureBox, 2004).

must be some conception at work of how you frame the relation between your own creative effort vis-a-vis the existing music, or?
DN: Hmmm, I think of music as being representable in all sorts of ways. Look at Oskar Fischinger, or Kandinsky, or Hipgnosis' Led Zep covers. Does it "quote" from music? No, but that's just a fact, not anything to really worry about. You can create images and visual worlds that come close to the tone and feel of the music.

V: Many listeners seem to feel that birth and rebirth are resonant themes on the two previous Wilco records, and Tweedy agrees in interviews, I have seen. When I visited Wilcoworld.net recently, I saw the nest, and I thought, this hatching and rehatching – in a way, the viewer is brought into yet another world, the wilcoworld, and so the egg seems to invite yet another narrative of rebirth as well: that of re-mediation as rebirth. Tweedy recently met up with Lawrence Lessig at the NYPL and discussed how music travels – as bytes and files – and it made me think of music as almost having an embryonic quality that the egg images now seem to illuminate. What is your response to that?
DN: I'm not sure I agree. To me, that record was about daily life and daily feelings more than anything else. The egg is an iconic, simple image that jibed with the title and had a bit of the grounded-yet-ethereal beauty of Wilco's songs. In that sense, it worked, but I'm not sure that its relation to music in general goes beyond that. For me, music is expansive, open, and not thematically linked to any one notion. That's what I like about *A Ghost is Born*: it feels like a record made by people who notice a million things every time they walk down the street. It is observant, sharp, and still beautiful.

G&V: Many people would claim that album graphics became less important when the compact disc was introduced some twenty-five years ago. What are your thoughts on the implications of that change of format for the function of the visual vis-a-vis the music? Do you think the continuing demand for LPs is as much a response to the desire for the artwork as it is for the vinyl itself?
DN: I think CDs offer plenty of opportunities, just look at the work of Stefan Sagmeister. He uses CDs as a medium, rather than seeing them as a lesser form. That's the way to approach it. CDs have a harder time making an impression because of the scale, yes, so they are less graphically present in the culture than

LPs were, but they can still be thrilling. As for the second question, yes, I think that's partly it, as well as the warmth of the vinyl sound.

G: One measure of the success of an album cover may be the extent to which one cannot actually listen to a particular record without immediately calling to mind its graphic representation. I have that experience with a number of records, for instance *Wish You Were Here* or Zeppelin's *Presence* (randomly chosen despite the obvious connection between the titles). What do you think may account for the fact that some sleeves can become so intimately associated with the music, while others just can't do that?
DN: I think that you're really just talking about the power of images. If an image is potent, it stays with you, whether it's a record cover or a painting. In the case of those covers, they're potent images regardless of the music, and once that's burned into your brain, it's hard to forget it when the music comes on.

G&V: You say that Wilco didn't have a concrete visual identity at the time when you first got in touch with them. How important would you say that identity is to an artist's success and sense of self in the current musical climate?
DN: It's very important to me, but I'm not sure it's very important otherwise. Videos, sure, but given how much music is immaterial these days, visuals are perhaps less commercially important. But for me, as a fan, they can make a huge difference. There's nothing quite like inhabiting both an aural and a visual world. It offers a rich experience and can lead to new connections within the music. It's just that extra push into new sensations.

G&V: Do you plan future collaborations with Wilco or other bands?
DN: If Wilco would have me, I'd love to do that again. I am publishing two other books with bands in the next year, but can't reveal their names right now. Each is very different from Wilco and each involves unusual approaches to music, pictures, and book making.

G&V: Would you want to design more sleeves?
DN: I'm less interested in that and more interested in books right now.

G&V: Which album covers in recent years have impressed you, and why?
DN: All three Lightning Bolt record covers are fantastic examples of Brian Chippendale's design and drawing. He uses patterns and lines to create images that vibrate at the same frequency of his music. The covers to the DFA compilations (1 and 2) are fantastic examples of minimal design to maximum effect – kind of like the music they hold. Also, Pulp's *Different Class* and *This is Hardcore*: two narrative approaches to music packaging that enhanced the stories told on each disc like illustrations in a book.

G&V: How 'reliable' is the album cover in indicating what the music on a record may be like? For instance, are there patterns of correspondence between sleeve imagery and, say, musical genres or periods? And would you buy a CD solely on the strength of its cover, on the assumption that the style of it somehow certifies the music?
DN: I don't think it's very reliable at all. Look at Hipgnosis – it would never occur to me to like the music clothed in the *Houses of the Holy* package! But there it is. Sometimes, as with, for example, the packaging for the Sex Pistols and the Buzzcocks, the graphics really match the feel of the music. Rude and raw in the case of the Sex Pistols and angular and electric for the Buzzcocks. So there's an obvious sensibility and moment that one could key into. That seems particular to "movements" in music – you're buying into a style that really signifies. But that's different than just randomly buying a CD because of the art. I don't buy music on the strength of covers. It's not enough of a reason for me to plunk down my dollars (I'll confess to having bought a bunch of old and cheap vinyl just for the covers, but that's more in the interest of just owning a piece of graphic design – I had no hopes for the music). I've bought plenty of records because of the label it's on (and in some cases that means assembling a wonderful graphic portfolio, as with Blue Note records or 4AD or Factory), but great graphic style can easily mask music I just don't care about.

V: Maybe you could say a few words about *The Ganzfeld*? How did you come up with the idea for this beautifully eclectic magazine (if indeed "magazine" would be the word)? Like, say, *McSweeney's*, it seems to be a bit of a con amore project, expensive in terms of production I suppose? I noticed that the first editions of *McSweeney's* went for more than $100 when I lived in Seattle last spring. Do you aim at a select audience, where you consider the journal a kind of laboratory?

Obviously you're not reaching for a mass audience. Certainly you have been able to present some great artists to your readers. As I write this I have #2 in front of me and I'm looking at what you have there by Chris Ware. Do you know many of the artists, so that there is an environment around *The Ganzfeld*? (Drinking coffee with Jeff Tweedy and Chris Ware every other week seems quite a privilege – if that's how it works). Did you bring along many of your ideas from *The Ganzfeld* to the Wilco project? Moody, for example, seems to have been involved in both the journal and the book.

DN: *The Ganzfeld* was conceived as an eclectic annual book that would contain art, design, illustration, comics, and historical writing that places all of those mediums in a broad context. It is not a cheap production, but I want to present art of all kinds and that means printing in color. So, it is not really that elaborate. I aim to find anyone interested in visual culture – ideally that would mean a large audience, but realistically it means, yes, a more "journal"-like audience in the end.

There is not really a "scene" around *The Ganzfeld* or PictureBox. I work with some artists who are also my friends, and others that I barely know at all. The point of contact, though, is always the art – it's not a social thing. And most everyone I deal with works pretty hard – the cafe life, alas, isn't really the thing. There isn't time. What it is great for, though, is leading me to all kinds of creators. Many of the contributors have arrived at *The Ganzfeld* through other contributors – like one long game of "telephone" or something. So, there is a kind of loose aesthetic community around *The Ganzfeld* that has friends and collaborators in common. That's fun and keeps it feeling friendly.

The Wilco Book evolved out of *The Ganzfeld*, actually. The idea was to apply the visual book model of *The Ganzfeld* to a rock and roll band. Wilco was and is a favorite, so I thought, why not? The particular lesson applied was how to make a cohesive whole out of disparate visual parts. It had to read like a whole document, not like an anthology. So, *The Ganzfeld* as applied to Wilco meant coming up with subtle, unannounced graphic and literary themes to tie the whole thing together, as well as reaching out to a variety of different kinds of artists and writers in order to give the book an unmistakable – but also uncategorizable – identity.

Notes on Contributors

Nicole R. Brown is Associate Professor of English at Western Washington University, where she teaches courses in writing, rhetoric, and professional and technical communications. Much of her scholarship explores the influence that computers and communication technologies are having on academic, social, and professional contexts. Other interests include community-based learning, sustainable design, cyber-cultural studies and music.

Ian Chapman is Executant Lecturer in Popular Music at the University of Otago, Dunedin, New Zealand. A professional performer and songwriter, his primary academic research interest is glam rock, 1970-1975, and in particular the exploration of image creation. His first book, a broad social history of New Zealand in the 1970s titled *Glory Days: from Gumboots to Platforms* (Harper Collins New Zealand), was published in 2009. He is also nearing completion of his Ph.D. thesis, an iconographical analysis of David Bowie's album covers. His performance work as glam-rock alter-ego, Dr Glam, can be seen at www.drglam.co.nz

Anne Galperin is Associate Professor of Graphic Design at the State University of New York at New Paltz. She heads the BFA program in graphic design and teaches courses including theory and criticism, history, and research methods. Her practice is comprised of editorial art direction and design, theoretical and empirical research, and writing. She is currently writing and designing a communication design textbook entitled *Page to Screen, Still to Motion*. She holds an MFA in 2D design from Cranbrook Academy of Art.

Asbjørn Grønstad is Professor of Visual Culture in the Department of Information Science and Media Studies at the University of Bergen, Norway, and director of the research project/center *Nomadikon: New Ecologies of the Image*. His most recent publication is *Transfigurations: Violence, Death and Masculinity in American Cinema* (Amsterdam University Press, 2008).

Eve Klein is a mezzo-soprano and electronic musician working in Sydney, Australia. She has worked as an Associate Lecturer at Macquarie University, teaching music technology, digital music cultures and DJing practice, and has written on the connection between diaspora, music and language within the Maltese Australian community, and heterosexual femininity in Australian country music. Her current work explores the hybridization of opera and ambient electronica; this forms the basis of her Ph.D. research at Queensland's University of Technology. She also works for the Music Council of Australia, coordinating the Music in Communities Network and managing the National Instrument Bank.

Sigrid Lien is Professor of Art History at the University of Bergen, Norway, where she teaches modern art and visual culture, specializing in the history of photography. Her Ph.D. was about the construction of music industry stardom through photography, focusing on punk photography. Recently, in collaboration with professor Peter Larsen, she has written the first extensive Norwegian history of photography (2007) and *The Art of Reading Images* (2008). In 2009 she published *Pictures of Longing – Photography in the history of the Norwegian US emigration*.

Hilary Moore graduated with a Ph.D. in ethnomusicology from the University of Pennsylvania in 2004. She has presented papers at numerous conferences, including the Society of Ethnomusicology, the British Forum of Ethnomusicology, the Society for Education, Music, and Psychology Research, and the Leeds International Jazz Conference. She is the author of *Inside British Jazz: Crossing Borders of Race, Nation, and Class* (2007). She is now a consultant and trainer for international communication, based in London.

Dan Nadel is the founder of PictureBox, Inc. (www.pictureboxinc.com), a Grammy Award-winning New York-based packaging and publishing company. Its most recent releases include *Gary Panter* and *The Ganzfeld 6* (www.theganzfeld.com). He is the author of *Art Out of Time: Unknown Comic Visionaries 1900–1969*.

Colleen Sheehy holds a Ph.D. and is director of Plains Art Museum in Fargo, North Dakota. In her former position as a curator and director of education at the Weisman Art Museum at the University of Minnesota-Minneapolis, she curated the first major Bruce Springsteen exhibition, *Springsteen: Troubadour of the Highway*, which examined links between the singer's lyrical imagery and his photographic and video imagery. She writes about music and visual culture and has curated several other exhibitions on intersections between music and the visual. She is editor, with Thomas Swiss, of *Highway 61 Revisited: Bob Dylan's Road from Minnesota to the World* (University of Minnesota Press, 2009).

Jonathan Silverman is Assistant Professor of English at University of Massachusetts Lowell, and received his Ph.D. in American Studies from the University of Texas at Austin. He recently served as the Fulbright Roving Scholar in American Studies in Norway. He is completing a manuscript, *Nine Choices: Johnny Cash and American Culture*, for University of Massachusetts Press. He is the coauthor (with Dean Rader) of *The World is a Text*.

Gavin Steingo is a Ph.D. candidate in Anthropology of Music at the University of Pennsylvania. He has published articles in several journals, including *Popular Music and Society*, *Black Music Research Journal*, *African Music*, *African Identities*, and *The Review of Disability Studies*. He recently received a grant from Merck Pharmaceuticals to conduct research on the use of medical equipment at a hospital in Cameroon.

Øyvind Vågnes is a Postdoctoral Fellow connected to the project *Nomadikon: New Ecologies of the Image* at the University of Bergen, Norway. He is working on a book, *Images from the Dark Side: Picturing the War on Terror*, on non-fiction narratives that concern the ongoing war on terror (with chapters on Errol Morris, Joe Sacco, and Nina Berman, among others). He has published two novels in Norwegian, *Ingen skal sove i natt* (2003) og *Ekko* (2005); a third will be out in 2009.

Andrew Warnes is a Senior Lecturer in American Literature and Culture at the School of English, University of Leeds. He writes about music and food in the cultures of the African Diaspora and the transatlantic West. His latest book is *Savage Barbecue: Race, Culture and the Invention of America's First Food* (2008).

Jeffrey Andrew Weinstock is Professor of American Literature and Culture at Central Michigan University. He is the author of *Scare Tactics: Supernatural Fiction by American Women* (2008), *The Rocky Horror Picture Show* (2007), and *Vampires: Undead Cinema* (forthcoming); he is the editor of six academic collections of essays including the *MLA Approaches to Poe* volume and a scholarly volume on the animated program South Park. He is currently working on a book-length study of American Gothic author Charles Brockden Brown, and is the general editor for the *Ashgate Encyclopedia of Literary Monsters* project.

Select Bibliography

Adams, Laurie Schneider, *The Methodologies of Art: An Introduction* (Colorado: Westview Press, 1996).

Ake, David, *Jazz Culture* (Berkeley: University of California Press, 2002).

Anderson, Benedict, *Imagined Communities: Reflections on the Origin and Spread of Nationalism* (London and New York: Verso, 1990).

Baddeley, Gavin, *Goth Chic: A Connoisseur's Guide to Dark Culture* (London: Plexus, 2002).

Baraka, Amiri, *Blues People: Negro Music in White America* (New York: William Morrow, 1999).

Barthes, Roland, "Death of the Author", in *Image, Music, Text* (Glasgow: Fontana/Collins, 1977).

Barthes, Roland, *Camera Lucida: Reflections on Photography*, trans. Richard Howard (New York: Vintage, 2000).

Barthes, Roland, *Mythologies* (London: Vintage, 2000).

Baudrillard, Jean, *Simulations* (New York: Semiotext[e], 1983).

Baxandall, Michael, *Patterns of Intention: On the Historical Explanation of Pictures* (London: Yale University Press, 1985).

Belk, Russell W., *Collecting in a Consumer Society* (London: Routledge, 2001).

Benedict, Brad and Linda Barton, *Phonographics: Contemporary Album Cover and Art Design* (New York: Collier Books, 1977).

Benjamin, Walter, "Unpacking My Library", *Illuminations*, ed. Hannah Arendt, trans. Harry Zohn (New York: Schocken, 1969).

Berger, John, "The Changing View of Man in the Portrait", in *Selected Essays and Articles: The Look of Things* (London: Vintage Books, 1972).

Bhabha, Homi K., *The Location of Culture* (London: Routledge, 1994).

Bolter, Jay David and Richard Grusin, *Remediation: Understanding New Media* (Cambridge, Mass.: The MIT Press, 2000).

Buchanan-Smith, Peter and Dan Nadel, *The Wilco Book* (New York: PictureBox, 2004).

Cardinal, Roger, "Nadar and the Photographic Portrait in Nineteenth-Century France", in Graham Clarke (ed.), *The Portrait in Photography* (London: Reaktion Books, 1992).

Cook, Nick, "The Domestic Gesamtkunstwerk, or Record Sleeves and Reception", in Wyndham Thomas (ed.), *Composition-Performance-Reception: Studies in the Creative Process in Music* (Aldershot: Ashgate, 1998).

Daley, Mike, "'Why Do Whites Sing Black?': The Blues, Whiteness, and Early Histories of Rock", *Popular Music and Society,* 26:2 (2003).

de Certeau, Michel, *The Practice of Everyday Life* (Berkeley: University of California Press, 1984).

de Ville, Nick, *Album: Style and Image in Sleeve Design* (London: Mitchell Beazley, 2003).

De Vries, Lyckle, "Iconography and Iconology in Art History: Panofsky's Prescriptive Definitions and Some Art-Historical Responses to Them", in Thomas Heck (ed.), *Picturing Performance: The Iconography of the Performing Arts in Concept and Practice* (New York: University of Rochester Press, 1999).

Dean, Roger and David Howells, *Album Cover Album 4* (Surrey: Dragon's World Ltd, 1987).

Deleuze, Gilles, *Francis Bacon: The Logic of Sensation* (London: Continuum, 2004).

Derrida, Jacques, *The Truth in Painting*, trans. Geoff Bennington and Ian McLeod (Chicago: University of Chicago Press, 1987).

Devereaux, Leslie, "An Introductory Essay", in Leslie Devereaux and Roger Hillman (eds.), *Fields of Vision: Essays in Film Studies, Visual Anthropology, and Photography* (Berkeley: University of California Press, 1995).

Devlin, Diana, *Mask and Scene: An Introduction to a World View of Theatre* (Hampshire: MacMillan Publishers Ltd, 1989).

Drew, Rob, "Mixed Blessings: The Commercial Mix and the Future of Music Aggregation", *Popular Music and Society* 28, no. 4 (2005).

Forss, John, Jo March, Graham Coxon, and Scott Burnett, "Creative Design and Packaging: Wear Your Art on Your Sleeve", *Music Week*, 2 (October 2004).

Foucault, Michel, *This is Not a Pipe*, trans. and ed. James Harkness (Berkeley: California University Press, 1983).

Frith, Simon, *Sound Effects, Youth, Leisure and the Politics of Rock'n'Roll* (New York: Pantheon, 1981).

Genette, Gérard, *Paratexts: Thresholds of Interpretation*, trans. Jane E. Lewin (Cambridge: Cambridge University Press, 1997).

Gibson, Chris, "Appropriating the Means of Production: Dance Music Industries and Contested Digital Space", in Graham St John (ed.), *FreeNRG: Notes From the Edge of the Dancefloor* (Alton, Victoria: Common Ground Publishing, 2001).

Gilroy, Paul, *After Empire: Melancholia or Convivial Culture?* (Abingdon, Oxfordshire: Routledge, 2004).

Gilroy, Paul, *Between Camps: Nations, Cultures and the Allure of Race* (London: Penguin, 2001).

Gladney, Marvin J., "The Black Arts Movement and Hip-Hop", *African-American Review* 29:2 (Summer 1995).

Goldstein, Robert (ed.), *Desecrating the American Flag: Key Documents of the Controversy from the Civil War to 1995* (Syracuse, NY: Syracuse University Press, 1996).

Hebdige, Dick, *Subculture: The Meaning of Style* (London: Methuen, 1979).

Heble, Ajay, *Landing on the Wrong Note: Jazz, Dissonance, and Critical Practice* (London: Routledge, 2000).

Hermes, Will and Sia Michel (eds.), *SPIN: 20 Years of Alternative Music* (New York: Crown Publishers, 2005).

Intro, *Radical Album Cover Art: Sampler 3* (London: Laurence King, 2003).

Jameson, Fredric, *Postmodernism, or, the Cultural Logic of Late Capitalism* (Durham, NC: Duke University Press, 1991).

Jeffords, Susan, *Hard Bodies: Hollywood Masculinity in the Reagan Era* (New Brunswick, NJ: Rutgers University Press, 1994).

Jenkins, Henry, *Textual Poachers: Television Fans & Participatory Culture* (New York and London: Routledge, 1992).

Jones, Mablen, *Getting it on: The Clothing of Rock'n'Roll* (New York: Abbeville Press, 1987).

Jost, Ekkehard, *Free Jazz* (New York: Da Capo Press, 1994).

Karmel, Pepe (ed.), *Jackson Pollock: Interviews, Articles, and Reviews* (New York: Museum of Modern Art, 1999).

Katriel, Tamar and Thomas Farrell, "Scrapbooks as Cultural Texts: An American Art of Memory", *Text and Performance Quarterly*, 11.2 (1991).

Kellner, Amy, "Hey DJ, Fuck You! (Anyone Can Rock the Party)", *Vice* 11 (2002).

Krims, Adam, *Rap Music and Poetics of Identity* (Cambridge: Cambridge University Press, 2000).

Kruse, Holly, "Subcultural identity in alternative music culture", *Popular Music* 12:1 (1993).

Leppert, Richard, *Art and the Committed Eye* (Colorado: Westview Press, 1996).

Lévi-Strauss, Claude, *Myth and Meaning* (London and New York: Routledge, 2002).

Litweiler, John, *The Freedom Principle: Jazz After 1958* (New York: Da Capo Press, 1990).

Lunenfeld, Peter, *Snap to Grid: A User's Guide to Digital Arts, Media, and Cultures* (Cambridge, Mass.: The MIT Press, 2000).

Manovich, Lev, *The Language of New Media* (New Haven, CN: The MIT Press, 2001).

Marcus, Greil, *In the Fascist Bathroom: Punk in Pop Music* (Cambridge, Mass.: Harvard University Press, 1993).

Marsh, Dave, *Glory Days: Bruce Springsteen in the 1980s* (New York: Pantheon Books, 1987).

Marsh, Graham and Barrie Lewis (eds.), *The Blues: Album Cover Art* (London: Collins & Brown, 1996).

Marsh, Graham, Felix Cromey, and Glyn Callingham (eds.), *Blue Note: The Album Cover Art* (San Francisco: Chronicle Books, 1991).

Matsui, Takumi, *In Search of the Lost Record: British Album Cover Art of 50s to 80s* (Tokyo: Graphic-Sha, 2001).

McKay, George, "DIY Culture: Notes Toward an Intro", in George McKay (ed.), *DIY Culture: Party and Protest in Nineties Britain* (London: Verso, 1998).

McKnight-Trontz, Jennifer and Alex Steinweiss, *For the Record: The Life and Work of Alex Steinweiss. Inventor of the Album Cover* (New York: Princeton Architectural Press, 2000).

McLeod, John, *Postcolonial London: Rewriting the Metropolis* (London: Routledge, 2004).

Melton, J. Gordon, *The Vampire Book: The Encyclopedia of the Undead* (Detroit, Washington, D.C. and London: Visible Ink, 1994).

Miller, David, *A Theory of Shopping* (Ithaca, NY: Cornell University Press, 1999).

Mitchell, W.J.T., "There Are No Visual Media", *Journal of Visual Culture* 4.2 (2005).

Mitchell, W.J.T., *Picture Theory: Essays on Verbal and Visual Representation* (Chicago: University of Chicago Press, 1994).

Morrison, Toni, *Playing in the Dark: Whiteness and the Literary Imagination* (New York: Vintage, 1992).

Ochs, Michael, *1000 Record Covers* (London: Taschen, 1996).

Oldenburg, Ray, *The Great Good Places: Cafes, Coffee Shops, Community Centers, Beauty Parlors, General Stores, Bars, Hangouts, and How They Get You Through the Day* (New York: Paragon House, 1989).

Pacht, Otto, *The Practice of Art History: Reflections on Method* (Munich: Harvey Millar Publishers, 1999).

Palmer, Robert, *Rock and Roll: An Unruly History* (New York: Harmony Books, 1995).

Parkes, Adam, "A Sense of Justice: Whistler, Ruskin, James, Impressionism", *Victorian Studies* 42:4 (2000).

Percy, Walker, "The Man on the Train", in *The Message in the Bottle: How Queer Man Is, How Queer Language Is and What One Has to Do with the Other* (New York: Farrar, Straus, and Giroux, 1975).

Pesch, Martin, *Techno Style: The Album Cover Art* (London: Collins & Brown, 1995).

Poyner, Rick, "Information Sculpture", *Eye*, vol. 4, no. 13 (Summer 1994).

Pressing, Jeff, "Free Jazz and the Avant-garde", in Mervyn Cooke and David Horn (eds.), *Cambridge Companion to Jazz* (Cambridge: Cambridge University Press, 2002).

Prince, Gerald, *Narratology: The Form and Functioning of Narrative* (Berlin, New York, Amsterdam: Mouton Publishers, 1982).

Radano, Ronald, *New Musical Figurations: Anthony Braxton's Cultural Critique* (Chicago: University of Chicago Press, 1993).

Rheingold, Howard, *The Virtual Community: Homesteading on the Electronic Frontier* (Reading: Addison Wesley, 1993).

Rivers, Charlotte, *CD Art: Innovation in CD Packaging and Design* (Hove: RotoVision, 2003).

Rose, Tricia, *Black Noise: Rap Music and Black Culture in Contemporary America* (Hanover, NH: Wesleyan University Press, 1994).

Saul, Scott, *Freedom is Freedom Aint: Jazz and the Making of the Sixties* (USA: President and Fellows of Harvard College, 2003).

Scott, Guenter, *The American Flag 1777–1924: Cultural Shifts from Creation to Codification* (Cranbury, NJ: Associated University Presses, 1990).

Seiler, Burkhardt (ed.), *The Album Cover Art of Punk* (London: Collins & Brown, 1998).

Shuker, Roy, "Beyond the 'High Fidelity' Stereotype: Defining the (Contemporary) Record Collector", *Popular Music* 23.3 (2004).

Shuker, Roy, *Key Concepts in Popular Music* (London: Routledge, 1998).

Shusterman, Richard, "Critical Response: Rap Remix: Pragmatism, Postmodernism and Other Issues in the House", *Critical Inquiry* 22 (Autumn 1995).

Solomon-Godeau, Abigail, *Male Trouble: A Crisis in Representation* (London: Thames and Hudson, 1997).

Sontag, Susan, "Notes on 'Camp'", in *Against Interpretation* (London: Vintage, 1994).

Spellman, A.B., *Black Music: Four Lives in the Be-Bop Business* (New York: Limelight, 1967).

Spiegelman, Art, "Drawing Blood: Outrageous Cartoons and the Art of the Outrage", *Harper's* (June 2006).

Such, David, *Avant-garde Jazz Musicians Performing 'Out There'* (Iowa City: University of Iowa Press, 1993).

Szwed, John, *Space is the Place: The Lives and Times of Sun Ra* (New York: Da Capo Press, 1997).

Taylor, Joshua C., *Learning to Look: A Handbook for the Visual Arts* (Chicago: The University of Chicago Press, 1981).

Thorgerson, Storm and Aubrey Powell, *100 Best Album Covers* (New York: Dorling Kindersley Publishing Inc., 1999).

Thornton, Sarah, "Exploring the Meaning of the Mainstream (or Why Sharon and Tracy Dance around Their Handbags)", in *Club Cultures: Music, Media and Subcultural Capital* (Cambridge: Polity Press, 1995).

Tofts, Darren and Murray McKeich, *Memory Trade: A Prehistory of Cyberculture* (Sydney: Interface, 1997).

Tomato, *Process: A Tomato Project* (London: Thames and Hudson, 1996).
Townsend, Peter, *Jazz in American Culture* (Edinburgh: Edinburgh University Press, 2000).
Truax, Barry, *Acoustic Communication* (Norwood, NJ: Ablex, 1984).
Walker, John A. and Sarah Chaplin, *Visual Culture: An Introduction* (New York: St. Martin's Press, 1997).
Walser, Robert, *Running with the Devil: Power, Gender and Madness in Heavy Metal Music* (Connecticut: Wesleyan University Press, 1993).
Ward, Brian (ed.), *Media, Culture, and the Modern African-American Freedom Struggle* (Florida: University of Florida Press, 2001).
Whiteley, Sheila (ed.), *Sexing the Groove: Popular Music and Gender* (London: Routledge, 1997).
Wilentz, Sean and Greil Marcus (eds.), *The Rose and the Briar: Death, Love, and Liberty in the American Ballad* (New York: Norton, 2005).
Wilmer, Val, *As Serious as Your Life: John Coltrane and Beyond* (London: Serpent's Tail, 1992).
Yanker, Gary, *Prop Art: Over 100 Contemporary Political Posters* (New York: Darien House, 1972).
Young, Neil, *Greendale* (London, U.K.: Sanctuary Publishing, 2004).

LPs were like the force of gravity. They had covers, back and front, that you could stare at for hours.
– *Bob Dylan*